Praise for *The Soft Edge*

"As we shift from the rigid 'ladder world' of scale efficiencies to the nimble 'lattice world' of scale agility, mastering the soft edge becomes a hard reality. Karlgaard sharpens our grasp of this elusive though vital topic and offers pragmatic, accessible solutions."

—**Cathy Benko,** vice chairman and managing principal,
Deloitte LLP, and bestselling author of *Mass Career Customization*

"As a teacher and student of leadership, I've long believed the relevance and power of 'soft side' economics. (Trust, for example, is a measurable economic driver that makes organizations more profitable and people more promotable.) With *The Soft Edge*, Karlgaard joins the conversation and makes the bold statement that *the soft side is now the only remaining competitive edge* in our new economy. Leaders, I recommend that you take full advantage of Karlgaard's advice—so you can start to reap the dividends."

—**Stephen M. R. Covey,** *New York Times* bestselling author of
The Speed of Trust and *Smart Trust*

"At a time when the stakes couldn't be higher, many leaders are searching for new ways of competing—with resilience as a top priority. Forbes publisher Rich Karlgaard, a longtime voice for 'hard edge' business practices, argues that 'soft edge' advantages have enduring power in our knowledge economy. Anyone with a stake in tomorrow's bottom-line outcomes should take a close look at Karlgaard's cutting-edge book."

—**Amy Edmondson,** Novartis Professor of Leadership and
Management, Harvard Business School, and author of *Teaming:
How Organizations Learn, Innovate, and Compete in the Knowledge Economy*

"*The Soft Edge* is an eye-opener: Rich Karlgaard makes the utterly convincing argument that the soft side of business makes all the difference to a company's ability to thrive in the long run. Leaders, it's time to stop polishing your strategy and fine-tuning your execution. Instead, read this critical book—then start investing in the very soul of your company."

—**John Gerzema,** bestselling author, including
The Brand Bubble and *The Athena Doctrine*

"Leaders have never had so many opportunities—and pressures. Get to the heart of it with Rich Karlgaard, who has distilled his significant experience into a single argument that works for every organization in today's times: if you want innovation and lasting success, you must develop your 'soft edge.' Exactly. The soft edge is truly as vital now as strategy and execution. So whether you're a tireless chief, a rising star, or a 'hard-edged' business veteran, you owe it to yourself to get a copy of Karlgaard's compelling new book. Why? Because *The Soft Edge* will help you find the future—and the future is now."

—**Marshall Goldsmith,** Thinkers 50 Top
Ten Global Business Thinker and top-ranked executive coach

"Management and leadership thinking has reached a crisis point. The great irony of our age is this: the faster technology progresses, the more crucial it is to organize around timeless human truths. Rich Karlgaard shows the way in his compelling new book, *The Soft Edge*."

—**Gary Hamel,** director of the Management Lab
and author of *What Matters Now*

"At a time when strategy and execution can be bought, your company's core values are the very accelerators you need for differentiation and innovation. Forbes publisher Rich Karlgaard knows which organizations are now winning the endurance race, and why. He shines a light on an often-overlooked driver: values. *The Soft Edge* is for forward-thinking leaders dedicated to rising above the competition."

—**Sally Hogshead,** author of *How the World Sees You:
Discovering Your Highest Value Through the Science of
Fascination* and creator of HowToFascinate.com

"The best companies enchant us with purpose, affection, empathy, coolness, and grit. Rich Karlgaard's book shows you how to achieve this lofty goal."

—**Guy Kawasaki,** author of *APE: Author, Publisher,
Entrepreneur* and former chief evangelist of Apple

"Rich Karlgaard puts the entire subject of culture and corporate character into a totally new context—a powerful framework proven with example after example. A great read for any business leader."

—**John Kennedy,** senior vice president of marketing,
IBM Global Business Services

"For decades I have witnessed the power of teams, trust, and smarts in the most disruptive startups in Silicon Valley. *The Soft Edge* makes a powerful argument for why great businesses and products repeatedly derive from the creative friction, small teams, and minimally invasive management which the best leaders employ to achieve breakout success. I want to thank Rich Karlgaard for a wonderfully readable and actionable exploration of these too often overlooked skills."

—**Randy Komisar,** partner, Kleiner Perkins Caufield,
and Byers lecturer, Stanford Business School

"*The Soft Edge* is crystal clear, deeply substantial, and alarmingly concrete. It illumines what an organization might be—what it must be if it is to impact the world and elevate the human spirit (and run a profit). To read it is an exercise in conviction."

—**John Ortberg,** senior pastor of Menlo Park Presbyterian
Church and author of *Who Is This Man?*

"I love this book. From the first page to the last it's a real pleasure to read, and without a doubt the most enjoyable business book in a very, very long time. It's smart, intelligent, and fun. That's because Rich Karlgaard understands the craft of writing and the art of business. He treats us to great stories and in-depth case studies that often read like edge-of-your-seat thrillers. And don't let the title fool you. Sure, it's about things like trust and teams and taste and stories, but it's rich in tangible, hard evidence that proves the power of these qualities. *The Soft Edge* is on my short list of best business books of the year. I think it'll end up on yours, too."

> —**Jim Kouzes,** coauthor of *The Leadership Challenge* and Dean's Executive Fellow of Leadership, Leavey School of Business, Santa Clara University

"The workplace is facing unprecedented global challenges. Tomorrow's leaders must inspire their teams across a host of new boundaries—geographic, generational, economic, cultural, and technological—to name a few. The greatest will be those who can leverage their soft skills to motivate. In the world of big data, human skills will be the big differentiator! Learn more about twenty-first-century leadership in *The Soft Edge*—a wonderful, easy-to-read, and insightful corpus by longtime business innovator Rich Karlgaard. It's hard to find a more experienced, intelligent guide to help you and your company make the necessary leaps."

> —**Ross Smith,** director of test, Skype Division, Microsoft

"Entertaining, magnificent, enlightening, and so relevant to the future."

> —**Vivek Wadhwa,** vice president of research and innovation at Singularity University; fellow at Stanford University's Center for Corporate Governance; research director at Duke University's Center for Entrepreneurship and Research Commercialization

"There has never been a more challenging (but potentially rewarding) time to lead. As is often the case, Rich Karlgaard once again successfully 'zigs' with his clever premise of *The Soft Edge*. Flush with innovative ideas collected from his unique vantage point, he offers countless refreshing tips for tomorrow's leaders. Net—a terrific blueprint for a wide range of executives who are serious about leading teams to victory in the new frontier. A must-read!"

> —**Greg Welch,** senior partner, Spencer Stuart, marketing and board recruiting practice

THE
SOFT
EDGE

WHERE GREAT COMPANIES
FIND LASTING SUCCESS

Rich Karlgaard

FOREWORD BY TOM PETERS

AFTERWORD BY
CLAYTON M. CHRISTENSEN

JB JOSSEY-BASS™
A Wiley Brand

Published by Jossey-Bass
A Wiley Brand
One Montgomery Street, Suite 1200, San Francisco, CA 94104-4594
www.josseybass.com

Jossey-Bass books and products are available through most bookstores. To contact
Jossey-Bass directly call our Customer Care Department within the U.S. at 800-956-
7739, outside the U.S. at 317-572-3986, or fax 317-572-4002.

Wiley publishes in a variety of print and electronic formats and by print-on-demand.
Some material included with standard print versions of this book may not be included
in e-books or in print-on-demand. If this book refers to media such as a CD or DVD
that is not included in the version you purchased, you may download this material at
http://booksupport.wiley.com. For more information about Wiley products, visit www
.wiley.com.

Library of Congress Cataloging-in-Publication Data
Karlgaard, Richard.
    The soft edge : where great companies find lasting success / Rich Karlgaard.
    —First edition.
        pages   cm
    Includes bibliographical references and index.
    ISBN 978-1-118-82942-4 (cloth); ISBN 978-1-118-89803-1 (pdf);
    ISBN 978-1-118-89807-9 (epub)
        1. Organizational behavior.   2. Organizational effectiveness.
3. Strategic planning.   4. Management.   I. Title.
HD58.7.K3764   2014
658.4—dc23
                                                            2014001623
Printed in the United States of America
FIRST EDITION
HB Printing   10 9 8 7 6 5 4 3 2 1

This book is dedicated to . . .
Great coaches and overachieving teams
Employers who give dignity with pay
All who show courage and grace

Contents

Foreword
  by Tom Peters   xi

Preface: *A Tale of Transformation—and Lasting*
  Productivity Gains   xvii

1   A Wellspring of Enduring Innovation:
  The Soft Edge   1

2   Hard Versus Soft: *The Fight for Resources*   20

3   Trust: *The Force Multiplier of All Things Good*   36

4   Smarts: *How Fast Can You and Your*
  Company Adapt?   66

5   Teams: *Great Things Come to the Lean*
  and Diverse   100

6   Taste: *Beauty Made Practical, Magic*
  Made Profitable   137

7   Story: *The Power of Story, Ancient and New*   173

Conclusion: *The Sweet Spot of High Performance*   209

Afterword
   by Clayton M. Christensen   219
Notes   223
Acknowledgments   233
About the Author   237
Index   238

Foreword

Tom Peters

Bob Waterman and I were hard-nosed guys. Both McKinsey consultants. Both engineers (Bob, mining; me, civil). Both Stanford MBAs. Life for us began and ended with beady-eyed analysis. We also had a McKinsey-ite's view of corporate America. Among other things, we worked in McKinsey's San Francisco office, on the forty-eighth floor of what was then the Bank of America headquarters. A couple of floors above us were the palatial offices of the bank's CEO. Oaken doors, as I recall, that reached into the city's fabled fog. The chief was protected from humanity by a phalanx of underlings in Savile Row attire.

Nonetheless, we found ourselves one afternoon in 1977 driving thirty miles down U.S. 101, turning onto Page Mill Road, and turning in to another corporate headquarters. That of Hewlett-Packard. HP had just crossed the $1 billion revenue threshold at the time. We had an appointment, gained without the least bit of bureaucratic folderol, with HP president John Young. Upon our arrival, John trotted out to greet us and ushered us to his office. Or is that the wrong word? It was in fact a half-walled cubicle, about ten feet by ten feet, that he shared with a secretary.

Hmmmm.

A half hour later, lightning struck. Mr. Young introduced us to what became a life-altering idea. Within the scope of the fabled HP Way, it was a notion fondly called "MBWA." Or Managing By Wandering Around. Get the hell out of the office, hang out with the engineers (or purchasing guys or whomever), exchange ideas, and take the pulse of the enterprise where the work was actually done.

Now jump ahead five years. Bob and I have written a book titled *In Search of Excellence*, and though it was the early days after publication, a lot of folks seemed to be buying it. We were in New York, heading for an early morning Bryant Gumbel interview on the *Today Show*. In the so-called green room, Bob looked at me with a wry smile and said, "Okay, who gets to say 'MBWA' on national TV?" He was my senior and I demurred.

We called MBWA part of the "soft stuff." It stood for being in touch with your customers, in touch with your employees in even a big firm. It stood for high-speed innovation fueled by a willingness to cobble together a quick prototype and get everybody playing with it at a fast clip. It was a long way from those mighty BofA oaken doors and assistants to assistants who still resided two floors above us in our San Francisco digs.

We were still engineers. We still analyzed the hell out of any data we could unearth. But now—thanks to HP and 3M and Johnson & Johnson and about forty others of their ilk—we had a fuller picture of sustaining excellent performance. Yes, the "hard stuff" damn well mattered. But it turned out, to horridly mix a metaphor, that the "bedrock of excellence" was that "soft stuff."

The values around engaging 100 percent of our staff's effort and imagination, of intimately hooking up with and co-inventing with our customers, trying out cool stuff in a flash without a thousand pre-clearances and shrugging off the inevitable screw-ups and getting on with the next try posthaste.

Bob and I had discovered things we hadn't expected and that messed with our preconceptions. The ideas and stories from *In Search of Excellence* were hardly "the answer," but we did help nudge a new model of enterprise management toward the forefront.

Times have changed—or have they? To be sure, the HP Way took a wrong turn with a succession of CEOs that managed by the numbers and strangled the essence of HP. As illustrated in the 1990s by Enron and WorldCom, and then in the early 2000s by sub-prime fiascos, and now by too many reality-free, numbers obsessed, models-r-us gangs, companies can ascend high up the economic pyramid before it all collapses.

Time for a reset?

I think it is high time for a reset, and that brings me to the delightful task of cheering on the birth of a new and necessary revolution heralded by Rich Karlgaard's magisterial *The Soft Edge*. As publisher of *Forbes*, Rich, not unlike Bob Waterman and me, brings impeccable logic and hard economics credentials to his task. And also like Bob and me, or even more so, in *The Soft Edge* he hardly runs away from the analytical side of things.

Rich offers and defends a balanced triangle of forces: "hard edge" (the systems and processes that guide complex execution tasks); "strategic base" (you stumble and tumble fast if you don't have a clear strategic direction); and, his focus in this book, "soft edge" (oft ignored or underplayed, it provides human values and resilience in a mind-bogglingly nutty world).

The heart of the book, not unlike the "eight basics" at the heart of *In Search of Excellence*, consists of chapters that examine in colorful and instructive detail the principal components of the soft edge:

- Trust
- Smarts
- Teams
- Taste
- Story

Of the five components that make up the soft edge (or five pillars as Rich calls them), the basic element labeled "taste" (which clearly underpins the likes of Apple's mind-warping success), is where Rich offers an example that pulls the entire book together for me. Though the author lives and plies his trade at the center of Silicon Valley, he purposefully reached out to every corner of the economy. Consider this telling remark by Robert Egger, the chief designer of Specialized Bicycles. Egger calls "taste" the "elusive sweet spot between data truth and human truth. . . . You want something that works great and is really emotionally charged." The hard edge and strategic base are indeed required—but they amount to little more than a piffle without the more-or-less sustainable differentiation contributed by the soft edge.

I must admit, in the softest of language, that I nothing less than love this book. I have been fighting the "soft edge war" since 1977—that is, thirty-seven bloody years. It is in fact a war that cannot be won. I fervently and unstintingly believe in balance (as embodied in Karlgaard's triangle of forces). But I also believe that the default position will always favor the strategic base and the hard edge, and that the soft edge, without constant vigilance, will always be doomed to the short (often very short) end of the resource and time-and-attention stick. And yet, as is demonstrated here so brilliantly, in general and perhaps today more than ever, only a robust and passionately maintained commitment to a vibrant soft edge will up the odds of sustaining success and, yes, excellence, in these days of accelerating change.

In short, ignore the argument in this marvelous book at your peril.

Preface

A Tale of Transformation— and Lasting Productivity Gains

In business, marginal gains add up. That's why we spend so much time looking for them. If we can reduce costs by 2 percent here and cut development time by a month there, it makes a difference. Good companies relentlessly seek these kinds of improvements and never stop. But great companies do more than that. They dig deeper to find transformative gains. Let me illustrate this by way of an amazing story of one person's transformation.

In October 2001, Roberto Espinosa, a thirty-one-year-old resident of San Antonio, Texas, stepped onto the platform of the service elevator at Manduca, his restaurant in the city's fashionable River Walk district. It was like stepping into air. The platform suddenly gave way. It plunged thirty feet to the basement and slammed onto concrete.

Dazed, Espinosa crawled out of the elevator shaft. He slipped in and out of consciousness. He barely remembers the arrival of first responders. They carefully immobilized Espinosa's neck, strapped him onto a gurney, and drove him the five miles to Brook Army Medical Center. Six hours of intensive care followed. Espinosa survived, but his road to recovery proved long and painful.

Espinosa had always sought an independent life. He had a natural predisposition for business. His family ran a furniture shop called De Firma in Mexico. It soon expanded into San Antonio under the name Home Emphasis. Growing up, Espinosa assumed he would go into the family business. But as time passed, he had an urge to prove himself outside the family cocoon and take on new risks.

So he started Manduca. This declaration of independence was either brave or dumb. Restaurants, with a three-year failure rate of 60 percent, are among the riskiest of businesses. Espinosa's wife, Lourdes, insisted they mitigate their risk by purchasing life and disability insurance for Roberto. "I didn't know much about insurance. So I called somebody I knew, Fernando. I trusted Fernando."

The trust paid off. After Espinosa's elevator crash and near death, Fernando Suarez was a frequent visitor to the hospital, visiting almost as often as Espinosa's family. "He was always there," said Espinosa. "As a friend, not a salesman."

Selling would have been futile, anyway. Espinosa had no money to buy more insurance policies. The 9/11 terrorist attacks had turned a mild 2001 recession into something worse. The travel and hospitality business was particularly hard-hit. In 2002 the physically fragile Espinosa was forced to close Manduca. He had never experienced failure like that.

Suarez noticed the drain on Espinosa's wallet, the decline in his confidence. He invited Espinosa to try out as a representative at his insurance company, Northwestern Mutual. Espinosa accepted.

But what does it mean, really, to accept a job selling insurance? These jobs pay only on commission. Is this a real career? Or is it a foolish gamble at a vulnerable point in one's life? "The first three years were very difficult," admitted Espinosa. "I had trouble making the sales phone calls. My prospects sensed my lack of conviction. I was so discouraged that I cleaned out my desk three times."

Coaching and mentorship got Espinosa through that rough beginning. Income started to trickle in. Still, it was tough to survive, to pay the bills and keep going. Then came a turning point that changed Espinosa's career forever. "I was at a funeral for a client," he said. "The deceased man's eight-year-old daughter got up and said she missed her daddy. Then she said her family would be okay. I got tears hearing that from an eight-year-old girl. I suddenly knew that what I was doing was very important work."

That day, Espinosa found his conviction. In a few short years he became one of Northwestern Mutual's top recruiters of new reps in San Antonio. Espinosa estimates his productivity increased roughly *fivefold* when his conviction switch turned on. That is not a marginal gain. It is something far bigger. For Espinosa and the company he represents, the gains are still adding up, still compounding.

Most companies hope for transformative events like these. Great companies, I've observed, know where to plant the seeds.

Palo Alto, California   Rich Karlgaard
February 2014

1

A Wellspring of Enduring Innovation

The Soft Edge

Innovate or die. The choice is not optional. The clock is ticking. If this sounds a bit melodramatic, it is also the truth. Disruptive waves seem to hit our companies more frequently than before. If we are to survive and prosper, innovation needs to be more than a one-time event. It must be perpetual, built-in, an automatic response to challenges and changes.

The "innovation response" in companies is very much like a healthy immune response in living organisms. People who enjoy long-term health don't have episodic bursts of health. They are healthy nearly all the time. Their immune systems routinely fight off most threats. Can the same be true of companies? The analogy fits. In great companies, innovation is a natural response to threats.

Why, then, do some companies have a more robust innovation response than others? From where does such vitality come? From the chief executive? This might be true in a small percentage of companies. But even for those relatively few, it is worth noting that CEOs don't stay on the job forever.

From clever strategy? If you think so, then you must believe your strategy will always be the correct one. But in all of industrial history, you will not find a single company that has always had a great strategy. History is littered with apparently solid companies suddenly undone by wrong strategic assumptions and bad bets. Eastman Kodak, Digital Equipment, MySpace anyone?

From flawless execution? Dell, with the fastest-growing stock in the 1990s, is legendary for its tight control of costs, mastery of supply chain, speed of delivery, and other flawlessly executed skills. Dell's smooth operations worked brilliantly in an era of PCs and laptops and corporate information technology departments that purchased both types of product for company employees. Then Dell's perfect execution model was suddenly not enough to sustain greatness. It was trumped by a shift toward smart phones and tablets and by employees' bringing their own technology to work.

Maybe it comes from large bets on research and development? That's certainly implied when you read an annual report and the company brags about the size of its R&D budget. (What company *doesn't* brag about this?) But R&D, while critically important to an innovative response and future health, is not sufficient by itself.

Finally, how about having an army of technology wizards to apply the latest cutting-edge advantages in big data, cloud, mobile, social, and so forth? Ah, that must be it! Think again. A technology advantage doesn't last as long as it once did. Consider weeks and months, not years and decades.

A healthy innovative response comes from a deeper place within your company. But it begins somewhere, and that somewhere is what I call the *soft edge*.

HOW A SIMPLE TRIANGLE CAN PREDICT LONG-TERM HEALTH

In the biological world, we know that a healthy organism has a better chance of surviving and adapting to change than an unhealthy one. No news here. Now let's suppose we want to predict any person's chances for long-term health. Can we do it? One framework for doing so is a simple equal-sided triangle like the one in Figure 1.1.

A person with the best chances of enjoying long-term health is one who is healthy on *all* sides of the triangle. Such a person will possess *physical* health—robust energy, few illnesses, and easy

Figure 1.1 Health Triangle

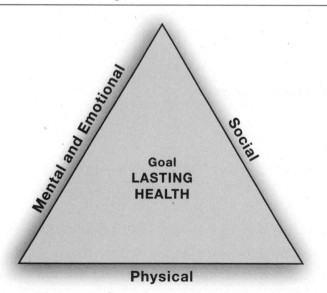

mobility, whether for work or leisure. Good *mental and emotional* health is a second component of well-being. This does not equate to a life of bliss, of course. It means a person will have a balanced perspective, understand cause and effect, have the ability to plan ahead, and be able to function even in difficult circumstances. The triangle's third side, *social* health, implies that people have a better shot at living a healthy life when surrounded by family, friends, and colleagues, in environments with low crime and stable rule of law, social cohesion, and economic opportunity. Remove any of these social pillars—live in a war-torn country, say—and your health prospects will be jeopardized, even if you're currently physically and mentally strong.

Seen this way, a trip around the health triangle can quickly reveal *where* a person would be at risk of not enjoying long-term health.

THE TRIANGLE OF LONG-TERM COMPANY SUCCESS

Now let's get down to business. Suppose we drew a triangle similar to the one that predicts long-term personal health. Only this triangle would predict a company's chances for lasting success. In its most basic form, it would look like Figure 1.2.

Here's a quick trip around the triangle, starting with the bottom, the *strategic base*. How important is getting your company's strategy right? When I visited Fred Smith, the founder, CEO, and chairman of FedEx, at his Memphis headquarters, he said it was his company's top priority.

The Strategic Base—Fundamental

As Fred Smith told me: "The number one thing that every organization has to get right is strategy. You can have the best

Figure 1.2 Triangle of Long-Term Company Success

operations. You can be the most adept at whatever it is that you're doing. But if you have a bad strategy, it's all for naught. Think Digital Equipment. Think Wang. Think Lockheed in the commercial airplane business. There were forks in the road where these companies chose the wrong strategy. Absent a viable strategy, you're in the process of going out of business."

This isn't a book on strategy. But you won't be able to understand the difference between the soft edge and strategy unless you have a clear understanding of what strategy really is. So let's take a quick look. When you talk to the best CEOs—who, like Smith, have proven themselves over several business cycles and market shifts—and when you further read classic business strategy books such as (to name only three of the best) *Competitive Strategy* by Michael Porter, *The Innovator's Dilemma* by Clayton Christensen, and *Playing to Win: How Strategy Really*

Figure 1.3 Strategic Base

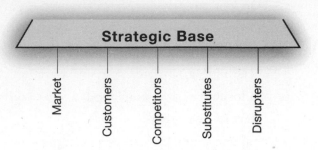

Works by A. G. Laffley and Roger Martin, you keep coming back to the five pillars of strategy illustrated in Figure 1.3. To take them each in turn:

Market: What markets are you in now? Are they the right markets for your business? Should you enter some or exit others? What are the adjacent markets? What are the forces shaping these markets? Which of your markets are growing, and which are stagnating?

Customers: Who are your customers? Why do they buy your product? Who are your potential customers? Why have they *not yet* bought your product? Are your products priced right for your customers? How would your customers respond to higher prices? Lower prices?

Competitors: Who are your direct competitors? How do your competencies and products match up to theirs? Where are you better and where are you worse? What is your market position relative to theirs?

Substitutes: Who are your indirect competitors? Where would your customers go if you didn't exist? Do these substitutes threaten to become direct competitors? Or do they suggest an opportunity for you to expand and acquire?

Disrupters: What are the technological game changers in your industry? Do you see new emerging players offering vastly cheaper or more convenient products than you can offer, even if these disrupters are not yet your direct competitors? Are these disruptive products finding new customers who were previously ignored? Are you losing valuable employees to these disrupters? When will you start to lose them?

These are vital considerations for your company, but they're not the questions that get asked at the soft edge. As important as they are, I must leave them now, because—as I said—this isn't a book on strategy. (For my top picks of great strategy books, please go to my website, richkarlgaard.com.)

The Hard Edge—Precise Execution

When Apple became the world's most valuable company in September 2012—a title it lost a year later, but may yet claim again—its CEO was Tim Cook, who had been in the job for only thirteen months. Prior to that, Cook had been Apple's chief operating officer since 2007.

Cook was widely considered the best large company COO in the world. What made Cook so effective? One, he was (and is) a workhorse. He typically begins e-mailing colleagues at 4:30 AM. He often skips meals, munching on energy bars throughout the day. On Sunday night, he convenes an Apple managers' meeting (by phone, thankfully) to talk about the week. Cook pushes himself to excellence and expects the same of his colleagues. For example, when an Apple manager described a problem with a factory in China, Cook's response was to stare incredulously. *Why, then, are you here?* Cook asked. *Go to the airport now, get on a plane, and solve the problem.* The manager didn't even bother to pack.[1]

Figure 1.4 The Hard Edge

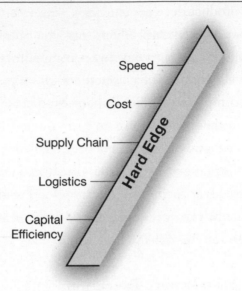

The second reason Cook was such a great COO is that he was a master of what I call the *hard edge* of business, as shown in Figure 1.4.

Cook himself calls it the execution side. Hard-edge execution is all about managing exactly to the numbers. The people who live on the hard edge of business are good at making the trains run on time. They focus on profit. Their language is time, money, and numbers. Every company in the world needs these employees, these Tim Cook types. Companies that fail to execute precisely on the hard edge of business will ultimately fail.

These are the five pillars that undergird the hard edge:

Speed: When FedEx promises overnight delivery, it has to make it happen or the brand will suffer. The same thing goes with Amazon, which now is offering daily delivery in certain markets. The execution needed to make this happen is the sum of a lot of numbers. Are the airplanes on time? How fast is each plane unloaded? How fast are the conveyor belts moving? Speed is also crucial to new product development. In Chapter Five, I describe how giant software firm SAP blew up and then reconfigured its team approach to cut product development time by 60 percent.

Cost: Not all companies compete on having the lowest price, but no company will succeed for long if it continually leaves money on the table because its costs are poorly managed. That's money not available for R&D, for more salespeople, for higher bonuses for deserving employees, and for shareholders.

Supply Chain: Harvard Business School professor Michael Porter, the dean of strategy thinkers, would put suppliers into the strategy category. In his most famous book, *Competitive Strategy*, he asks two related questions: What leverage do your suppliers have over you? What leverage do you have over them? What has changed since Porter's seminal 1980 book, of course, is technology that can monitor and report supply chain changes in real time. That's why I put supply chain on the hard-edge side.

Logistics: Norman Schwarzkopf, who was commander-in-chief of the U.S. Central Forces Command in the Persian Gulf War, told a TV interviewer, "Armchair generals talk strategy. Real generals talk logistics."[2] Logistics overlaps with supply chain, but logistics is really the *how* of the supply chain. Where are the trucks? What is fuel availability? How much is this costing? Are we operating fast enough? All great companies have a firm grip on their logistics.

Capital Efficiency: This hard-edge advantage is crucial to success. Are you using your capital to the best advantage? Say you are Southwest Airlines. How should you hedge your fuel purchases? This one decision can make or break airline profitability for the next five years. Or say you are a fast-growing start-up but not yet profitable. Should you raise money by issuing stock?

By expanding your credit line with your bank (assuming you can)? Should you go the high-yield-bond route? Great companies think about their capital structure. Tax strategies would also fall under capital efficiency.

I discuss the hard edge more in the next chapter. But now it's time to introduce the central theme of this book—the *soft edge*.

The Soft Edge—Expression of Your Deepest Values

The soft edge is the most misunderstood side of business. It also tends to be neglected and underfunded in too many companies. Several reasons explain this: One, the soft edge is harder to measure. Two, because it is tough to measure, it's more difficult to attach an ROI (return on investment) figure to any investments made in it. Three, most CEOs and board chairmen are not comfortable talking in the language of the soft edge.

Figure 1.5 sets out the soft edge as this book describes it.

Figure 1.5   The Soft Edge

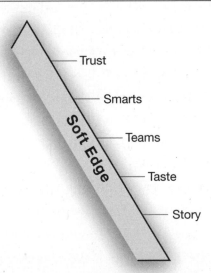

The rest of this book, with the exception of Chapter Two, focuses on the soft edge and the enduring company advantages to be found there. Here are the five pillars of the soft edge, along with some of the lessons presented later in the book:

- Trust
- Smarts
- Teams
- Taste
- Story

Trust

Trust is the foundational soft-edge advantage. It starts with two questions: Does your *external* market, your customers and share-holders, trust you? And two, does your *internal* market, your employees and suppliers, trust you? Let me illustrate the importance of trust by asking you to imagine a career that most people would be loath to try. That would be a commissioned sales job, selling to people who balk at buying your product. Life insurance fits this description. Yet Northwestern Mutual has built a $25 billion revenue juggernaut on that one word, *trust*. Remember Roberto Espinosa from the Preface? He saw his productivity jump *fivefold* when he began to trust his career.

Within an organization, trust begins with culture and values. There are reasons why companies that make the best-places-to-work lists published by magazines actually do perform better than their peers. Companies that develop trust have a recruiting advantage. They have a retention advantage and a productivity advantage. Externally, trust means that your product or service is authentic and robust enough to withstand the immediacy of today's media. When things go wrong, customers and stakeholders believe you'll do the right thing. Trust buys grace.

Trust may seem like a blurry concept in terms of ROI. But research and market results have proven that deep trust creates measurable real-world returns. Trust underlies effective working relationships. It improves group effectiveness and organizational performance. Maybe most important, trust underpins innovation by facilitating learning and experimentation. Chapter Three discusses ways to create an environment that engenders this kind of trust, including keys for developing a higher purpose and building a safe organizational culture.

Smarts

In most technical fields, from medicine to software, formal education quickly becomes out of date. How do you keep up? How do teams and entire companies learn and become smarter over time? What is *organizational smarts*, anyway—processing speed, memory, pattern recognition? Chapter Four discusses how Mayo Clinic, Stanford University women's basketball, and others stay on top by relentlessly pursuing an advantage through smarts.

But what, exactly, does it mean to be smart in the world of business? Unlocking knowledge and supporting learning are pivotal to success. But there's another dimension to being smart: one that relates to a few old-fashioned-sounding concepts like grit, perseverance, and hard work. These traits are fundamental to accelerating learning and helping you adapt more quickly to disruptive trends.

Chapter Four ventures to deepen understanding of what it means to be smart in today's complex world. It also explores a group of habits—like establishing beneficial relationships, learning from mistakes, and thinking laterally—that are sure to help you gain an edge over your competitors.

Teams

How does FedEx's Fred Smith manage 300,000 worldwide team members who move more than 2.5 billion packages in a year? What balance of central authority and peripheral autonomy works in such a logistically complex organization? Or why, in an entirely different industry, did German software giant SAP blow up the management framework for its 20,000-person development department and replace it with small teams?

Since collaboration and innovation are a must in the global economy, effective teamwork is vital. Yes, we humans are imperfect. We have different needs, roles, and perspectives that we bring to every interaction or team effort. But when we work together, we make each other better. We increase accountability, passion, and effort: we facilitate learning and catalyze innovation.

In Chapter Five, the focus is on small, high-performing teams of eight, ten, or twelve people. By exploring the best ways to identify optimal team members, as well as how to push those chosen few to the next level of performance, the chapter offers a powerful framework for managing flexible, fast, and creative teams.

Taste

Taste is the word Steve Jobs used when he described Apple's unique but universal aesthetic appeal. Jobs felt taste came from his own understanding of the yin-yang of science and humanity. The chief designer of Specialized Bicycles, Robert Egger, called it "the elusive sweet spot between data truth and human truth."

Nest Labs co-founder Tony Fadell said, "If you don't have an emotionally engaging design, no one will care."

During the last few decades, good design has become an increasingly valuable competitive asset. But taste is much more than just good design. It's a universal sensibility, an emotional engagement, that appeals to the deepest part of ourselves. It's wonderment and desire, power and control. We see it in those magical products that not only show us at our best but also make us feel and perform even better.

What kind of company can consistently make products or services that trigger these emotional touchpoints? And can you do it, too? Those are the subjects of Chapter Six. My goal is to illustrate how a flicker of imagination is transformed into a physical, tangible object that surprises and delights. In the process, I discuss how geometry, familiarity, selfishness (yes, selfishness), consistency, and simplicity all contribute to the mechanics of attraction.

Story

Companies that achieve lasting success, I've found, have an enduringly appealing story. But now in the age of social media, the challenge has become: How do you tell your company's story *your way* when customers, fans, and critics insist on telling your story *their way*? What if you dislike—or really hate—how outsiders tell your story?

Used both internally and externally, stories create purpose and build brand. Purpose may be a soft attribute, but it's what gives you steel in your spine, especially when cutting corners might temporarily boost the bottom line and delight shareholders. Externally, stories are used to launch new brands and enhance the image of existing brands—a task made more difficult by today's many new forms of communication.

Humans have evolved as storytellers—that's old news. But how you tell your company's story—that's a still-evolving discipline. Chapter Seven introduces an oddly contentious yet strangely fruitful story-shaping relationship between a company and its customers. Additionally, it sets out some practical do's and don'ts of effective storytelling, including ways to better understand your audience, dial up the verisimilitude, and refine your storytelling technique.

THE PRIZE IS CONTINUAL INNOVATION AND LASTING SUCCESS

Now that you have a snapshot of the three separate sides of the triangle, I can put all the pieces together. If your goal is to build a company that can continually innovate, be healthy in volatile times, and enjoy lasting success, you want a triangle that looks like the one in Figure 1.6.

Keep in mind, however, that this book is focused on the most misunderstood and maligned side of the triangle—the soft edge. And in detailing the benefits, challenges, and practices of soft-edge mastery, the book's chapters are intended to be read in order. As mentioned earlier, trust is foundational. It's the basis upon which learning occurs and great teams are built. Trust, learning, and great teams all contribute to a more defined sense of taste. Taste, along with smarts, leads to more engaging stories, which, in turn, help to better develop trust, and so on.

But if you want to dig into only a few of the soft-edge advantages, don't worry. Each of the chapters is also designed to be self-contained, with its own narratives, techniques, and well-defined terms. If you're fascinated by teams and teamwork, jump to it. If you need to sharpen a few storytelling techniques before next

Figure 1.6 Complete Triangle of Long-Term Company Success

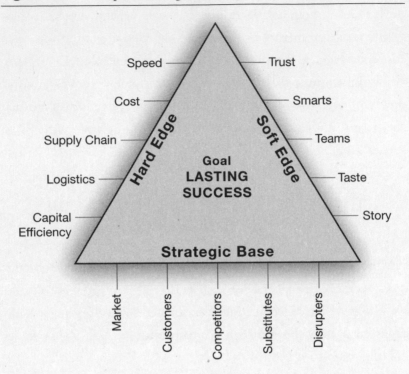

week's big presentation, have at it. In fact, if you go to my website, richkarlgaard.com, you'll find a comprehensive (and free) assessment for determining your soft-edge strengths and weaknesses. Your results can help guide your reading or identify chapters that may be worth revisiting.

Each of the individual chapters on trust, smarts, teams, taste, and story ends with a glimpse into the future, a look at what's new or on the cutting edge in that individual field. Often, these focus on how technology or data is being incorporated into soft-edge tasks. To the possible surprise of readers who have preferred the hard edge, the soft edge represents one of the final frontiers for numbers and statistics; for bits and bytes. These days, many great thinkers, futurists, and scientists are finding new, fascinating ways to get the best out of an organization. And these are real, tangible tools that can help you do things that were previously believed to be the realm of intrinsic genius.

Additionally, Chapters Three through Seven present a few recurring themes that are closely tied to soft-edge excellence: grit, courage, passion, and purpose. I admit that ideas like grit and courage may not sound so soft, but no one ever said soft is easy. Rather, as Tom Peters and Bob Waterman wrote in their seminal book *In Search of Excellence*, "Soft is hard."[3] The fact is, dictating strategy or crunching numbers is a lot easier than building trust or driving learning. You need grit and passion to build an enduring culture of innovation. And in today's markets, taking a long-term perspective over a short-term profit requires nothing if not an abundance of courage.

So make no mistake: excelling at the soft edge is not easy. That's why only the excellent companies do it.

WHY THE SOFT EDGE NOW?

Many colleagues have asked me why I'm writing a book called *The Soft Edge* now.

I believe the business world is at a crossroads, where hard-edge people are dominating the narrative and discussion. For example, Wall Street is about the hard edge. It's driven by speed, execution, and short-term capital efficiency. It dominates the way we think about free enterprise and capitalism today. Has this been good? (I'll let you answer.)

Also dominating the discussion are trends like big data and analytics. These are tremendously useful tools. But they are the brain, not the heart and soul, of your company. Some companies—many of them located in Silicon Valley, where

I live—have forgotten that. These companies command cutting-edge technology and brilliant 800-math-SAT employees. These companies can succeed for periods, often spectacularly. But they won't thrive for long if they suffocate their soft edge. Hewlett-Packard lost its way after years of neglecting the cultural values given to it by its founders, Bill Hewlett and Dave Packard. The so-called HP Way was universally understood by HP employees as a set of inspirational and ethical standards. For decades, the HP Way guided the company's enduring excellence. But successive CEOs, straining too hard for top-line growth, chipped away at HP's core values. Eventually the HP Way was lost—and with it, creativity, talent retention, brand value.

Finally, growth and profit were lost, too.

Too many businesses leaders today, pressured by a tough economy, badgered by shareholders, find it tempting to neglect their employees' and customers' deeper values. Alienation and distrust are on the rise. A majority of people around the world hate their jobs. This capitalism-leads-to-alienation argument is often made by critics of capitalism. As publisher and columnist for *Forbes*, let me make the same point as a free-market enthusiast. We can and should do better in the way we run our companies. It will profit us in the long run if we do.

Now, I want to be clear that this book is not an academic study. It's a collection of observations and anecdotes. As a thirty-year veteran business observer, at *Forbes* and as a participant in various Silicon Valley start-ups, I feel qualified to share these observations. You may agree or not, but I hope you will.

I have chosen a wide spectrum of companies—large and small, makers of products and services, located inside Silicon Valley and outside, privately held and publicly traded (and even a company owned by its customers). I chose this variety to see if I can derive some universal principles of lasting success.

While I chose variety in size, products, and ownership structures, there's one constant: they are enduring leaders in their industries. The companies described here are industry leaders in revenue or market share, and most have been around for four decades or more. Two have lasted for more than a century. Most have faced big challenges and setbacks. Many, even now, face big disruptive threats. I purposely left out younger superstars like Google and Facebook because of their youth and because neither company has been severely tested. It's true that Google and Facebook look more like Apple than Eastman Kodak, but time will tell.

With a few definitions freshly in mind and a strong grounding in the hard and soft edges of business, let's next take a look at how our conceptions, or misconceptions, affect things like organizational priorities and resource allocation. The following chapter explores this tension between the hard and soft edges by placing both within a historical context and examining their current utility.

Machine rationality versus hippie humanism?

Is that even a fair fight?

Let's see.

2

Hard Versus Soft
The Fight for Resources

As FedEx CEO and Chairman Fred Smith points out, the right strategy is foundational to any company's success. Your strategy may evolve, of course. But if it isn't there in the first place, or you fail to constantly review it and recalibrate it, your company has set itself up to make disastrous decisions.

No serious CEO or manager would debate the need for a smart, strong, and flexible strategy.

Rather, the battle for money and attention boiling inside most companies and among most managers is that between the hard and soft edges. Here is the key question: In a fight for limited resources, which side—hard or soft—should get the most money and attention? There is a right answer for every company and it will vary from year to year. But from my perch, far too many companies invest too little time and money in their soft-edge excellence. In the long run, they will pay for this mistake.

This mistake has three main reasons:

- The hard edge is easier to quantify. The metrics around speed, cost, supply chains, logistics, and capital efficiency are well understood. The data is relatively easy to come by, search, analyze, and manage.
- Successful hard-edge investment provides a faster ROI. Buying technology that trims costs or cuts time in a supply chain seems like a no-brainer.
- CEOs, CFOs, COOs, boards of directors, and shareholders speak the language of finance. These people—the company's hard-edgers—are experienced and comfortable with numbers. To these left-brained business titans, the soft edge looks like a realm of artists, idealists, hippies, poets, shrinks, and do-gooders. It's almost like Mars versus Venus.

Does the hard edge, therefore, have the more convincing case in the fight for time and money? No—just the easier case. Here's the case for investing time and money in your company's soft edge:

- Soft-edge strength leads to greater brand recognition, higher profit margins, more loyal customers, and more committed employees. Soft-edge excellence is the ticket out of Commodityville.
- Companies strong in the soft edge can often survive a big strategic mistake or cataclysmic disruption that would sink companies without a sturdy soft edge. Loyalty, passion, and commitment are the dividends of a strong soft edge.
- Hard-edge strength provides a fleeting advantage. The hard edge is easier to clone than the soft edge, especially as technology and software become cheaper and more widely accessible.

For example, Apple's great design and loyal fan base—soft-edge advantages—are the essence of its enduring appeal, more than its supply chain and capital efficiency, great as those are. And what gives Starbucks its ultimate edge? Better coffee? Not so, say people who love coffee! Cheaper locations? Quite the opposite. It is soft-edge excellence—which includes trust, brand, and cheerful employees—that creates a consistently satisfying experience.

THE HARD EDGE GREW FROM RESOURCE SCARCITY

The hard edge of business is often said to have started during the early Renaissance with the advent of double-entry bookkeeping. But intriguingly, it turns out that many hard-edge practices actually predate industrialization, the advent of math, and even civilization. The goal of cost-effectiveness surely started when mankind realized that resources are limited—a fact Cain grasped and his brother Abel did not. The very first "databases" appeared about thirty thousand years ago on cave walls in what is now the South of France. These Paleolithic hunters and gatherers used cave paintings to record the comings and goings of deer, elk, and other large animals that were harvested for food and clothing.

As our earliest instincts to track and record resources blossomed, tools to assist calculation soon followed. The oldest counting tool is thought to be a Babylonian abacus from 500 BC. The Roman hand abacus, the first portable calculating device, ruled from 27 BC to 400 AD. Its main use was to count currency, presumably allowing Roman emperors like Caligula to rob their citizens faster than before. The Suanpan, or 2/5, abacus—a device capable of addition, subtraction, multiplication, division, and even determining square roots—appeared in Chinese culture around 1300 AD.

The late Renaissance in the 1600s offered a veritable boom for calculating devices and machines. An astounding number of new and varied contraptions to assist with computation appeared across Europe, but the two that really mattered were William Oughtred's slide rule, a device used by science and engineering wizards well into the 1970s, and Blaise Pascal's mechanical calculator, a forerunner to industrial-age adding machines.

In 1886, the adding machine gained widespread use when William Seward Burroughs, the grandfather of beat writer William S. Burroughs, started American Arithmometer Company, later known as Burroughs Corporation. Just four years later, Herman Hollerith, one of the founders of IBM, created a punch card system that reduced the time to calculate the 1890 United States census from seven years to six weeks.

"IN THE FUTURE, THE SYSTEM MUST BE FIRST"

But the hard edge of business really hit its stride at the beginning of the twentieth century with Frederick Taylor's theory of scientific management, also often referred to as Taylorism. It was the age of political Progressivism: science was in. Lone heroes were out. "In the past, man was first; in the future, the system must be first," Taylor wrote in his introduction to *The Principles of Scientific Management*, published in 1911.

Taylor put forth a simple and appealing idea: you could increase labor productivity by measurable amounts if you could spot, then eliminate, all the irrational time wasters. To do that, managers had to watch, record, measure, and analyze the actions of their workers. No more employee freelancing on the factory floor. No more make-it-up-as-you-go. Taylor wanted to reduce complex manufacturing processes to the smallest, repetitive steps that any worker could do.

Taylorism, predictably, required an almost dictatorial level of control over workers and their work practices. Taylor, of course, saw his movement in a better light. Taylorism would be the savior of workers, since more productive workers could earn more money.

Taylor's peak of influence came in the first few decades of the twentieth century, with his theories finding their greatest realization in the auto assembly plants of Henry Ford. And indeed, just as Taylor had predicted, Ford paid his most productive workers up to four times the going rate for factory work.

Though Taylorism was soon eclipsed by other efficiency theories, Taylor had let a hard-edge genie out of the bottle. Taylorism spawned many new timing, bookkeeping, and accounting methods, as well as workflow charts, machine-speed slide calculators, motion studies, and assembly pacing metrics. He gave managers permission to observe, measure, analyze, act—and control. That was the core of scientific management, and it was hard to argue against its value.

Taylorism, in its strictest sense—stopwatches and all that— became obsolete by the Great Depression of the 1930s. But a form of Taylorism made one last run in the 1950s and 1960s, an organizational era born of World War II. This era was defined by a brilliant man with, alas, no clue of how to connect his beloved data and systems analysis to the softer, muddier world of human agency.

His name was Robert McNamara, and he was wired for the hard edge from the beginning. With degrees from the University of California at Berkeley and the Harvard Business School in hand, McNamara spent World War II devising routes and logistics for American bombers. In 1947, Henry Ford II hired McNamara and some military statistics geeks to save the Ford Motor Company, now getting clobbered by General Motors. The young men were called the Whiz Kids, and their analytical methods quickly proved successful at Ford. The most successful Ford car born of the Whiz Kid era was the utilitarian Ford Falcon. It generated no passion, but it was cheap to buy, fuel, and maintain. In that sense, the Falcon was the perfect Whiz Kid car.

McNamara didn't stay long at Ford. In 1961, the new U.S. president, John F. Kennedy, appointed McNamara the Secretary of Defense. One of McNamara's job priorities was to analyze U.S. involvement in the Vietnam conflict. He did, and decided to increase U.S. troop presence in South Vietnam from 900 to 16,000. After Kennedy's assassination, McNamara and President Lyndon Johnson pursued a strategy they called aggressive escalation. They bumped up U.S. troop presence from 16,000 to more than 500,000. McNamara's systems analysis had concluded that the United States could win a war of attrition against the Viet Cong.

As we now know, McNamara was wrong. Terribly so. In a 2003 documentary, *Fog of War*, McNamara admitted that his systems analysis approach had failed to account for human nature: specifically, the resourcefulness of the Viet Cong and the lack of support from traditional U.S. allies and the American media.

But even as McNamara's rigid idea of systems analysis died in the jungles of Vietnam, the 1960s and 1970s saw the rise of a new class of tools for business that reflected a passion for quantitative analysis.

When IBM's 360 mainframe became the first affordable corporate computer—affordable if you were a big corporation—computerized databases quickly followed. One of them was

SABRE, which American Airlines used to manage its reservations. This was a transformative event for commercial airlines.

Then, in 1978, analytics went small. Dan Bricklin and Bob Frankston co-created VisiCalc for the Apple II home computer. VisiCalc became an instant success and sold over a million copies during its product run. But VisiCalc's reign of glory was short, as rival Lotus 1-2-3 came to own the 1980s. Lotus couldn't hold its position, either, for next up was Microsoft's Excel. Released in 1984, Excel was originally written for the 512K Apple "Fat" Macintosh. It may be hard to believe now, but many people bought a Mac just to use a product created by Bill Gates.

Up at the higher (that is, more costly) realms of business computing, data management systems became a huge commercial success, creating one of technology's first billionaires, Oracle's Larry Ellison. The use of these tools created yet more billionaires, such as Wal-Mart's Sam Walton, who could thereby discern what was selling on every Wal-Mart shelf in the world. Slower to use these tools were many older discount retailers, such as Sears, which went into relative decline.

By 1989, Howard Dresner, an analyst for the Gartner Group, coined the term "business intelligence" to describe how fact-based support systems were even capable of making predictions. Sam Walton used this knowledge to stock his stores, city by city, and to price Wal-Mart products based on likely customer response.

The new millennium brought an explosion of faster and cheaper analytical tools, touching every aspect of our digital lives: point-of-sale, online sales, medical records, social networks, and mobile apps. As we've moved from measuring data in kilobytes to measuring it in zettabytes, our ability to create predictive models and use information as a strategic asset has increased exponentially. Costs have dropped exponentially, also. Who in Robert McNamara's day could have predicted that a media company with a goofy name, Google, would build the first planetary supercomputer?

While today's technology and advanced analytics may seem centuries removed from Fredrick Taylor and his stopwatch, many of his theories of business and management still dominate business discourse. Even today, most managers are driven by the beliefs popularized by Taylor and McNamara. These include a cold-eyed emphasis on efficiency and the elimination of waste, a secret belief in top-down management, and an almost reverent focus on metrics and bottom lines.

BACKLASH GROWS AGAINST LIFELESS RATIONALITY

Even as scientific management and its variations have flourished over the last hundred years, a parallel backlash against what many people see as lifeless rationality and ruthless efficiency has emerged. The yin and yang of effective management has always been about the search for the right spot between data truth and human truth. At any given time, academic fashions and cultural winds will tilt more one direction than in another. One year, a hard-edge concept like return on assets will dominate management thinking and magazine articles. The next year it will be a soft-edge craze like the war for talent. Of course it's pointless to argue whether hard or soft, yin or yang, Mars or Venus, is superior. Both are always needed. The best companies master the conundrum of embracing hard-edge discipline while also avoiding the more extreme Tayloristic dangers inherent in hard-edge-only analysis.

Taylor's flaw was a fatal one. He saw employees as lazy, uneducated, and lacking curiosity. He urged managers to think of them as replaceable components. He promoted an extreme level of predictability and managerial control that made the working life of employees both menial and tedious, even as it raised their pay. Taylor saw the trade-off as worth it. So did Henry Ford, who would never forgive his well-paid factory workers for not being more grateful when they began to unionize in the 1930s.

Perceiving the downside of Taylor's quantitative-only-driven management, James Hartness, a mechanical engineer and machine tool inventor, encouraged a better relationship with workers in *The Human Factor in Works Management*, published in 1912. Likewise, Henri Fayol, a French mining engineer, developed a general theory of business that was in direct opposition to Taylor's scientific management. Calling his theory "administrative management," Fayol promoted equity, team spirit, and unity.

As economic conditions deteriorated across the United States in the 1930s, Hollywood joined in bashing the machine rationality encouraged by Taylor. In 1936's *Modern Times*, Charlie Chaplin's iconic Little Tramp bumbles his way through the machine-paced realities created by modern industrialization.

But the tyranny of efficiency and execution wasn't limited to the blue-collar workforce. Chaplin's hapless factory worker can be seen as a forerunner to the 1950s "organization man," a term coined by sociologist William Whyte. The dehumanization of labor wasn't that far removed from the dehumanization of white-collar work. Much like the assembly-line worker, the office-bound manager was choked by processes and tethered to mechanisms of rationality and efficiency. Sapped of initiative and creativity, many executives were experiencing the same cog-in-the-machine tedium as their counterparts on the factory floor.

In response to a growing corporate malaise, Abraham Maslow published his hierarchy of needs, a taxonomy of fundamental human desires, in his 1954 book *Motivation and Personality*. Providing a framework for gaining employees' commitment, Maslow's theories painted people as much more complex than Taylor's "replaceable components." Instead of being happy to just collect a paycheck, the employees Maslow depicted were longing for higher, more abstract levels of reward such as self-esteem and self-actualization.

But the image of the unhappy organization man wasn't solely propagated by social scientists like Whyte and Maslow. Novelists portrayed work in large organizations as mind numbing and monotonous. American literature has long portrayed corporate executives and managers as somber drones crushed under the weight of empiric minutiae and authoritarian hierarchy. Notably, the writings of Sloan Wilson, Richard Yates, and John Cheever depict men for whom the grind of business eventually leads to alienation, detachment, and alcoholism.

Who, then, would guess the answer to America's corporate rut in the 1970s would come from Japan, a country steeped in traditional and hierarchical culture?

HOW EDWARDS DEMING FOUND THE MAGICAL BALANCE

Japan's rapid rise from the ashes of World War II was a shocker to American business managers and investors. The rising sun hit full force during a period of American stagnation in the 1970s and early 1980s. So it was even more of a surprise when it turned out that Japan's most influential management guru was a small-town American, a man born in Iowa and educated at the University of Wyoming.

His name was W. Edwards Deming. Though he had once taught statistics, Deming's love—his religion, almost—became quality. Deming was able to show that an emphasis on quality would cut expenses and increase productivity. The big surprise turned out to be the way it would also lift employee spirits, reduce alienation, and elevate a company's market share and brand.

Deming's ideas about quality were so good that most American businesses refused to believe him. His ideas ran *completely* counter to Western logic. They seemed about as far-fetched and fantastical as time travel or perpetual motion. How could quality *cut* costs?

But you have to start somewhere, said Deming, and quality was the magic key that would open the door to other advantages. Deming's best-known disciple was Sony's co-founder Akio Morito, who led Sony to electronics dominance in the 1980s. But Deming's influence is seen even today. Toyota takes quality so seriously that it invests billions of dollars in its internationally famous University of Toyota where employees become students and learn the deeper philosophies of quality and continuous improvement before they set foot on the factory floor. Deming was one of those rare geniuses who saw the magical power of harmonizing the hard and soft edges.

The 1980s also saw the publication of two truly landmark books. Tom Peters and Bob Waterman's *In Search of Excellence* and Terry Deal and Allan Kennedy's *Corporate Cultures: The Rights and Rituals of Corporate Life* were both published in 1982. These books challenged the idea of business as exclusively a rational enterprise and promoted the importance of organizational culture, organizational health, and humanistic management. Both books debunked the cult of pure rationality—blasting those managers who always defaulted to an empirical business model—and called for a greater emphasis on creativity, autonomy, and the celebration of ideas.

In particular, *In Search of Excellence* helped set the stage for future management experts like Warren Bennis, Rosabeth Moss Kanter, Gary Hamel, Jim Collins, and Patrick Lencioni. By highlighting past managerial failures, these authors have been instrumental in bringing leadership, teamwork, and innovation to the forefront.

In my view, however, the most important managerial book of the last twenty years is *The Innovator's Dilemma*. Written by Harvard Business School professor Clayton Christensen, *The Innovator's Dilemma* shows how relentless hard-edge rationality and fixation on numbers can blind managers to the innovation happening all around them, often right at their feet.

Let me stop here to answer a question that I expect many readers will have.

Why all the history? Can't we just get on to the soft edges and the promise of lasting success therein? Well, sure, but I think it is important to show that management thinkers, corporate leaders, and even novelists have long debated the proper roles of the hard and soft edges in human organizations. These are legitimate debates, by the way. The proper balance between hard and soft is always changing. Some organizational challenges will demand solutions that are mostly on the hard edge; others are primarily soft problems.

To demonstrate the balance and flexibility required, I need to return to the history. I've described the extraordinary gains in productivity from Taylor's theories, which were proven on the factory floor by his foremost disciple, Henry Ford, in the 1910s and early 1920s.

But now to the rest of the story. Taylorism didn't suffice as Ford's sustainable edge. The other automakers soon caught up. Then they kept going. Alfred Sloan, the CEO of General Motors during its mid-twentieth-century ascendance, ran circles around the aging and cranky Henry Ford, both in organization and marketing. Ford got stuck in his ways. He became so angry about unions—how dare his well-paid workers betray him like that!—that he doubled down on dictatorial control. Suddenly Ford's assembly lines were seen as an evil force. Ford could never accept that he'd gone from national hero to national goat. He died a bewildered and unhappy man. Times had changed. Rigid Taylorism had stopped being an advantage.

The lesson: Business evolution will always change the relative value of hard and soft skills. But the hard edge is more vulnerable to change because it is the side more influenced by technology and numbers.

HARD-EDGE ADVANTAGES ARE WONDERFUL BUT FLEETING

Don't misunderstand me: I'm not disputing the importance of the hard edge. Apple, a brand with soft-edge hippie roots that border on a quasi-religion, has taken operational hard-edge excellence to a level never seen before. Companies like Siemens, Novartis, and Citigroup are cutting billions a year in costs by embracing cloud, virtualization, and other new technologies.

Look closely at the leader in any industry that makes or moves things—companies like Samsung, Wal-Mart, FedEx, and

Amazon—and you'll see a strong correlation between hard-edge supply-chain mastery and category leadership.

Yes, numbers work. But their utility isn't the problem.

Instead, the problem in business today is that our methods and tools continue to be strongly biased toward the hard edge, even though the hard edge cannot promise a sustainable market advantage on its own. Today the lure of data and analytics seems irresistible. We are attracted to what we can measure. We feel safety in data. We can tinker with analytics. We can clock the speed. We can record throughput and utilization rates in a way that Fredrick Taylor and Henry Ford never could have imagined.

But those hard-edge advantages get competed away, and faster than before.

As tools of the digital age—bandwidth, storage, and computation power—continue to trend in the direction of infinite and free, they also level the playing field. The arms race is over. Everybody can be fully armed. This exponential increase in the number of people who have access to the same tools and knowledge creates enormous market shifts and new, disruptive trends.

Last decade, manufacturing and supply chains were revolutionized by low-cost, mostly Asian labor. This decade, it's robotics. Today's disruption for the knowledge industry isn't Asian outsourcing, it's competing against free labor. The encyclopedia companies weren't brought down by low-cost labor and low-cost production from China and India. They were killed by Wikipedia, by a volunteer effort.

So no matter how fast, efficient, and low-cost your company becomes, technology and competition will cook up a way to leapfrog you with products that are even better and cheaper. And with today's technology, customers can instantly compare price, features, quality, and service. The normal innovation-to-commoditization life cycle is shortening. Hard-edge mastery, therefore, is no longer enough. Think of hard-edge mastery as table stakes—necessary to compete, but not sufficient to win.

Consider the following: only seventy-four of the original five hundred companies in the S&P Index were still on the list forty years later, a mortality rate of more than ten per year. The average life span of an S&P 500 company has steadily decreased from more than fifty years to less than twenty-five. Looking forward, it's likely that only about one-third of today's major corporations will survive as significant businesses during the next quarter-century.[1]

Considering these realities, the natural temptation is to hunker down and stick to the quantifiable, the rational, and the provable—the stuff I call the hard edge. Your investors will practically demand you do so. But here is where the hard edge gets slippery. The trajectory and pace of hard-side evolution is mostly outside our control. If anyone controls it, it is a handful of engineers at places like Qualcomm, ARM, and Intel, who make chips for our phones, tablets, and laptops. Or a few engineers at Google, Cisco, or Huawei, working day and night to expand the Internet's bandwidth capacity. You get the idea. Unless you are deep into the research of computer science or fiber-optic code division multiplexing, the odds are you don't control the pace of technological evolution. Therefore, while you should always try to optimize your company's hard-edge advantages, you can't predict how long they'll last. You can only adapt when the technology changes. But so can others.

So, to conclude, hard-edge advantages are necessary but fleeting. At worst, hard-edge success can also trap you into legacy technology, techniques, and thinking.

THE SOFT EDGE IS THE KEY TO
ENDURING COMPANY HEALTH

Having assessed many great companies and superb leaders over my years at Forbes, as well as while researching this book, I can make three statements with confidence:

- Great, enduring organizations are masters at both the hard and soft edges.
- Top performance depends on finding the right balance of hard and soft skills for any given situation.
- On balance, the soft edge is gaining currency. In this tough, global Great Reset economy, mastery of the oft-neglected soft edge will become as critical as (or even more critical than) mastery of the hard edge.

It's now time to dive deeper into the soft edge. I've defined five core pillars. The next five chapters cover each one in detail.

3

▲

Trust

The Force Multiplier of All Things Good

Not long ago at the Four Seasons Hotel in Palo Alto, California, I overheard a conversation between two Silicon Valley venture capitalists. Both were thirty-something men with Stanford and Harvard degrees. They wore slim-cut tailored blue suits and open-collared shirts, the very models of modern major moguls. I paraphrase:

So the cloud strategy is a Trojan Horse, ya think?

So totally true, dude. The game is still the same. Lock customers in!

Let me pose a question. Are the men's snarky banter and predatory tactics related? The first time I heard a serious businessperson start every sentence with the word *So*, it was during the ethically dodgy dot-com boom in the late 1990s. That's also the time, if my ear and memory are correct, when investment bankers on Wall Street started aping the linguistics of teenaged girls from shopping malls near Los Angeles, a patois captured by Frank Zappa in his 1980s song, "Valley Girl."

What explains this strange turn of language? One theory is that the 1980s television hit *Seinfeld* introduced a mocking irony into the culture and language. It caught on with tail-end baby boomers and Gen Xers sick of their elders' self-importance. By the 1990s this "been there, done that, got the T-shirt" worldly cynicism had become the hip lingo of the business and financial worlds on the East and West Coasts.

But snarky lingo also serves remarkably well to trivialize the gravity of bad behavior. A Merrill Lynch dot-com analyst, educated at Yale, spoke for all aspiring cool kids when he e-mailed: "LFMN at $4. I can't believe what a POS [piece of sh*t] that thing is." The analyst, of course, had recommended the stock he was dissing privately. He was signaling his fellow cool kids what he really thought of LFMN and the gullible masses that bought on his recommendation. *Wink, wink.* In the new millennium, the hippest moguls mocked and snickered, blogged and tweeted. To speak with any degree of straightforward earnestness was a social faux pas that marked you as a Boy Scout or a dork.

So what shall we make, in our own snarky day, of a CEO and executive VP who say things like:

"We're in business for one reason. And that's to answer yes when someone calls us and asks, 'Am I going to be okay?'"

"These are our friends, our families, our clients. I always felt that if you're going to make a living in this community, you've got to give back."

"You're always on a mountain when you climb."

I decided to take a closer look at this self-consciously unhip company—Northwestern Mutual, a 157-year-old, $25 billion-revenue-per-year insurance and financial services company based in Milwaukee, Wisconsin.

TRUST IS WORTH $25 BILLION IN SALES

The first thing I noticed was the ribbons. Half of Milwaukee's BMO Harris Bradley Center—the city's largest indoor arena and home to the Milwaukee Bucks professional basketball team—buzzed with Northwestern Mutual financial reps walking the arena floor, jabbering with colleagues, shaking hands. Hanging from their suit jacket lapels were ribbons and more ribbons signifying their achievements for the year. Several men and women were walking about with ribbons hanging and flapping all the way to their pants cuffs.

It was shortly before 8 AM—apparently by some legal decree the start of the Midwestern business day—when the 8,400 financial reps took their seats. Spouses and children added another 3,000 people in the audience. Promptly at 8 AM a middle-aged woman with Wisconsin blonde hair and a red dress took the stage to sing the "Star-Spangled Banner," followed by "God Bless America."

After some announcements, and a respite of oddball entertainment from a magician and a country guitarist who played Queen's "Bohemian Rhapsody"—quite a feat for one guitarist—Northwestern Mutual CEO John Schlifske took the stage. A big man who looks like an ex–Green Bay Packer, he began to speak about Northwestern Mutual's values. Suddenly I had a vision of being transported back in time—to a mid-twentieth-century America, when business salesmen (nearly all men then) would read books like Napoleon Hill's *Think and Grow Rich*, Dale Carnegie's *How to Win Friends and Influence People*, and Norman Vincent Peale's *The Power of Positive Thinking*. The language of those books was wholesome and wholly without irony. They sound like a foreign language now. But this is the language of Northwestern Mutual's CEO, John Schlifske.

It almost seems too earnest. Where are the sardonic punch lines? In New York or San Francisco, a CEO might be howled and tweeted off the stage if he talked like this. Or maybe not. Schlifske, his company, and his financial reps in their goofy ribbons and plain suits represent an ethic and spirit that many of us laugh at with our cool kid friends but secretly miss: trust and earnestness. In a culture of rising cynicism and distrust, Northwestern Mutual dares to be the old-fashioned George Baileys of the financial services industry. Steady as she goes for over 157 years, always taking the call when the accident occurs or the cancer diagnosis comes in, this company has become the largest life insurer in the largest insurance market in the world, the United States.

In the movie *It's a Wonderful Life*, Jimmy Stewart's character, banker George Bailey, never got rich. But many of those Northwestern Mutual financial reps have become middle-class millionaires by showing up, sticking to it, and mainly trusting.

TRUST IS THE FOUNDATION OF GREATNESS

Trust has many definitions, but I like to think of it as confidence in a person, group, or system when there's risk and uncertainty. When we trust, we feel comfortable that the other party will serve our needs fairly and competently. There is no guarantee our trust will be returned. Trust always involves the risk of betrayal—the possibility that our trust will be taken advantage of by another person or organization.

But we do it anyway. Trust is the risk we must take to move ahead. Trust is the key to relationship building. Trust is the price we pay when we want to enable engagement, creativity, and great work. As Warren Bennis so aptly put it, "Trust is the lubrication that makes it possible for organizations to work."[1]

For organizations, trust has two primary dimensions. One is the *external* trust between an organization and its customers. Will a company stand behind its products? If something goes wrong, will its people do the right thing? Since the beginning of time, business has depended on external trust and goodwill in order for commerce to flourish. In fact, the word *credit* has its origins in the Latin word *credere:* "To give trust to, to have trust for."

The second dimension is the *internal* trust among employees, managers, and top-level management. Embodying organizational systems and culture, this form of trust is created through management's credibility and the respect with which employees feel they're treated. Not surprisingly, this dimension of trust is the defining principle of great workplaces.

By now, we're all familiar with the many published lists of the best and greatest places to work. The magazines that publish these lists love to show off perks like jars of free gourmet cookies, espresso machines, trampolines, and climbing walls. This is an unfortunate image, as it leads readers to believe that a great workplace somehow equates to a Club Med. I've talked with a number of companies that routinely make these great-places lists, however, and I want to correct that impression. Those perks are fun—and they certainly attract magazine readers—but they're marginally important, at best. The real foundation of a "best places" workplace is dirt simple. It's trust.

As Jim Davis, the chief marketing officer of SAS Institute, a data analytics software firm that always makes those best-places lists, told me: "Magazines like to play up the benefits. It's always a picture of people jumping in a room full of balls or something. But that's a fraction of what makes a best place to work."

What are the important issues? Davis answers with a set of questions. "Does the management convey strategic direction? Is there room for advancement? Have you created an environment that lets employees do their best work? That's where innovation comes in."

Tom Georgens, the CEO of NetApp, asserted something similar: "Magazines want to hear about these great perks, about pet massages and free food. But we don't have anything like that. Which is fine, because the primary concern is really around trust and building a strong, supportive culture. So, for us, we're not a great place to work because we goof off. In fact, I make it very clear that the culture of trust that gets us on those lists also lets us win in the marketplace. No company was a great place to work the day before they went out of business."

Trust may seem like a fuzzy concept when it comes to financial value. But as research and market results have proven, dignity, respect, pride—and the sense of trust those feelings engender—create real-world returns and measurable increases in productivity.

BUILDING TRUST IS STRATEGIC—AND RARE

In any economic climate, building trust is not just a nice thing to do—it's a strategic thing to do. You can make a strong business case for investing in trust. Trust underlies effective working relationships. It improves group effectiveness and organizational performance. It underpins organizational credibility and resilience. All these factors contribute to creating a lasting competitive advantage—because trust attracts talent, strengthens partnerships, and retains customers.

Now, these aren't just my opinions. Decades of research have highlighted the central role of trust in organizations. At the micro level, trust has been linked to outcomes like employee satisfaction, effort and performance, office citizenship, collaboration and teamwork, leadership effectiveness, and negotiation success.[2] At the macro level, trust has been credited as a driving force in organizational change and survival, entrepreneurship, strategic alliances, mergers and acquisitions, and even national economic health.[3]

Pause here: trust appears to underlie nearly every aspect of managing a business. So much so, you'd think building trust would be at the top of every leader's to-do list or tip sheet.

But no.

Trust in companies is significantly lower than just a generation ago. According to the latest Edelman Trust Barometer, a comprehensive yearly survey of public sentiment, only 19 percent of people trust business leaders to make ethical or moral decisions. Sounds pretty bad, right? It gets worse. Only 18 percent of those surveyed trust business leaders to even tell the truth. And while misconduct on Wall Street surprises no one, only one in five Americans, according to a recent Gallup poll, trust their primary bank. That's about half the level it was before the 2008–2009 financial crisis.[4]

Is it too much to say that trust has reached a low point? Maybe. But trust certainly has a long way to go to make a comeback. Oddly enough, the perks aren't helping. Evidence suggests we remain suspicious of companies that talk a good game about trust and even back it up, at a surface level, with perks such as foosball tables, espresso bars, maternity leave, flex time, and even opportunities to work from home.

Those things are nice, but they don't appear to build trust. What does?

"When information can flow easily and it's expected to flow easily—*that's* what builds trust. It's the substrate for all the interactions in a company," Jay Kidd, chief technical officer of

NetApp, explained. "Then you can have fluid teams because organizational boundaries are extremely porous and political fiefdoms don't form."

Kidd's colleague, NetApp's co-founder Dave Hitz, put it a slightly more illustrative way: "Think back in your life. It might have been a sports team, or a particular small group. Think of a time when you accomplished more than any other time in your life. Why did that happen? I've been on teams that worked hard and didn't get results: goals weren't met. And I've been on teams that were working hard but they were having fun, people respected and trusted each other, and they did amazing stuff. It's not a 10 or 20 percent difference, when you look at it. It's an enormous difference, maybe two or three times greater in terms of the results."

That's not marginal. It's transformative. And it emanates from this deeper definition of trust. A number of great books have been written that extol the virtues and benefits of trust, from Edward Marshall's *Building Trust at the Speed of Change* to Stephen M. R. Covey's *The Speed of Trust*. Covey, in my opinion, offers one of the best ways to illustrate the power of trust. When trust is low, he explains, it places a tax on every transaction, communication, and decision. This brings down speed and increases costs. The lower the trust, the higher the tax. On the other hand, individuals and organizations that foster a culture of trust get a performance multiplier—a dividend in Covey's analogy. Trust, in this sense, greatly improves the chances that employees will succeed in their daily interactions with customers and with each other.

TRUST IS THE BEDROCK OF INNOVATION

If I haven't yet convinced you that trust is worth the risk, let me try a little harder: let's talk about innovation. Today, innovation is important, right? It's on lips, minds, and PowerPoint decks everywhere.

By now, thanks to people like Clayton Christensen, it's conventional wisdom that organizational culture is a key to innovation. More and more, the best-places-to-work methodology correlates tightly with companies that are also innovative, and especially innovative over the long term. Why? Because trust has implications for knowledge sharing and learning outcomes. Shared interpersonal trust among employees facilitates engagement, learning, and experimentation, all of which are vital to innovation.[5] In fact, a PricewaterhouseCoopers study of corporate innovation among the Financial Times 100 showed that the number one differentiating factor between the top innovators and the bottom innovators was trust.[6]

Ideas can't be pulled from heads—they must be offered willingly. And, yes, those great ideas are only given to those we trust. Not surprisingly then, creativity and innovation are likely to flourish in climates of trust and wither when distrust is rampant.

Externally, trust and transparency are more critical now than ever. According to the Edelman survey, for the first time in history, impressions of openness, sincerity, and authenticity are more important to corporate reputation in the United States than the quality of products and services.[7] This means trust affects tangible things such as supply chain partnerships and long-term customer loyalty. People want to partner with you because they've heard you're a credible company built through a culture of trust. In a sense, being a great company to work for also makes you a great company to work with.

And when customers trust an organization, they're more likely to have a stronger impulse to purchase products, as well as have a higher level of customer satisfaction. They're also more likely to cooperate with your organization by sharing personal information or contributing to a marketing study. When your customers trust you, you can charge higher prices than your competitors do, offer a higher-profit-margin feature set than your customers are looking for, and require a longer wait for delivery—and they'll *still* buy from you.[8]

Simply put, trust sells.

And yet, when you look at every study, every poll and indicator, it suggests that trust has fallen through the floor. Therefore, for the handful of players in any industry that have built a culture of trust, it's almost a magical quality. Trust is one of those soft-edge advantages that separates the enduring organizations from those that may produce a flashy or convenient product but lack credibility and authenticity.

TROUBLE IN PARADISE: NETAPP

NetApp, the $6.5 billion vendor of computer network storage solutions, occupies a small world of elite companies. It manages to make both the *Forbes* list of the World's Most Innovative Companies *and* a number of the best-places-to-work lists. Tom Mendoza, president of NetApp from 2000 to 2008, was instrumental in building NetApp's culture on the paired principles of innovation and trust. I had a chance to ask him, as well as current CEO Tom Georgens, how they did it and how they maintain it.

"You quickly find out if you truly have a great culture, if you have that essential trust, when you go through tough times," Tom Mendoza said. "Anybody can have a great culture when things go well. But when times get tough, you find out if you're willing to live your values."

Being named one of the best places to work is always a point of pride at NetApp. But what happens when the top award comes just a month before a large layoff?

"The year we were named the number one best place to work was, ironically, very tough for us," said Georgens. "In January we ended up number one. In February, we were doing a reduction in force. And we thought to ourselves, could the timing be any worse?"

Let's stop here and assess. NetApp's financial model was never in danger. Started in 1992, the company had grown to nearly $4 billion in revenue by 2009 and was still profitable. The threat, rather, was to NetApp's culture. Should that have mattered? Was a soft-edge culture threat (as opposed to a hard-edge financial threat) worthy of top-brass attention? A shareholder might say no. A board director might say no. The financial press might say no. But NetApp's leaders disagree. They believe culture is the very source of NetApp's ongoing innovation, its ability to compete with both larger, entrenched companies as well as numerous Silicon Valley start-ups. Making the best places to work list, therefore, is a predictor of future innovative capacity. Thus the question, "How do you carry a great culture through those tough times?" is not really about making a list. It's about making a future.

"Here's what I think we did right," Mendoza offered. "We thought long and hard about what percentage of the company the reduction would affect. We decided to be aggressive in our forecast, so we wouldn't have to disclose more bad news later, which is how a lot of companies do it.

"Pay special heed to how you treat the people who leave," he continued. "You have to be fair, you have to be clear. You should do it as quickly as possible. You don't want to drag it out.

We made sure the people affected understood it was an economic situation, not dissatisfaction with them as employees. We were very clear about that messaging."

But the *way* the message gets delivered is as important as the content of the message. Which means, when you're faced with a tough economic climate and the necessity of letting people go, you need to be transparent: you need to provide those affected with a face-to-face opportunity to ask questions.

"We got together as executive teams and we traveled the world," Mendoza explained. "We made it to 80 percent of our employee offices within a one-week period. Everybody on the executive team said, 'Let's get in front of our employees, tell them what we're doing, and tell them what we believe the future looks like. Let them ask us anything they want.'

"You know, what's astounding to me," he added, "when we had to do it in 2009, there were very few questions about why. Instead, it was all about, 'What can we do to help this company win?' We left those meetings energized. In fact, we said, 'You know, we should do this every year or every other year regardless of the economic situation.' It's just such a good employee communication vehicle."

A commitment to culture, and its implicit emphasis on trust, really does come through the loudest during hard times. For Tom Mendoza and the rest of the leadership at NetApp, that culture has been very deliberately built. But it's still a challenge to maintain it through good and bad, through leadership changes and corporate reorganizations. "People ask me all the time, 'How do you keep the culture?'" Mendoza said. "I tell them, 'It's hard work.' If you claim people are your most important asset, act like it. Think like it. Spend time on it. Get in front of your people so they know what you're saying is true."

DOES TRUST STILL WORK WHEN SALES REJECTION IS THE NORM?

Let me offer a personal story: I was in my mid-twenties, a few years out of college, and I had gone back to my hometown in North Dakota to visit my parents and high school friends. It was a warm feeling to be home, to see the people with whom I had grown up. My other feeling was relief. I was glad to be out of California for a few days, glad to be free of the nonstop gray drizzle of anxiety that haunts a life not going anywhere. I didn't have a steady job yet. Now and then I would get a freelance ad copywriting job. But when the chips were down, I would take anything for a paycheck. Temporary typing jobs. Security guard work at a trucking company. Washing dishes in a company cafeteria.

But at least I wasn't selling insurance. I hadn't sunk that low.

I still remember vividly the following scene: I was standing around the concession area of a basketball game with some old high school friends. We were laughing it up, retelling old war stories with new embellishments. About a hundred feet away was Andy Anderson, who was part of our group back in the high school days. But Anderson had a new look about him. He was wearing real grown-up clothes, his hair was trimmed, and he was clean-shaven. He walked toward our group with a friendly look about him.

"Oh, oh!" said Stroh, one of our laughing group. "Look out. Here comes Andy Anderson to sell us insurance!"

The mortification! The embarrassment! To be outed as the insurance salesman before you even get to say hello. I decided then and there that being an insurance salesman had to be the most embarrassing of jobs. I might have sunk to the level of being a security guard and dishwasher, I told myself, but as least I'm not some Earnest Andy who hits up his old friends on term life insurance.

Decades later, I am at ease in corporate life myself. I wear pressed slacks, at least in public, and I try to greet my colleagues and customers with an earnest and friendly demeanor. But, Lord, I still can't imagine what it must be like to sell insurance. What kind of person can do this, to face rejection every day? To build a life and a career on commission sales, selling a product most people would rather not think about?

I put this question to a highly successful Northwestern Mutual managing partner. We were enjoying a fine lunch at the Capital Grille in Milwaukee. What's it like to sell insurance, I asked. How do you overcome rejection? How can you tell if a new recruit is going to succeed or fail?

Scott Theodore jumped in. Theodore is a Northwestern Mutual managing partner out of Denver. He's built his own business to the point where it now supports 120 financial advisers and 32 employees. "I was not looking to be in sales," he started. "My background is a degree in petroleum engineering and a degree in geology. I moved to Colorado to be in the oil business back in '87. A couple years later my company was sold. It was a national oil and gas company, and nine thousand people lost their jobs. I had just gotten married, bought a house. So I got called on by a Northwestern Mutual rep and when I told him that I might be losing my job, he gave my name to a recruiter and they tricked me into this deal." Theodore laughed.

"If you didn't want to be in sales," I asked, "why did you do it?"

"I went to five of my closest friends, and four of them were already Northwestern clients," Theodore said. "The way they talked about the company in reverent terms, almost like it was a national treasure. I'm like, 'Really? This is just an insurance company.' But I met with the managing partner. He gave me a picture of what that future could look like."

HOW TRUST CREATES GRIT (AND VICE VERSA)

A picture of a great future is one thing, I think. But it still comes down to those dreaded phone calls. Earlier in the day, Todd Schoon, who is Northwestern Mutual's executive vice president of agencies—which makes Schoon the company evangelist who oversees the company's national sales force—stood before the BMO Harris Bradley Center audience and reminded the reps of the simple mathematics that determine success or failure at Northwestern Mutual. Schoon called it the 10-3-1 rule. Make ten calls to get three meetings. Out of the three meetings, on average, get one new customer.

Trust the process, Schoon, said. Make those ten calls.

At lunch, Scott Theodore expanded on Schoon's formula: "Each new rep has a mentor that works with them. The two meet three times a week for ten minutes a day to ask, 'What did you do yesterday and what are your goals today?' Also, once you're in the business for a month, you meet monthly with seven or eight of your peers who have been in the business about the same time as you. Each month they talk about their activity, production results and goals. How many calls did you make? How many appointments did you set? How many referrals did you get? We have a point system that shows any gaps. Say if you called a lot of people and didn't get a lot of appointments. We know there's a part of the sales process that's broken. We can work on your phoning language or maybe the referral wasn't as strong as it could've been. Let's work at pre-engaging that appointment. We can see that before the meeting even happens."

It's painstakingly hard to onboard a new Northwestern Mutual rep. Some of the best-looking recruits, at least on paper, wash out because they can't or won't make the calls. "It takes grit to succeed," said Theodore. "Grit and trust. They have to trust the process." Echoing Theodore, Conrad York (Northwestern Mutual's vice president of marketing) added, "This is a simple business, but a hard business. Trust gives you conviction. Conviction gives you commitment."

Northwestern Mutual spends an average of $20,000 to onboard each new rep, one West Coast leader told me. But four out of five will fail, which is to say, they will not commit. Most of them fail within the first three months. That's $100,000 invested in each new rep who makes it past the three-month mark and is willing to dig in for the long haul. After that, it takes from several months to a few years for most reps to get a decent income stream established. And once the income starts rolling in, the rep must avoid the temptation to spend too much of it. The successful reps like Scott Theodore have learned to plow their income back into building an office with assistants to book calls and other reps to build even more income. The goal is to build a business within the business.

Through diligence and patience—and never fearing to make those ten phone calls a day per Schoon's formula—a successful Northwestern rep can clear several hundred thousand dollars a year or more by the midpoint of a productive career. And it gets better after that. Some top Northwestern reps truly are the millionaires next door.

But for that happy result to occur, it's not only the sales process that has to be trusted. If Northwestern Mutual itself isn't trusted, none of this will work at the rep level. This is where the facts say Northwestern Mutual has three significant trust advantages. One is its sheer longevity. The company has been around since 1857—a period that covers a civil war, two world wars, and two dozen recessions. Two, Northwestern Mutual is owned by its customers. "We can afford to make payouts that will hurt our earnings in the short run," said CEO John Schlifske. "A shareholder-owned insurance company will always face a trade-off between customer interests and shareholder interests." A third advantage, and related to the second, is the strength of Northwestern Mutual's balance sheet. The company has $215 billion of assets and $1.5 trillion in life insurance contracts. This 7:1 ratio of insurance contracts to assets is among the lowest— thus the safest—in the life insurance industry.

So when I talk about trust as a soft-edge advantage, it really means two things. The first is the internal cultural trust between company managers and employees. *Can you trust your career with this company?* The second is external and applies to the trust between the company and its customers. *Will the company be there when I need it to be there?*

Northwestern Mutual has spent 157 years trying to figure this out. The results speak for themselves. The company has done an admirable job of building trust in both vectors: internal and external.

How important is trust? Think of it this way. Insurance is both a big business—as shown by Northwestern Mutual's $25 billion in annual revenue—and an algorithmic one based on actuarial odds. You might imagine, therefore, that some 800-math-SAT wizards in Silicon Valley or on Wall Street could disrupt the insurance business by eliminating the need for Northwestern Mutual's middlemen, that army of George Baileys in their plain suits and ribbons. But this has not happened. You see, the sharpest brains in the world have not figured out a way to beat trust.

HOW TO BUILD A CULTURE OF TRUST, INSIDE AND OUT

Understanding and managing trust—how it's built, supported, and even recovered—is a critical competency for any organization. A trustworthy organization is one that operates effectively, acts with concern for the interests of its stakeholders, and conducts itself according to principles of honesty and fairness.

In trustworthy organizations, coworkers believe that others are ethical and the organization as a whole is true to its values and commitments. Jennifer Brase, vice president of diversity and inclusion at Northwestern Mutual, has turned down numerous job offers because of how much she trusts her employer: "I've been recruited by several other companies, but the reason I don't move is because I know Northwestern has my back. This is such a regulated industry. It's hard for any single person to keep up with the compliance issues. But Northwestern does, and they watch out for us."

How can you create an environment that engenders this kind of loyalty and trust? How do you build a culture that can perform in headwinds as well as tailwinds? The recipe for developing those things is not as elusive as you may think. The very first step is understanding that trust isn't based on what the company is doing; it's based on what its leaders are doing.

Trustworthy Leadership

Engaging in moral behavior is one the easiest ways for any leader to demonstrate trustworthiness, while also creating a trusting climate. If you're a leader—whether a CEO or a helpful coworker that others turn to for guidance—you need to understand that all your actions are being interpreted by employees and team members. So living and breathing those deep core values, as Tom Mendoza and John Schlifske do, is critical. If there's one gospel or guiding light here, it's that trustworthy organizations and insincere leadership are incongruous. Leaders must, as the saying goes, walk the talk.

Back in the 1990s, I spent a week on the road with Microsoft's Bill Gates. He was touring cities to drum up enthusiasm for Microsoft's latest version of Office, then called Office 4.0. One late night, as we flew in the coach section of a Delta flight between Boston and New York, I asked Gates, "You're worth billions. Why are you flying coach?"

"I defer to Steve Ballmer on this," Gates said. "Ballmer says Microsoft employees can fly first class if they want, but it's on their own dime. Microsoft pays for coach. Microsoft pays for Hiltons, not Four Seasons. Microsoft pays for a Ford rental, not a Cadillac. I have to abide by Ballmer's cost limits, or no one will."

Unfortunately, many of us can't seem to shake the top-down model of management that abides by the notion that authority—and a glitzy show of authority—creates trust. In reality, trust creates authority.

A big part of realizing this change is to cultivate a strong sense of self-awareness. Do you stop to consider how your actions, including your words, affect others, or do you function in a cloud of self-absorbed cluelessness? It shouldn't surprise you, but your answer is closely tied to your current trust-building capacity. Those who operate with thoughtful self-reflection enable trust. Those who don't undercut it.

Here are some other things leaders can do to gain trust. One is to demonstrate real concern. We tend to trust people we believe will care about our welfare. So demonstrate to others that you'll do the right thing for them even if it's uncomfortable or puts you at risk. Another behavior that helps build trust is being predictable. Think about it—unpredictability is anathema to the concept of trust. The couches of psychotherapists are filled with people whose parents were unpredictable, often because of addictions. An important part of predictability is integrity. By this, I mean honoring your word.

By the way, predictability in the matter of trust is different from predictability in tactics. Good leaders and coaches will shake things up. Legendary basketball coach Phil Jackson once held a Chicago Bulls practice in the dark. He wanted to see how well his players really knew the plays he was teaching.

But good leadership isn't just a list of things you can do, and trust isn't just an atmosphere in which we operate. Trust is something we do, something we make. "I believe in leadership rather than management," Tom Mendoza of NetApp explained. "You can be loud, you can be quiet, but leadership is what you are, not what you say. So my overriding principle of leadership is people don't care what you know unless they know that you care. All industries have one thing in common, which is people come through for their leaders not because they're afraid, not because they're intimidated, but because they just don't want to let them down."

Trust Begets Trust

I know this is a broad generalization, but in business we don't seem to trust other people very much. Indeed, entire industries have grown out of offering everything from honesty tests to ethics training. This makes it seem like we don't trust our employees to manage their own talents and aspirations, to be self-motivated and do great work. This is profoundly sad when you think about it. Your employees are the same people running community charities, parenting children, creating apps, or figuring out new product ideas in their spare time. But when they come to work, we still treat them like kids who need a list of chores to get anything done.

Some examples? While it may not seem like a big deal to some, the banning of social networking sites like Facebook and Twitter is a sign that management doesn't trust employees to use those sites for business purposes. Jim Goodnight, the founder and chairman of SAS Institute, told me, "We do keep track of the websites that people visit and maybe how much time they spend on each site. But other than that, we don't keep a whole lot of data on what employees are doing inside the company. It gets to be a question of trust. Trust is probably the most important factor in a great place to work; that they trust you. And if you do too much snooping, they're not going to trust you anymore."

When it became public knowledge that Marissa Mayer, CEO of Yahoo, had ended the company's popular work-from-home policy, Richard Branson, founder of the Virgin Group, offered this perspective in a blog post: "To successfully work with other people, you have to trust each other. A big part of this is trusting people to get their work done wherever they are, without supervision. We like to give people the freedom to work where they want, safe in the knowledge that they have the drive and expertise to perform excellently, whether they are at their desk or in their kitchen. Yours truly has never worked out of an office, and never will."[9]

Simply put, trust begets trust.

This means one of the keys to creating trust is to return workers and employees on all levels to self-respecting, self-determining adulthood. This mindset builds an environment of shared respect. Behavioral scientist Ernest Fehr (at the University of Zurich, Switzerland) confirmed, through a number of experiments, "If you trust people, you make them more trustworthy." And, conversely, "Sanctions designed to deter people from cheating actually make them cheat."[10] So, not only is banning Facebook sending the message that you don't trust your employees to use their time wisely, it might actually encourage them to use the site more.

The big lesson: you can pay for someone's time at work, and people will show up and do what they need to do. But you can't wrench ideas, extraordinary effort, and innovative solutions from their minds. Instead, if you give trust and respect, you'll find those great, innovative ideas readily offered.

Find Your True North

Recently, I spoke with a handful of people from Northwestern Mutual about what makes employees happy to work there. "We're not driven just by dollar signs, money, and the brass ring," said Michael Pritzl, a vice president of leadership development. "That fulfillment comes from a life's work of helping people. What we talk about is as important or more important than the financial reward. It's the true north feeling that's strong with Northwestern Mutual."

A good way for increasing trust in any organization is to identify your greater purpose, your true north. Why do you exist? What meaningful value do you offer to employees, customers, or society? A great purpose should be aspirational, not merely financial. It should create a common cause and promote a collective effort. It should answer all the tough questions of *why:* Why commit? Why persist? And, most important, why trust?

Great organizations have great purposes. This isn't news, of course; you know it in your heart. But do you live it?

According to Jennifer Aaker, professor of marketing at Stanford Graduate School of Business, communicating a strong purpose and cultivating meaning has its own set of benefits. "New research shows there is a strong correlation between happiness and meaning. In fact, having a meaningful impact on the world around you is actually a better predictor of happiness than many other things you think will make you happy," Aaker contended. "When we can cultivate mindfulness and meaning in all that we do, including our work, we have the opportunity to influence not only our own well-being, but also the well-being of our family, friends, coworkers, and wider community."[11]

Make It Safe

As a leader or manager, you have two choices. You can consciously build organizational trust, or you can allow petty issues and misperceptions, both signifiers of a fear-based culture, to erode trust. Fear kills curiosity. It quells exploration, dulls creativity, and stunts growth. In a climate of fear, people are afraid to make mistakes. Fear saps performance, synergy, teamwork, and morale.

While some managers believe that fear is a necessary part of achieving goals and objectives, researchers from Abraham Maslow and W. Edwards Deming to Edgar Schein and Harvey Hornstein have warned against the subtle but profound effects of management-by-fear. Deming argued that fear makes people hesitant to share their best ideas, expand their capabilities and skills, admit mistakes, suggest process improvements, question the underlying purpose and reasoning of decisions or procedures, or even to act in the best interest of the company.[12]

Instead of inculcating an environment of fear, build a culture of trust. Everyone should feel confident that they can participate in meetings and projects, say what's on their mind (if they are prepared), and be respected for their opinions and ideas. Innovative cultures are safe environments for honest inquiries. Let it be said that innovative cultures can be decidedly unsafe places for faking and posturing. Amazon's Jeff Bezos harbors a special dislike of poorly reasoned or random comments. So did Bill Gates at Microsoft and Steve Jobs at Apple. Great companies never confuse a safe environment with kindergarten. Rather, they aim for an authentic adult safety that builds trust, helps fuel a robust dialogue based on facts, not grandiosities or grudges, and allows great new ideas to surface. Researchers call it "psychological safety."[13] The goal is to support frank conversations and the tolerance of honest mistakes.

Here the skeptic may ask: *Won't the absence of fear lead to complacency?* That may be true, but it would only show that you recruited the wrong kind of people. If your people require fear for motivation, you've already blown it as a manager.

It all sounds simple enough, right? Lead with integrity. Trust your people. Provide a true, meaningful purpose. And make it safe to experiment and speak up. But it's not as simple as the words make it seem. Actions and follow-through never are. Fortunately, new tools and technologies that can help measure, analyze, and strengthen trust are becoming available.

USE DATA (WISELY) TO BUILD TRUST WITH CUSTOMERS AND EMPLOYEES

Brands are about creating trust. In fact, a brand is simply a promise a business or organization makes to its customers. Just think about that for a second. . . .

Levi's, with its rivets and heavy denim, promises its products will be tougher than other pants. Nordstrom's promises that you can return any of its items, no questions asked. McDonald's promises consistency and cleanliness. That's why we tend to buy brand names over generic products.

So making and keeping promises creates trust, while breaking promises destroys it. This dynamic isn't so much about what a brand says as it is about what a brand does. Humans are naturally skilled at subconsciously discerning what's authentic. If it's not true, we'll know, soon enough. Mediocre brands or passing fads fail to gain any real loyalty with customers because their leaders pay too much attention to what their brands *say* but demonstrate little concern for what they actually *do*. And therein lies a significant danger for any brand.

The way I see it is we tend to anthropomorphize businesses, treating them in the same way we treat our friends. If our friends betray us by not acting with honesty, we lose trust. And we may even cease to be friends. Similarly, if businesses engage in practices that don't follow a code of conduct we consider acceptable—if they break their promises—we'll usually cease supporting them. And, of course, with the Internet and social media, this dynamic has been greatly amplified.

In this sense, your customers are the ultimate reality check. They allow you to get a better sense of whether your reputation is moving up or down. In today's web-based economy, companies are using applications and social networking tools like LinkedIn, Facebook, and Twitter to solicit consumer feedback and measure customer satisfaction.

Companies like SAS Institute, the data analytics software developer, provide a broad array of such tools. According to SAS chief Jim Goodnight, social analytics operates in two primary dimensions: as social media analysis and as network analysis. "One of the best ways for any brand to be able to determine what people are thinking or saying about it," Goodnight explained, "is to analyze all the tweets and the blogs." That's the role of social media analytics. Basically, on an hour-by-hour basis, you gather all the tweets and search all the blogs that pertain to your product or brand. And then you run this mass of data through a social analysis engine like the one SAS has created to determine whether what people are saying is good or bad, positive or negative.

With the second dimension, network analysis, a firm like SAS would assign a value to each customer of your company, determining which people in the network are, as they term it, *influencers*. "If we get somebody that's an influencer," Goodnight said, "we want to make sure we don't lose them as a customer. Or we might want to pump some special offers at them, because we know they'll influence a lot of the other customers."

So both dimensions—identifying public opinion and classifying customers who have additional sway—help in recognizing a brand's current standing and future potential. With its granularity and continuous view of individual consumers, this type of data can also help you begin to understand what true customer loyalty and trust look like. But as you deploy these various types of customer analytics, you need to keep in mind that there's a fine line between using information to create value or using it to erode trust. This type of data mining can easily be interpreted as invasive.

The utility of social media analytics doesn't stop with gauging your company's public reputation. Something similar is happening *inside* companies. "If you want to start looking inside your organization, a lot of companies are using text mining and social media analytics to follow the internal conversation; to evaluate the satisfaction of the employees and determine the overall health of the company," offered Jim Davis of SAS. "We have a hub called Socialcast, and that's an internal mechanism for employees to talk amongst themselves about various topics. Salesforce has a similar application called Chatter."

The rise of these internal company-wide social networks provides a great opportunity to check the pulse of your workforce. But, echoing earlier cautionary messages, it's a tricky balance between getting to know your employees and coming across as invading their privacy. Some companies may be tempted to capture every keystroke on every keyboard—Taylorism for the digital age!—but keep in mind that trust begets trust.

It might seem a bit old-fashioned in comparison, but simply asking your employees how they feel can also provide a useful picture of morale throughout your organization. For example, when Northwestern Mutual asked its financial reps in a survey, "If I had the opportunity to do this career with this company all over again, I would do it," and 92 percent responded emphatically with "yes," the Northwestern Mutual leaders could be confident that they're doing something right.

Similarly, as Dave Hitz, a co-founder of NetApp, explained, "One of the reasons we do these great-place-to-work programs is because they're a feedback mechanism." NetApp leadership can see whether they're down in a certain category compared to other organizations, or whether they're down compared to past years. "It's real live data we can work with," Hitz explained. "We'd rarely go off and try to tackle something on the soft side, like trust, without some hard data to give us insight as to what might make a difference," Jay Kidd (the current CTO) elaborated. "From that data, we can then put programs in place to boost numbers we feel aren't acceptable and that should help increase trust."

So even in the age of big data and advanced analytics, one of the best ways to understand your level of organizational trust is still through a simple survey. "There's not enough data that I'm aware of that you can really get a feel of how everybody thinks about things without doing a survey," Jim Goodnight, the SAS Institute CEO, admitted. "Things like trust—you trust your managers, you feel appreciated—are really hard to measure just from the data that's around," Jim Davis added.

But these limitations certainly haven't stopped companies from trying to find new, innovative ways to evaluate the mood and health of their organizations. Australian software company Atlassian has placed flat-panel screens at every exit. And each day, as you leave, you're asked to answer four questions. While the questions are presented in a goofy way to make them fun and feel like a game, they do have a serious purpose. And that's to capture the energy level and degree of trust within the company. Just imagine, soon we'll be able to do something similar with a smartphone app or digital sensors embedded in ID badges.

DATA VISUALIZATION: A CATALYZER OF TRUST

Some of these new technologies can be used for more than measuring and analyzing trust within a company. They can also be used to build trust. But first you must find a *language* of trust that is widely understood throughout your organization.

"We're going through our last employee survey," Keith Collins, chief technology officer of SAS, explained. "We put all the data up in visual analytics for everyone to see. What's really powerful is to be able to compare myself to all of the other divisions. And that's about having openness and the trust across all the executives—we actually allow everybody to see everybody else's information."

A big part of what makes data and data visualization so valuable—and this really gets to the point of creating trust—is that they offer a common language that spans the company; one that bridges jobs, expertise, and training. To be honest, most of us don't absorb spreadsheets easily. We don't naturally think in numbers and statistics. Instead, most of us are less naturally analytical and more visually inclined. This means large quantities of data can confuse us or put us on the defensive, causing us to consciously or subconsciously resist the underlying message.

But with data visualization, companies and organizations can create a shared language, a common set of understandings, so that employees don't feel manipulated. Why do some of us distrust, say, lawyers? It's because they'll lapse into legal speak. Being the distrustful souls we are, we'll wonder if the lawyers are doing it to manipulate us instead of to inform us. So I see visual analytics—the plain language of images, story, and context—as a huge driver of consensus, as a catalyzer of trust. With data visualization, you have a more easily understood way for people to *see* a situation the company is facing.

Putting issues into context across divisions and teams is a powerful tool. If you can understand issues and problems within a shared context, you accelerate decisions and you accelerate execution. The visual depiction of data gives you context, whether you're from a soft-edge area like human resources or a hard-edge area like finance. By creating this easily understood framework, you're establishing trust across these different groups of people. Which, in the end, means it's a new way of getting the best out of the entire organization.

GAINING THE EDGE

- Trust is becoming more valuable for the very reason it's declining in society.
- Trust has two key components: external trust (customers, suppliers, shareholders) and internal trust (employees). Great companies invest in both.
- Trust, more than pay or perks, is the secret to making a best-places-to-work list.
- Trust is the bedrock of innovation, because ideas can't be forcibly pulled from people's heads.
- Trust is also the bedrock of sales productivity. Salespeople thrive when they trust the purpose of their career and their company.
- Trust is easily destroyed by executive hypocrisy.
- Trust can be improved with visual analytics, because this creates a common language for diverse groups.

4

Smarts

How Fast Can You and Your Company Adapt?

In 2012 CBS Sports, which has televised the NCAA men's basketball tournament for thirty-three years, ranked the best college teams of all time. Atop the list—ahead of the 1967–68 UCLA Bruins and the 1995–96 University of Kentucky Wildcats—was the 1975–76 Indiana University Hoosiers. That team went 32–0 that season and crushed the University of Michigan in the 1976 NCAA title game.

Indiana was coached by Bobby Knight, a tough leader from the old school. Knight liked to curse at officials and throw chairs. He tolerated no dissent, not even spoken words from players during practice. Knight's conditioning workouts were brutal. They included running up and down the 109 stairs of Indiana University's Assembly Hall arena. "Our freshmen couldn't believe it," said a senior center, describing the intensity and occasional vomiting. "Neither could I. When we began last year, I almost went into shock."

Knight also insisted on his players going to class and graduating. "If a kid comes to Indiana and all we teach him is basketball, then we've really fouled up," Knight told a sportswriter. *Fouled up?* It's almost certain that Coach Knight did not use the words "fouled up." Knight's well-known extravagant use of profanity would embarrass a drill sergeant.

"Just because Indiana University Coach Bobby Knight, that mellowing maniac, has not punched a player, strangled a referee, pistol-whipped a writer or howled at the moon in the last few minutes, is no reason to ignore his team," *Sports Illustrated*'s Curry Kirkpatrick wrote in a 1975 story. Knight confided to Kirkpatrick that he had tried his best to put a lid on his profanity—for a while—but that the effort wasn't worth it. "I'm not getting any more *bleeping* mellow, you son of a *bleep-bleep*," he finally conceded. "I'm only getting *bleeping* smarter." Of course, he didn't say "bleep."

Along with Knight's players, assistant coaches, and trainers, only one other person—a female student—saw Knight coach in every single Indiana University home game, and every practice, during Indiana's greatest season. This young lady would arrive each day and sit in the stands, a few rows behind the bench. Day after day, she showed up like that to watch the Hoosiers play or practice. She kept her eye on Coach Knight. She studied him closely and took notes.

Her name is Tara VanDerveer. And while Knight was "getting *bleeping* smarter," so was she. Her notes about Knight's practices were bulky enough to fill multiple metal file drawers. Soon, VanDerveer became a coach herself. Within ten years, she had embarked on one of the most successful head coaching careers in NCAA women's basketball history.

By examining Coach VanDerveer's development, as well as the thoughts and stories of other great leaders, this chapter aims to deepen your understanding of what it means for both individuals and organizations to be smart in today's hypercompetitive world.

WHAT, EXACTLY, ARE SMARTS?

When we use the word *smart*, we're usually talking about intelligence. In research literature, intelligence is described a number of different ways. Most commonly, it's described as—and I'm paraphrasing here—a general mental aptitude that involves the ability to reason, plan, solve problems, think abstractly, and learn quickly. For greater clarity, this description can be parsed into two major components:

- The ability to learn new things and solve novel problems—call this intelligence-as-process.
- The ability to apply outcomes of learning—call this intelligence-as-knowledge.[1]

This overall aptitude for learning, thinking, and application is recognized through the term *general intelligence*, which is usually designated by the symbol g. Going back over a century, many people believed we're born with a predetermined intelligence, our g, which is not significantly alterable. Our individual differences in g are measured using psychometric tests, most commonly an IQ test, that cover cognitive areas like reasoning, processing speed, memory, and spatial ability. Although these areas are sometimes considered independent, most research has established that they're not—meaning, if you perform well in one domain, you also tend to perform well in the others.[2]

But when it comes to measuring smarts, *g* isn't the only game in town. Developmental psychologist and Harvard professor Howard Gardner in 1983 introduced the theory of Multiple Intelligences (MI). Another theoretical framework called Emotional Intelligence, or EI, was popularized in 1995 by psychologist and *New York Times* science writer Daniel Goleman. Both theories say there is not just a single intelligence, as defined by *g*, but a number of different dimensions and layers to intelligence. While all three approaches—*g*, MI, and EI—offer valid points and specific advantages, I'm here to tell you something very important: when you get right down to it—

None of them matter.

That's right. General intelligence, Multiple Intelligence, Emotional Intelligence—and all the other types of "intelligences" theorized and promulgated by academia—just don't matter much in business. Now, don't get me wrong: I'm not saying frameworks like *g*, MI, and EI are irrelevant. They're not. They're incredibly useful as vehicles for study, research, and discussion. Cognitive testing, with all its faults and biases, has been instrumental in creating and applying life-changing interventions. And I mention them up front because any valid discussion of smarts needs to at least acknowledge the most prominent theories of cognitive development.

But all these theories, as well as the lofty test scores and grade point averages that support them, get tossed out the window when it comes to actually being smart in the context of a complex organization or an individual career. In the real world, smarts isn't about looking for the next star student with a 4.0 or having an IQ that can boil water. Instead, it's about the importance of hard work, of perseverance and resilience. Call it grit. Call it courage. Call it tenacity. Call it a can-do attitude. These are such old-fashioned concepts, they're sometimes easy to miss.

Grit, and its associated friends, is hard to capture: it's not revealed by grades and honor societies and trumped-up résumé enhancers. Too often in places like Silicon Valley and Manhattan, in Boston and Seattle, we in business propagate this witless (and grit-less) idea that the only people fit to hire are those who scored 800 on their math SATs.

Grit, courage, and persistence are themes you'll run into throughout this book. But here, when discussing smarts in business, grit shows up not as a parallel advantage to g. Grit shows up as a form of g itself. Grit leads directly to faster learning. That's its hidden virtue.

What does it mean to be smart in the world of business? Most business leaders would think of it as an ability to get something done; to achieve, to weather the tough times, endure, and succeed. T. Boone Pickens is smart. So are Donald Trump and Madonna. They may not be mathematical geniuses like Facebook's Mark Zuckerberg or Google's Sergey Brin, but they're wily, clever, and capable. They'll survive good times and bad. They'll adapt to changing markets and win more than they lose.

While discussing smarts, Tom Georgens (CEO of NetApp, the $6.5 billion data storage company) had a very interesting observation: "I know this irritates a lot of people, but once you're at a certain point in your career—and it's not that far out, maybe five years—all the grades and academic credentials in the world don't mean anything anymore. It's all about accomplishment from that point forward." That's an important realization. About his own hires, Georgens offered, "There are members of my staff and I don't even know where they went to college or what they studied." To him and other CEOs, at some point, it just doesn't matter anymore.

Taking the idea in a more entrepreneurial direction, "Some of the better venture capital firms that I know," Greg Becker, CEO of Silicon Valley Bank, told me, "when they look for individuals, they want people who are scrappy, who have been through trials and tribulations. These people will figure out a way to make it work, no matter what."

Maynard Webb, chairman of the board for Yahoo and a board member of Salesforce.com, added, "What I'm looking for is a talent. And talent isn't just intellect. Talent is also what you did. If you're an entrepreneur trying to break through, it's hard work. You have to be tough, you have to be willing to take lots of body blows. So I'm looking for that grit factor."

For most of us, this should be good news: we're not limited or defined by the faculties and aptitudes we've inherited. Much of what makes us smart is due to what we learn or, put another way, what we've learned the hard way. Now, some people will say those things aren't technically being smart. Fair enough. I'm willing to concede that notions like effort and perseverance don't directly align with the scientific definition of intelligence. But before dismissing this book's definition of smarts, consider what some of today's great practitioners, including CEOs, consultants, financiers, sports coaches, and even a world-renowned chef have to say. Then, I suspect, you'll see how grit leads directly to being smarter and results in an ability to learn more and adapt faster.

GRIT ACCELERATES LEARNING

From the prenatal period to the very end of our lives, experiential factors shape the neural circuits underlying our behavior. These experiential factors include both involuntary influences like adversity, as well as intentional influences like learning and training. This means the human brain displays amazing neural plasticity—the ability to modify neural connectivity and function—even into our seventies. This is good news on many levels. It's hard to envision facing life's challenges with a brain incapable of adapting to its environment.

Moreover, the smartest people in business are not those with the highest *g*. Instead, they're those who regularly put themselves in situations that require grit. These acts of courage accelerate their learning through adaptation. Salespeople who make more calls, for example, will almost always outperform salespeople who make fewer calls. But here is the key point: this happens not just because the act of making more calls mathematically raises the chances of success. It turns out, making all those calls has additional benefits. The more frequent callers, by facing up to the gritty task of making a call, put themselves on a faster learning curve. They more rapidly learn what works and what doesn't. They more rapidly learn techniques to overcome rejection. Thus their success yield will improve—that is, double the calls, triple the sales. The act of making lots of calls also develops self-regulatory skills such as self-discipline, delayed gratification, and, maybe most important, self-regulated learning.

And speaking of self-regulated learning, remember that one person who watched Bobby Knight coach in every single home game and home practice? I visited Stanford University women's basketball coach Tara VanDerveer at her offices next to the Maples Pavilion basketball arena. "I loved watching Bob Knight's practices," VanDerveer recalled. Now sixty, VanDerveer grew up in Massachusetts, but she has the flat voice of a Midwesterner and the dry humor to go with it. "I didn't sit in the front row. I would sit up just a little bit behind the bench," she said, chuckling at the thought. She wanted to be out of Bob Knight's line of sight when Knight lost it, started kicking chairs, or cussing out God and the world. But there was another side to Knight, and that's why VanDerveer stuck around—and kept learning.

"Watching Coach Knight, I learned things I would do, as well as things that I wouldn't do," VanDerveer told me. "He was a great teacher and his practices were extremely well organized. Watching practice every day, it gave me a lot of confidence that I could go out and coach a team myself."

That's an understatement. VanDerveer, Stanford's coach since 1985, is the fourth most winning woman's basketball coach in NCAA history and has won two NCAA championships. Her head coaching résumé also includes an Olympic gold medal in the 1996 games, four Big Ten Championships while at Ohio State, eighteen Pac 10 and Pac 12 Championships, and a lifetime college winning percentage of 83 percent. If that's not enough, she's also currently one of only thirteen women to be inducted into the Basketball Hall of Fame along with male luminaries like Bill Russell, Magic Johnson, Larry Byrd, Michael Jordan, Pat Riley, and Phil Jackson.

But her education in coaching started much earlier than her college years at Indiana. To better appreciate the challenges VanDerveer had to surmount to become an elite-level coach, you need to understand that she grew up on the wrong side of Title IX, the educational amendment passed in 1972 that, among other things, required equal access to organized sports for women. This means there were virtually no opportunities for girls or women to play sports when VanDerveer was young.

So VanDerveer forged her own path to coaching greatness. She watched coaches from the time she was very young. The sixth-, seventh-, eighth-grade boys teams, the freshman high school team: she watched them every day. "I grew up watching boys practice," she said.

And that's really the key: intelligence is not just a thing we get from our parents, it's a continual process that's affected by our experiences and associations—both sought and imposed. Successful people just are more tenacious in seeking out those opportunities to accelerate their learning, as suggested by Tara VanDerveer with Bob Knight.

This value of accelerated learning isn't just limited to individuals like Coach VanDerveer. To better understand the challenges in getting and staying smart, here's a look at a truly exceptional organization operating in one of the most knowledge-intensive industries in the world.

THE KNOWLEDGE EXPLOSION: MAYO CLINIC

In January 1863, Abraham Lincoln signed the Emancipation Proclamation, freeing the slaves. Six months later came the Battle of Gettysburg, which tipped the course of the Civil War to the Union Army. During the same year, a doctor named William W. Mayo got as far away from the war as he could get, settling in a southern Minnesota town called Rochester. Mayo had two sons, William J. and Charles, who would join the elder Mayo's practice in the 1880s.

In those days, the prevailing attitude among American doctors was that of a guild. A young man—they were all men then—worked hard to become a doctor. Knowledge was a valuable asset. The last thing a doctor would do with such a money-making asset was share it or give it away. But the Mayo brothers saw it differently. Ahead of their time, they embraced innovation and teamwork. They traveled to Paris to learn the best surgical methods. They asked other doctors and researchers to join their practice. In 1889, they started the world's first private integrated group practice—what has become known worldwide as Mayo Clinic.

Mayo Clinic has been the "leading brand in medicine for more than a hundred years," said their latest CEO, Dr. John Noseworthy. Few would argue. Mayo Clinic has some thirty-two thousand licensed health care professionals. That's a vast army of smart people. The challenge is that these thirty-two thousand people also need to be educated, certified, recertified, and kept up to date with the latest techniques and practices in order to maintain the clinic's historic level of excellence.

To do so, Mayo has traditional schools like many medical centers. These include—and I'll try to get through them quickly—the Mayo Medical School, a traditional medical school just like at Harvard or any other major university. There's the Mayo Graduate School, which is focused on scientific fields outside medicine. Then there's a graduate medical education school for residents and fellows—these are people who've already graduated from medical school, but are learning a specialty. It's actually the largest post-doc school in the country. More physicians have trained at the Mayo School of Graduate Medical Education than at any other institution in the United States. In addition, Mayo has a school for nonphysicians. This school, called the Mayo School of Health Sciences, trains thirty different types of health practitioners, from nurse-anesthetists to cytotechnologists (the people who examine cell specimens) to phlebotomists (the people who draw your blood). Finally, there's the Mayo School of Continuous Professional Development, which keeps health professionals current on new research, practices, and technologies.

Whew! That's five schools. But I shouldn't forget to add the Mayo Clinic Online Learning Program, an extensive catalogue of digital courses and modules intended to help a worldwide workforce find the time to learn new skills and practices. To optimize digital instruction, Mayo blends these online courses with face-to-face time in classrooms.

For the more hands-on specialties like surgery, much of Mayo's learning is still clinical, but its additional training consists of practice and simulations utilizing a mix of cadavers and manikins. To take advantage of surgeons' natural competitive nature, Dr. David Farley, a professor of surgery, has created an event for interns that he holds every July called the Surgical Olympics. It's a decathlon of sorts, with events such as intravenous catheter placements, transverse incisions, and one-handed knot tying—all performed as the clock ticks and Dr. Farley observes—that help interns understand where they are in terms of basic surgical knowledge and procedures, as well as the ability to handle pressure.

So there's really no question that the people at Mayo take learning and continued education very seriously. In fact, I'd bet there are few if any other service organizations in the world that take such a rigorous and organized approach to providing career-long learning, training, and professional development.

But all is not perfect, even in the bucolic world of Rochester, Minnesota. One very real problem with medicine right now is the fact that there's just too much to know.

"Consider cardiology," began Dr. Doug Wood, Mayo's professor of cardiovascular disease. We were seated at a dining room table in a corner of the Mayo Clinic's main building called the Center for Innovation. Wood went on: "Back in the 1980s, there were three leading journals of cardiology. Each published once a month. You could keep up. But now, one of those monthly journals has been split into three separate journals that are published every two weeks. Another one of the journals has been split into four, though they're still all published monthly. So, in total, those three journals per month have now turned into eleven journals per month. That's a lot for anyone to read, much less someone who's already handling a heavy schedule of appointments, procedures, rounds, and staff meetings."

Now add the explosion of literature on drug and treatment trials. In 1960, approximately a hundred articles were published on randomized control trials, generally considered the authority for best practices in medicine. Today, more than ten thousand articles reporting on randomized control trials are published annually.[3] How can anyone hope to keep up with this exponential growth in knowledge and information?

They can't.

Huge challenges to learning exist with procedural practice, as well. Surgery especially. As Dr. Farley told me: "Repetition [in surgery] is crucial. You do have to do things over and over again. And you've got to have feedback. To fix a hernia, which is a relatively simple and straightforward procedure, it takes about 250 operations until we get a sense that the learning curve is flattening off and we're not going to get any better." I was sitting with Farley behind a one-way mirror as he watched a student practice catheter insertions on a manikin. He swallowed some coffee and continued. "So the scary thing for us in surgery and in education is, in five years of training, well, the student is not going to do 250 operations. Which means I have to send people out to Palo Alto and Tacoma and Mankato, and they're going to be general surgeons and they've done eighty, or fifty, or twenty operations."

Scary, right? But just hold on one second. It gets worse.

"In my world, I do a lot of endocrine surgery," Dr. Farley said. "Adrenal surgery is really sort of complex and challenging, and it's dangerous. The average resident in the United States rarely does one in five years. At the Mayo Clinic, they do four. 'Hey, way to go Mayo Clinic, you're the number one program in the country!' But we've done four. So when someone asks a surgeon, 'Hey, have you ever done this before?'—'Oh, yeah, I have.' Four, and you're an expert? That's tough."

With these challenges the question becomes, can technology accelerate this learning? Can online modules and the use of cadavers, simulators, and manikins help make up for the loss of repetition?

"I hope like hell it can," Dr. Farley said. "Because as I sit here in front of you, I don't want to—this is not utopia. Ten years ago, almost to the day, duty hours were passed across the country. These said residents can't work more than eighty hours a week and they've got to have one day off per week. Which are good and reasonable laws," Dr. Farley conceded, "better for family, better for sleep deprivation, better for education. But it has decreased the number of repetitions and created a decade's worth of people that didn't have the same training that I had the luxury to go through. That's a real problem."

This isn't just a problem for Mayo Clinic: this is a problem for everyone in health care. The system is getting bigger, the procedures more complicated, and the expectations higher. The classes, the online modules, the simulations and checklists, getting everything right before cutting into living, breathing people; yes, those things help. But they still leave Farley saying, "I'm nervous that the people I'm going to turn out aren't as good as the people that had to do the torture session for a hundred hours, and had to be sleep deprived, and that sort of thing."

Later in the chapter, I introduce a new kind of doctor, one that may well be an answer the challenge of keeping up. I also explore how Mayo Clinic has adapted its learning and training programs to meet these new challenges. But first, let's examine how we can all accelerate our learning, both individually and organizationally, to better adapt to today's fast-paced environment.

STRETCH YOUR NEUROPLASTICITY

If you talk about getting smarter with neuroscientists, you're sure to go down this path of discussion: brain scans, MRIs, gray and white matter generation, neurogenesis and neuroplasticity, and things like that. For example, research has shown that we demonstrate pronounced *neuroplasticity*—the ability to change cognitive structure—and *neurogenesis*—an ability to generate new neurons—throughout our adult lives. Both types of neural modification occur through learning a new skill, whether it's juggling, playing golf, or plucking a banjo.[4]

Exercise also improves cognition. Do it outside, in a setting scientists call an "enriched environment"—say, riding a real bicycle on a twisty road—and the benefit will be compounded over exercising in a closed, sterile environment like a gym. Add a social aspect to your exercise, and now you've turbocharged your cortical remapping and neural generation. You see, those lunchtime walks or bike rides with coworkers may be doing a lot more than just burning a few calories; they may actually be making you smarter.[5]

There's little doubt that these facts are important to your neural health. But does it have much do to with business?

While discussing this idea of smarts with business leaders, and other folks who've reached the apex of their chosen career, the discussion tends to follow an entirely different path. Business leaders are not worried about whether you learn to juggle or take a new, enriched route on your next jog through Central Park. To them, that's not what getting smarter is about. To them it's about effort. It's about work. It's about cultivating specific behaviors, including a willingness to search out mentors, see mistakes and failures as learning opportunities, and embrace ideas from outside your own field.

LEARN FROM THE BEST

Tara VanDerveer started her coaching career at the University of Idaho in 1978. While she was there, until 1980, Don Monson was the men's head coach. Monson was eventually voted the National Coach of the year in 1982. His great skill was getting a group of undertalented, barely recruited athletes to play as a team. The Idaho players under Monson routinely exceeded their expectations. While coaching women's basketball at Idaho, VanDerveer continued her habit of watching the men's team practice and taking notes, notes, and more notes.

After two years at Idaho, VanDerveer became head coach of the women's basketball team at the Ohio State University. Being in the Big Ten—with teams like Michigan, Michigan State, Wisconsin, Indiana, and Illinois—was a boon. All the great coaches, both men's and women's, would come to Columbus, the home of Ohio State, to practice and play. "I'd stay and watch the opponents practice," VanDerveer said. "I had a chance to see some of the best coaches in the country work and prepare their teams." At the same time, VanDerveer also took coaching classes from Ohio State men's coach Fred Taylor, who, it turns out, had been Bob Knight's former coach at Ohio State.

In 1985, VanDerveer moved to the San Francisco Bay Area to be head coach of the Stanford women's basketball team. At the same time, Pete Newell, the former basketball coach at the University of California at Berkeley, was running a widely respected "big man" camp for athletes who played the center position. Newell had won the NCAA championship in 1959 and was thought by his coaching peers to be one of the truly great minds in basketball.

"Yeah, well, I was always hanging around," VanDerveer told me. "And I'm standing there and Pete would say, 'I'm going to go get Chinese food. Do you want to come?' I said, 'Sure.' And then I got to know him." They spent hours and hours working and talking, with VanDerveer again taking copious notes. Many lunches later, she had a file cabinet full of notes she had taken from Pete Newell.

The point is likely clear by now: VanDerveer found people to learn from everywhere she went. In *Shooting from the Outside*, VanDerveer writes: "I never thought I'd be a coach, but just hearing the same things from Coach Knight over and over, day after day, and watching, watching, watching, my brain formed patterns for how the game should be played."

This brings to mind the ten-thousand-hour rule, made popular by Malcolm Gladwell in his best-selling book, *Outliers*. It's the idea that gaining expertise, and the resulting success, is a matter of practicing—and practicing more. Gladwell suggested that ten thousand hours was a useful starting point. He told the story of the Beatles playing tens of thousands of hours in dingy Hamburg nightclubs in the early 1960s, honing their rock-and-roll craft. And of Bill Gates, still in high school, spending night after night at the University of Washington computer center. Gladwell made the ten-thousand-hour idea popular, but it was originally conceived by Anders Ericsson, a professor at Florida State University. According to Ericsson, greatness requires time and effort. Lots of time. Lots of effort.

Well, so does smarts.

But with smarts, it's not just ten thousand hours of practice. It's also hours of observing, listening, and learning. It's absorbing other experts' years of experience and taking their guidance to heart. In *Outliers*, Malcolm Gladwell wrote, "No one—not rock stars, not professional athletes, not software billionaires—ever makes it alone."

It sounds so easy—learning from the other great minds, the Bob Knights and Pete Newells, in our own professions or industries—yet so few of us do it! So few of us take the time to search out the people who can show us a shortcut to greater knowledge and skill. It seems so obvious, the question each of us should be asking ourselves is, "Why don't we do the same thing?"

Because it takes time. It takes persistence. It takes being humble and admitting what we don't know. It takes getting out of our shy shells and reaching out, putting ourselves on the line, and opening ourselves up to rejection. Those are tough things to do. Take it from me; I understand. But people are surprisingly generous with their time. They want to help, they want to act like mentors, even if they don't want to be called a mentor. They want to make a difference by passing along knowledge and sharing the expertise they've developed during their ten thousand hours.

My personal theory on why this is so? We all long for eternity. Passing on our knowledge—our experiential DNA, if you like—is one way to achieve it.

VanDerveer's story echoes something that Fred Smith, founder, CEO, and chairman of FedEx, told me. Halfway through our interview in Smith's private conference room at his Memphis offices, I noticed that Smith kept citing history books on the Roman Republic, the American founding, and the U.S. Constitution. "You're a very well-read CEO," I said. Smith's response astonished me: "My dad died when I was four. I needed new mentors. I found them in books."

If you remember nothing else in this book, remember this: most successful people like to be asked how they became successful. So ask.

LEARN FAST FROM YOUR MISTAKES

David Chang is the chef and owner of Momofuku, a growing culinary empire that includes eleven restaurants located in New York City, Toronto, and Sydney, Australia. The Momofuku brand also comprises a growing media presence that includes a quarterly magazine called *Lucky Peach*, a best-selling eponymous cookbook, and a TV series called *The Mind of a Chef*. Talk about tough industries—restaurants and media! They probably have two of the highest failure rates of all businesses in the United States.

Chang sees success as a series of mistakes or, as he put it, "burning yourself." He told me that in the culinary world there's no such thing as a genius or a prodigy, because cooking requires a whole new set of skills that people just aren't born with. "I mean," he clarified, "someone might be more predisposed to being a better cook, but being a great chef, it's a process of who learns from their mistakes the fastest. It's about making mistakes, documenting them, dwelling on them." He defined this as the Japanese principles of *Kaizen* (the practice of continuous improvement) and *Hansei* (the acknowledgment of your own mistakes). "Western culture might be more allergic to documenting failure," he said. "Except for the scientific community."

Chang admitted to me his own weakness. With such a large number of creative and skilled people looking to learn and grow within the Momofuku family, Chang has discovered a need to be much more patient. This hasn't been easy. A recent example: one of his cooks put a new dish on the menu. Chang didn't hate it, but he didn't love it. In the past, as he explained to me, "I would have probably responded with, 'What the *bleep* is your problem? This is the dumbest *bleeping* thing I've ever seen. It's disgusting. It's stupid. What the *bleep?* Like why'd you even put it on the menu? You're wasting my time, you're wasting everybody's time, and it's just frankly embarrassing.'"

Then Chang added, "I probably would have said something like that, but much worse." Okay, I'll take his word on that.

But instead of going *bleeping* Bob Knight on the cook, Chang decided to leave the item on the menu. And guess what? The cook in question came back a few days later and told him, "I thought about it and I'm going to take it off the menu. Maybe it doesn't make it back on the menu, but it meant a lot to me to serve that dish because it reminded me of my heritage growing up." Instead of forcing it, Chang was able to create a situation where the outcome is much more healthy and organic. And that's a more instructive way for people to learn. "I have to let people make mistakes," he said, "in order to make the future better."

That's a great example of a one-on-one situation in which a tolerance of mistakes can lead directly to a more effective learning opportunity. But how do you incorporate these philosophies of Kaizen and Hansei into an organization? How do you scale it up, codify the practice, or embed it in the cultural DNA? Margit Wennmachers, a partner in the Silicon Valley venture capital firm of Andreessen Horowitz, offered a great approach.

Before working at Andreessen Horowitz, Wennmachers founded a public relations firm named The OutCast Agency. Even with Wennmachers gone, OutCast is still around and doing very well, which speaks highly of her ability to build a strong culture. During her CEO tenure, one of the key values at OutCast was the pursuit of excellence. *Good is a commodity*, she said. So how do you get to excellent?

"The way you get to excellence in a service business," Wennmachers told me, "is by making sure that people feel they can take risks." To encourage this risk-taking behavior, Wennmachers instituted a weekly meeting to talk about moments of excellence. Not that groundbreaking, right?

But, wait, she also did the flipside. So if you'd made a really goofy mistake at OutCast, if you'd really *bleeped* up, as Coach Knight or Chef Chang would say, you were strongly encouraged to share it. As Wennmachers explained, "Excellence takes risk. And you're not taking enough risks if you're not learning anything by making a mistake. It's essentially a failure. For risk to work, for people to do it, it needs to be okay to fail." Wennmachers knows that talking about failure in a group setting removes the sting of embarrassment faster, and thus allows learning to occur faster.

Generally, no one wants to admit failure and no one wants to look bad in front of peers. We all want to protect our image and our self-esteem. That's natural. We see failure as unacceptable. And we'd just as soon avoid it. Failure is tough to talk about, and too many organizations punish people for mistakes without extracting the valuable lessons contained in a mistake.

But to increase smarts, both on an individual and organizational level, we need to acknowledge our performance *bleep-ups*. As counterintuitive as it may sound, more *bleep-ups* lead to greater improvement and faster innovation. IDEO, the award-winning design firm, has a saying: "Fail often in order to succeed sooner."[6]

Mistakes, and the failures they cause, are opportunities for real learning, the kind that makes you smarter, as well as a little more courageous. The secret for both individuals and organizations, of course, is to figure out how to embrace mistakes, rather than ignore or hide them. Sometimes this means reaching out beyond our comfort zone. It means thinking differently or zigging while other people zag. And that leads to the next practice for getting smarter—thinking laterally.

But first, humor me for a few moments while I take a quick but illustrative detour through the worlds of football and battlefields.

HOW A GREAT COACH GOT HIS BEST IDEA

The story of Bill Walsh, Joe Montana, and the San Francisco 49er juggernaut of the 1980s is well known. What's not as well known is how Walsh came up with the West Coast Offense, an innovation that revolutionized football. Yes, I know the story of how Walsh first implemented the West Coast Offense with the Cincinnati Bengals in the late 1960s has been told. But I'm talking about the actual genesis of the offense—the spark that led to this radical new vision of field management.

To unravel the origins of one of the most remarkable innovations in sports, I need to jump ahead about a decade to the early 1990s and the dawn of the Internet. I began at Forbes in 1992, hired to start a bimonthly futurist magazine called *Forbes ASAP*. I wanted to have somebody in the magazine who excelled at discerning patterns: somebody who knew how to process information while trapped in what Prussian military analyst Carl Von Clausewitz called the "fog of war," an expression used to describe confusing situations frequently confronted on the battlefield.

What were the industries that already operated in a kind of fog of war?

I felt then, and I still do, that professional sports, particularly football, is one of those industries. And who better to contribute a column on innovation, I thought, than the man everyone called "The Genius," Coach Bill Walsh. In ten seasons that included three Super Bowl wins, Walsh had taken the 49ers from ruins to glory. He did it with a system that utilized precise passing routes and quick throws to pick apart the zone defenses and blitzing schemes designed to harass and confuse quarterbacks. And he did it with a quarterback few believed could survive, much less dominate, the NFL.

Joe Montana, a first-ballot Hall of Famer, was the fourth quarterback taken in the 1979 draft. Many experts believed Montana lacked the physical tools—the rocket arm, quick feet, and powerful core—that were considered critical for NFL success. Instead, he was tall and thin, with a high center of gravity. And despite a winning record at Notre Dame, most insiders dismissed Montana's chances in the much faster and harder-hitting NFL. But together, Walsh and Montana helped define a decade of sports.

In one of our early interviews, the question came up of why Walsh drafted Joe Montana. What did he see that all the other coaches and scouts missed? This led to a discussion of how he developed the West Coast Offense.

The invention came, according to Walsh, while he was sitting in the bleachers of a high school basketball game. It was 1967, and Walsh was head coach of a short-lived semi-pro football team named the San Jose Apaches. As Walsh watched the high school game from the bleachers, he noticed that one of the teams was running a full-court press, swarming and trapping the other team as it tried to inbound the ball.

But somehow the team being pressed was still able to consistently get the ball in play and move it up the court. Walsh marveled at the fact that even though the offensive players were outnumbered (with five defenders guarding four players) and getting harassed, they were still able to break the press more than 90 percent of the time.

How the heck did they do that?

And suddenly it clicked. They were able to do it because of screens and pick-and-rolls and short passes, the basic plays that had evolved in the sport of basketball as an answer to defensive systems designed to harass and confuse offensive players. These basketball plays morphed into the short slants, crossing patterns, and screen passes that came to define the West Coast Offense.

Walsh saw the common response to the full-court press as something he could apply in football and therefore what he was looking for was not the standard NFL quarterback. What he was looking for was the football equivalent of the player inbounding the ball to break the press in a basketball game. A player with great peripheral vision. A player able to track people in motion, read developing patterns, and get the ball to one of those four players being covered by five defenders. A player who, despite a skinny frame and an average arm, could read coverage, run a progression, look off his options, then lob a ball to the open man at the back of the end zone.

That was what Bill Walsh realized while watching a high school basketball game in 1967. That was the genesis of the West Coast Offense, as he explained it to me. And that was how he orchestrated one of the greatest success stories in the history of sports.

THINK LATERALLY

The story of how Bill Walsh revolutionized the NFL by observing a high school basketball game is a powerful metaphor for the concept of lateral thinking. By borrowing from the periphery, by looking for ideas and opportunities outside his own space, Walsh was able to reinvent a multibillion-dollar industry. This idea of being able to use lateral thinking to accelerate innovation aptly characterizes what it means to be smart in today's business climate.

Lateral thinking is what it sounds like—sort of. It's the ability to imagine how a good idea for one function might also be a good idea for another, separate function. The term "lateral thinking" was coined in 1967 by Edward de Bono, a physician, author, and consultant. In de Bono's model, lateral thinking is a process used to restructure old thought patterns and provoke creativity. No need to get too wrapped up in the actual process as defined by de Bono; it's enough to embrace his central insight: the habit of adapting great ideas from other areas. No matter what field you're in, there are always new and innovative ideas you can borrow from art, from sports, from other businesses and industries.

Chef David Chang of Momofuku exemplifies this capability. He has an incredible ability to see things from different cultures, draw from different experiences, and bring them into the offerings in each of his restaurants. When talking with Chang—a Korean American who was born and raised in Virginia—it's clear he had a great awakening in Japan. While working in backstreet Tokyo noodle bars, it dawned on Chang that "good food could be for everyone."

"In terms of the culinary world," he told me, "it's so insular. Japan has restaurants that are nearly eleven hundred years old. We don't have anything like that. In America, the food culture's so young and unsophisticated, I have to look elsewhere to understand where the food culture might go. For instance, I think the biggest parallel to the food world is actually fashion, and I've tried my best to understand what happens in the fashion world."

Fashion? Did he just say fashion?

He went on: "It's actually uncanny in terms of how similar they are. And fashion may be twenty or thirty years ahead of where the food world is." For Chang, this realization keeps him on the cutting edge of food and years ahead of other, less perceptive people in the culinary world.

It's similar for Tara VanDerveer. Her unconventional thinking, her borrowing from lateral fields, has given her a real advantage in the very competitive world of NCAA sports. "My dad taught me a long time ago, in athletics you don't have to have a patent for ideas. You can steal stuff. So I'm a really good thief. I go around and watch football practice. I watch water polo practice. I get ideas, I talk to coaches, I try to learn how to do my job better. It's talking to other people about what works for them and putting it together within the context of what I do."

After VanDerveer arrived at Stanford in 1985, one of the first people she looked up was Brooks Johnson, a track coach at the university. Throughout his career, Johnson had great success. A world record holder in the sixty-yard dash in the 1960s, he was an Olympic coach in 1984. Johnson had VanDerveer bring the basketball team down to the track, so they could work on their foot speed and vertical jump by doing things like toe raises, lunges, short sprints, and barefoot training in the grass. And Johnson got results. "We had kids improve their vertical jump eight inches in three months," VanDerveer said. "That was incredible to me."

In sum: search out mentors, embrace your mistakes as learning opportunities, and look for great ideas you can adapt from other fields. All those steps will help you learn more and innovate faster. Now, how about that new kind of doctor I mentioned earlier in the chapter?

DR. WATSON, I PRESUME

For a long time, it was thought that only humans and a few advanced species like apes and marine mammals possessed intelligence. But with the exponential development of computers, robots, software, and artificial intelligence (AI), what we think of as smarts may now also be embodied by machines. This means one of two things: either our race against the machines has become much harder and more heated, or our machines can now make up for human frailties and weaknesses, essentially plugging the holes in human cognition.

Which one is it?

To start, take a moment to reflect on the challenges at Mayo Clinic, as defined by doctors Doug Wood and David Farley: too much to learn and read and too few hours for hands-on practice. In many ways, health care is moving too fast and growing too big for even the most brilliant among us to handle.

Enter IBM's latest supercomputer, Watson. If you're a fan of the TV quiz show *Jeopardy*, you'll remember Watson's victory over Ken Jennings and Brad Rutter. How wide was the margin of victory? The word *drubbing* comes to mind. But there's no dishonor in losing to Watson. The earlier, and less powerful, incarnation of Watson was Deep Blue, the supercomputer that beat Gary Kasparov, considered by many to be the greatest chess player of all time, in a six-game match. That opened people's eyes to the growing power of AI. But now Watson has moved on to even bigger stakes, making decisions that are literally life or death.

As part of my research for this book, I attended a lecture at Singularity University by Chris Wicher, the IBM computer scientist responsible for the Watson project. Half mad scientist and half favorite science teacher, Wicher explained that the first big commercial application for Watson will be in health care.

To begin its career in medicine, Watson is currently working with oncologists, the doctors who diagnose and treat cancer, at Memorial Sloan-Kettering Cancer Center. Located in New York City, Sloan-Kettering is a leader in cancer treatment, so its doctors typically see the most complex cases in the world. That's why IBM chose Sloan-Kettering to train and test Watson. Much like those at Mayo Clinic, the doctors and nurses at Sloan-Kettering are brilliant, passionate people. As Wicher, no intellectual slouch himself, described it, "It's humbling to be around all the oncologists at Memorial Sloan-Kettering."

But, as you can imagine, there are no cookbook solutions, no simple answers, to these incredibly complex cases. In truth, it's almost impossible for a human being to absorb all the information on cancer, to go through every possible permutation and understand every piece of available literature.

This is where Watson enters the picture. Basically, the people at IBM and Sloan-Kettering sent Watson to medical school. It ingested medical textbooks, medical journals, important medical papers, and the results of all the salient clinical trials ever performed. And this is for each individual type of cancer. Now,

Watson doesn't take an article on blind faith, but instead weighs the validity of the information. Incredibly, Watson looks at different evidence, different clinical trials, and different articles and assigns them varying quality ratings.

And it's actually the Sloan-Kettering oncologists who determined Watson's "course load." The idea was if these oncologists had unlimited brain power and time, what would they want to read, study, and absorb to be the very best in their field. They gave it to Watson, which ingested millions and millions of documents related to every type of cancer.

Additionally, for each individual case, Watson absorbs the patient's entire medical record, which includes doctors' notes, nurses' notes, test results, blood work, and summary reports of various body scans.

Are you starting to sense of the power of Watson?

Watson has now gone to medical school and knows all the available facts of the individual case. And, of course, one of the big benefits of Watson is a big-data capability of easily jumping between discrete and seemingly disparate data sets and noting correlations that are hard—make that nearly impossible— to observe. You feed in someone's symptoms, along with their history, along with their genomics, and Watson is able to see how everything lines up compared to all the cancer research and trials in the world.

That's big.

Typically, an oncologist looking at an individual patient and following established protocol can narrow down treatment options to about twenty-five regimens, each of which has theoretically equal efficacy for the patient. But how do you choose the best of the twenty-five?

That's where Watson shines. It whittles down the number of optimal treatment options to a handful that will have the greatest efficacy for this patient.

And when you're talking about things like quality of life, debilitating side effects, and even death, this is an incredible leap forward. This is something that helps people under a death sentence to live longer and better lives. This iteration of Watson isn't going to replace doctors, but it's a terrific consultant.

So what's next? When you talk with AI experts like Chris Wicher and the people at Singularity, it's very clear that the next giant step forward, the real power in the future, will come when we have networks of cognitive systems like Watson. They'll be heterogeneous, with each machine focusing on a distinct discipline. Think of a vast network of cognitive systems able to interact, consult each other, and trade masses of information in an instant. Make all the jokes you want about Skynet—the fictional AI network in the *Terminator* movie series—but it's an amazing power; one that will change the world around us. Especially in historically slow-moving industries like health care.

CAN MAYO LEARN FAST ENOUGH TO AVOID DISRUPTION?

Medicine as we know it is about to be disrupted, big time, and not just by IBM's Watson. Many other cutting-edge technologies and new health care delivery models are gaining traction. Consider that in 2012 Qualcomm, the smartphone chip maker, sponsored a $10 million X-Prize competition to see which inventor can turn an ordinary smart phone into the closest approximation of the fictional *Star Trek* tricorder—a hand-held device that diagnoses diseases and injuries. And fiction is rapidly becoming fact: already you can buy an app and thumb pads for your iPhone that will let you measure your EKG. Vivek Wadhwa of Singularity, who suffered a heart attack in his forties, records his EKG on his iPhone every day.

Another kind of disruption is suggested by specialty hospitals such as Cancer Centers of America, which look like a replay of big box retailers' disrupting department stores. This time the old-style department store is an all-purpose hospital. Yet more disruption will arise from drugstores like Walgreens that provide walk-in health care services suitable for common illnesses, such as colds, fevers, ear infections, and the like.

In *The Innovator's Prescription*, authors Clayton Christensen, Jerome Grossman, and Jason Hwang note that the biggest disrupter of all could be large employers outside the health care industry. Facing untenable health care costs, large employers will soon take matters into their own hands and begin to fund their own clinics.

So the question for Mayo Clinic becomes, can its soft-edge excellence, particularly in smarts, help it adapt to what will be the mother of all disruptive waves about to crash over the health care industry?

"We think of technologies like Watson as having great value," said Dr. Doug Wood, the cardiologist who heads Mayo Clinic's Center for Innovation. "Having something like Watson would actually be a tremendous help in synthesizing a lot of that knowledge." So Mayo Clinic is not running from new technology and the disruption it promises. Like all great organizations, it's running toward it by actively thinking of ways to adapt to the coming changes.

"Fundamentally, we know we have to recreate Mayo Clinic," Dr. Wood explained. "We think an important part of that is being there for patients when needed." According to Dr. Wood, that doesn't mean being there from 8 to 5, Monday through Friday, or when a customer—note how Dr. Wood uses the word *customer*, not *patient*—needs a hospital room. Instead, it's being there every time the customer needs to make an important health decision. Do I really need to see a doctor or can I handle this myself? Dr. Wood puts it this way: "What can Mayo deliver that will help everybody be comfortable with their decision? Customers should feel comfortable, not threatened, not scared. Our job is to do it in a way that's simple and easy and meaningful for people, so that in turn we actually become a trusted partner in health."

As part of this reimagining of Mayo Clinic and its services, Wood has learned that people only need a doctor about 20 percent of the time. "A lot of the other things could be done by nurses, dieticians, physical therapists, or pharmacists," Dr. Wood revealed. "And 12 to 15 percent of people didn't need to be in a clinical setting at all. Instead, we could deliver the necessary service by computer, maybe by phone, maybe in a grocery store, maybe at work or school."

When the people at Mayo studied this issue, they realized they'd be more effective and efficient if they worked in small, high-performance teams. If that's a surprise to you, then just wait until you read Chapter Five. As Dr. Wood explained, "What would happen if we blew up the traditional model of one doctor and one nurse? And we said, okay, let's take one doctor, one nurse, and two or three people who are not as heavily licensed, and then bring in other specialists when we need to. We'll call that an optimized care team."

And guess what? Surveys and follow-up questionnaires revealed a higher level of satisfaction among patients (oops, customers) *and* providers. As a bonus, the people at Mayo Clinic also realized that with their optimized care teams, they could offer care to triple the number of patients. That's right—not a 5 percent or 10 percent increase, but three times as many. Mayo is effectively multiplying its doctors by three and improving health at the same time.

Increased convenience and increased efficiency: so far so good. But Mayo's new vision of itself stretches even further—reaching into surprising but familiar territory.

"We're trying to make Mayo Clinic a welcoming spot," Dr. Mark Warner, executive dean for education at Mayo, told me. "And it's not something that happens automatically. Ritz-Carlton and Disney probably do it about as well as anybody." So, to provide the same world-class service, Mayo Clinic has created programs with both Ritz-Carlton and Disney to train Mayo employees to be as welcoming and hospitable as possible. "It can be a simple thing," Dr. Warner explained, "like are you allowed to extend your hand to shake somebody's hand or not? In some cultures you are and in some cultures you aren't. It's offensive to some people if you extend your hand."

The point? At Mayo Clinic, accelerated learning goes beyond just science, medicine, and licensure: it also includes the culture. "That's one thing we do in education that goes beyond what you ordinarily think of as education," Dr. Warner pointed out. Empathy is part of delivering the whole package of excellence. You see it and feel it every time you walk into a Mayo Clinic, whether in Rochester or in any of its satellite locations. When you enter those facilities, you don't feel the anxiety you feel when you walk into most hospitals. Instead, you feel trust, confidence, and comfort.

We can learn a lot from how Mayo Clinic has dialed up its smarts in order to prepare for coming waves of disruption in health care. This includes focusing on creating greater trust, an advantage explored in Chapter Three. It also includes a shift toward using small, high-performance teams, as outlined in Chapter Five. But the true smarts advantage comes with Mayo's focus on hospitality and service—a clear move toward creating a complete, integrated experience (something discussed in much more detail in Chapter Six).

In taking this step toward creating a more complete experience, the smart folks at Mayo have embraced two of the most important techniques in this chapter. They've found their mentors by reaching out to two best-of-breed companies— Ritz-Carlton and Disney—in the hospitality game. Also, they've learned to think laterally by adapting techniques from the hotel and amusement park industries, two fields that clearly eschew the grim, sterilized feel of most health care settings. Because of these purposeful efforts, there's no reason why Mayo can't remain a force for good in health care.

It's a belief of mine that soft-edge excellent companies are better prepared to adapt to the type of disruption threatening the health care business. Soft-edge excellence—in trust, smarts, teams, taste, and story—tends to attract loyal customers and committed employees. That's one reason why I urge consistent investment in all the advantages that define the soft edge, even though the return-on-investment is not as immediately clear as it is on the hard edge of business.

GAINING THE EDGE

- Smarts—as defined by academics as g and measured by the IQ test—matters less in business than you might think.

- Smarts in business is more about tenacity and grit than IQ. Grit turns on the adaptive response, which accelerates learning.
- Smart leaders think laterally. They love to learn from innovative thinkers in different industries.
- Smart companies build alliances with other smart companies. They're known by the company they keep.
- Smart companies don't deny their challenges. They prefer to run a little bit scared—but not so much that they're paralyzed.
- Smart companies encourage people to talk about their mistakes and what they learned along the way.
- Smart organizations embrace transformative technology, even if it costs them in the short run.

5

▲

Teams

Great Things Come to the Lean and Diverse

In 1989, Jim Barksdale was scared. To know why this matters, let me first introduce you to Barksdale. The easiest way to do that is to jump in our time machine and briefly leap forward to August 9, 1995.

On that day, a young firm called Netscape was going public. This was the first major Internet initial public offering, and investors were eating it up. Shares were offered at $28, but demand was so backed-up that Netscape's price almost immediately tripled to $74.75. The price settled to $58.25 by the end of the day. Investors loved the Netscape story. Its co-founder was twenty-four-year-old Marc Andreessen, an apple-cheeked Wisconsin man fresh from the University of Illinois Supercomputer Center. The other co-founder was middle-aged Jim Clark, who had started Silicon Graphics years before. Neither Andreessen nor Clark could reliably run Netscape. Andreessen was young and untested as a CEO. Clark was a genius, but erratic. So the

Netscape CEO duties fell to an outsider, Jim Barksdale, who had been CEO of McCaw Cellular.

Barksdale, a southerner, was seen as a mystery man in Silicon Valley. But industrial America certainly knew of him. Born and raised in Mississippi, he attended the state university in Oxford and was elected senior class president. In 1979, Barksdale was named chief information officer of FedEx, and in 1983, Barksdale became the overnight delivery firm's chief operating officer. It's fair to describe Barksdale as having a dual fluency. He's somebody who had proved he could run a big industrial operation like FedEx while also knowing where technology was headed.

Now that you know Barksdale, let's get back in our time machine and return to 1989, when Barksdale was still COO of FedEx. At that point, he was facing a technology problem at FedEx that he solved with a new and highly unusual team member.

By 1989, Barksdale was seeing rapid changes to technology that could leave his employer, FedEx, in a bad spot. Throughout the 1980s, Barksdale had invested heavily in IBM mainframes to run FedEx. "We were a big mainframe shop," he told me. "In fact, by the mid-1980s, we were the largest IMS single image database in the world, keeping up with all those damn packages."

But now, in 1989, the old computer world was starting to crumble. The leading edge was swiftly moving to a new generation of networked computers. If FedEx didn't get the transition right, it had a lot to lose. In fact, FedEx had more to lose than its competitors, for the very reason that FedEx had invested so heavily in mainframe architecture. FedEx could be left saddled with old, slow technology—and be rendered uncompetitive—if it didn't act. What to do?

Barksdale called FedEx board member Phil Greer, a New York venture capitalist, for ideas. Greer had one. Years before,

Greer's firm—Weiss, Peck and Greer—had invested in a Silicon Valley company called Bridge Communications, founded by a husband-wife team of Bill Carrico and Judy Estrin. Carrico was the sales head and Estrin the technologist. While doing her master's at Stanford, Estrin had worked closely with Internet protocol language inventor Vint Cerf. That was a huge credibility test, and Estrin had passed it with flying colors, causing Greer to invest. In the mid-1980s, Greer had asked Barksdale to join Bridge's board. Both men were hugely impressed with Judy Estrin. "We loved her," said Barksdale.

That's how Barksdale and Greer decided to go to FedEx founder Fred Smith with their crazy Judy Estrin idea. *Now, Fred*—one can imagine Barksdale and Greer saying—*I know what you're thinking. She's only thirty-six. She's never been a CEO. She's never served on a large company board.* Estrin was summoned to Memphis where Smith pronounced her "blindingly bright." "We felt that having IT and audit in a single bucket [as board committees] was a mistake. It meant you were not looking at technology as a strategic issue," he said. Smith instantly grasped that Judy Estrin was the perfect person to head the FedEx Information Technology and Oversight Committee.

Estrin served on the FedEx Board from 1989 to 2010. In an e-mail, she described being asked to join in 1989: "I remember going to lunch with Jim Barksdale. Jim said he'd given my name to Fred and asked if I would consider joining the board. The first step would be to go talk to people in Memphis. I was surprised and honored. I knew what small company boards were like, but had never worked for a large company and certainly had never had experience in the board room."

I asked Estrin what her first board meeting in was Memphis was like.

"I remember feeling reasonably out of place—the only woman, significantly younger than anyone else in the room, the only one from the West Coast, one of the few technologists. But I knew Phil Greer and Jim Barksdale, so that made it a bit easier. I was also a bit intimidated by Fred—although he was very welcoming. He was, and is, so smart and such a strong leader. I hadn't met many people in business like him before."

After twenty-one years, Estrin's intense travel schedule led her to retire from the FedEx board in 2010. She still serves on the board of the Walt Disney Company. (She's also the person who coined the term "cloud computing" back in 2001.) As you think about building and managing your teams for lasting success, a good place to start is with this question: Who are your company's Judy Estrins?

TEAMS ARE OLD, TEAMWORK IS NEW

We humans are social by nature. If you look back through our history, we've always collaborated in families, tribes, or teams to survive. After all, you couldn't kill a ten-ton woolly mammoth on your own, right?

You might be surprised that our social nature, and our resulting inclination to work together, is primarily due to cognitive evolution. Essentially, we're hardwired to live, work, and excel in teams. Studies of perception and action in social situations show that the human brain contains an ability to recognize situations that require a team effort. In a team, we actually perceive our jobs differently than we would if acting alone. This type of recognition triggers specialized, coordinated cognitive abilities that are attuned, as Rutgers professor Natalie Sebanz and her colleagues put it, "to make common cause."[1] Through these adaptations, the neocortex—the higher-functioning, outer brain layer—has evolved as a "social brain" that pushes us to gain advantages by working as teams.[2]

Builders of the Egyptian pyramids understood teams. So has every military leader in recorded history. What's astonishing is how recent is the idea that teams can be more than the sum of their parts—far more, in fact. Readers with a long memory, or an itch to read back through decades of management literature, will know that terms like "teams" and "teamwork" didn't begin seeping into the organizational vernacular until the 1970s. Oddly late, don't you think? Why these appeared in the 1970s is anyone's guess. Maybe the turbulent economy, or the fracturing of social cohesion—conditions that exist today—caused researchers and management theorists to look deeper into why some teams fail and others succeed.

Today, the amount of research aimed at understanding effective team performance is overwhelming. Military, social, cognitive, and organizational psychologists have now been studying teams for the last few decades.[3] Thanks to the work of behavioral scientists like Chris Argyris, Amy Edmondson, Deborah Ancona, and Eduardo Salas, we can see what teams do, how they do it, and how to improve what they do.[4]

Teams, of course, come in all shapes and sizes. The precise configuration of any team is usually determined by its task. Production and execution teams can involve thousands of people in building an offshore oil platform or just two people in writing the melody and lyrics for a song. Some teams work together for years, creating strong bonds of familiarity and trust. Other teams—like those in hospitals, restaurants, or retail outlets—may need to change for each patient, patron, or client. Accordingly, teams exist for nearly every purpose and occasion, along with advice and theory on how to best build and manage each type of team.

But in this chapter, my focus is on small teams of eight, ten, or twelve people. Think of leadership teams, product teams, research teams, and design teams. In my experience, these types of teams are the most prevalent—and the most effective. To show how this works, let me return to FedEx, a stunningly complex global giant that relies on small teams to maintain its focus.

THE MIGHTY POWER OF THE TWO-PIZZA RULE

The big dance near the Mississippi delta begins each night at 11 PM. The glow of lights can be seen from the house of rockabilly singer Jerry Lee Lewis in Nesbit, Mississippi, six miles to the south. But we're not at a roadhouse. And the beverages of choice aren't beer and whiskey but coffee and Red Bull. We're at the Memphis International Airport.

Here, each night of the year, the world's largest air cargo company becomes the largest industrial operation of any kind. On a typical night, from 11 PM to 4 AM, the FedEx Express World Hub processes 1.5 million packages. During this five-hour window, some 150 jets arrive from as far away as Hong Kong. The jets don't make money sitting on the ground. They're offloaded, repacked, refueled, and sent back in the air within thirty minutes.

Except during Christmas season. That's when it gets busy. In December 2013, FedEx moved more than 22 million packages globally on its peak shipping day. That's nearly double the peak shipping day of 11.5 million packages in 2007.

Handling the holiday surge takes focus and teamwork. For example, during the busiest day in 2013 at the FedEx Express

World Hub in Memphis, package processing jumped from an average of 1.5 million to about 3 million during a twenty-four-hour period. The Memphis hub operates almost around the clock, with only a short break to perform equipment maintenance checks. Each package has its bar code scanned as it gets off one jet, is sorted onto a conveyor belt—there are 4.4 miles of conveyor belts at the Memphis hub—and ends up on another jet.

"If there were 'Seven Wonders of the Industrial World,'" wrote Jeffrey Rayport of MIT's *Technology Review*, "the FedEx Express World Hub would easily rank among them, right up there with Toyota's production centers, Google's data centers, and NASA's Mission Control."[5]

The hub occupies nine hundred acres—bigger than Central Park in New York City—on the northern and eastern side of Memphis International Airport. Tiny, by comparison, is the commercial terminal on the airport's southwest side. The Memphis hub employs 11,000 people and has its own fire department.

More astonishing is that the 11,000 Memphis hub employees represent a tiny fraction of FedEx's 300,000 total global workforce. FedEx operates more than 630 jets and turboprops around the world and 45,000 trucks for FedEx Ground. The logistics required to keep this near $50 billion revenue company going and growing are on a scale not seen in human history outside of war. The only equal is FedEx's rival, UPS, which operates a similar air hub it calls Worldport in Louisville, Kentucky.

The FedEx Express World Hub story is fairly well known. What is less known about FedEx is how it runs itself. I wanted to understand this firsthand, so I went to visit Fred Smith himself.

Smith explained the FedEx dynamic and dilemma: "In a big organization like FedEx, we can throw our weight around. We can buy paper cheaper. We can buy jet fuel cheaper. Our production capability can outdo your production capability. We're bigger, faster, and so forth. We have scale. But now comes the challenge. With scale comes a huge risk. And that is loss of focus."

The sixty-nine-year-old founder, CEO, and chairman of FedEx Corporation was wearing a white shirt and tie—all executive employees in Memphis dress formally—minus the coat. It was August in Memphis, after all. We were sitting in Smith's personal conference room. The ex-Marine and Vietnam veteran who founded Federal Express in 1971 spoke in the crisp language of a fighter pilot.

The most surprising thing about my meeting with Smith was the location. I had expected the FedEx Corporation global headquarters to be at the airport, in or near the World Hub. My alternative guess would have been in downtown Memphis near the FedExForum, home to the Memphis Grizzlies pro basketball team. But that's not where we met. We were in a brown, four-story building on South Shady Grove Road in sleepy suburban Memphis. This quiet location works just fine for Smith. It's the perfect symbol of how he balances FedEx's global scale with an intense focus built around small teams. To explain his small-team focus, Smith shoved a spiral-bound FedEx Corporate Operating Manual toward me and drew on a whiteboard.

At the top is a holding company called FedEx Corporation. Smith is the CEO and chairman. He has eleven direct reports, beginning with the CEOs of FedEx's four major operating companies:

- FedEx Express, the air cargo service, with $27.2 billion in 2013 revenue
- FedEx Ground, the small-package ground service, with $10.6 billion in 2013 revenue

- FedEx Freight, the large-package, long-haul trucking service, with $5.4 billion in 2013 revenue
- FedEx Services, which includes FedEx Office, the retail shops purchased from Kinkos in 2004, with $1.6 billion in 2013 revenue

Smith's other reports include the general counsel, the chief financial officer, the chief information officer, and the heads of sales, marketing, operations, and human resources. These seven reports make sure that the FedEx operating companies, in Smith's words, "operate independently, compete collectively, and manage collaboratively." The idea is to present a single FedEx face to customers and shareholders.

As more and more companies strive to stay agile and innovative, they've discovered that units of eight to twelve people, like Smith's core leadership team, work best as the natural size of high-performance teams. Jeff Bezos, founder and CEO of Amazon, calls it the "two-pizza rule," specifying that a development team should be small enough for two pizzas to feed. Bezos didn't invent the term; it seems to have first appeared at the Xerox Palo Alto Research Center (PARC) in the 1970s. Recall that Xerox PARC during the 1970s invented three of modern computing's key pillars: the graphical user interface, printer languages, and local area networking. This alone is a good reason to pay attention to the two-pizza rule.

The surface reason most often cited for using the two-pizza rule is that it keeps teams agile and fast. It does do that. But there's a deeper reason it works. When teams consist of a dozen people or less, each team member is more likely to care about the others.

At a dozen team members or smaller, people are far likelier to share information. They also are far likelier to come to one another's aid. If the mission is important enough, they'll even sacrifice themselves. It's no surprise that the basic unit of the U.S. Army's Special Forces is the twelve-person Operational Detachment Alpha. Soldiers will jump on a grenade to protect their teammates. The principle works in business, too. In a small team, marketing associates will stay up all night to sharpen another team member's presentation. Engineers will get their hands dirty to ensure the product is perfect at launch. This unity tends to fall apart as teams scale up. At a hundred people, you sort of care about your team members, but it's not top of mind. More than that, and team unity becomes a daunting challenge.

So the key question is always, "How many team members will be needed to accomplish a task?" To sum up the advice I heard in many of my interviews: Work your way to the smallest possible number you think you need, then subtract one. The "minus one" philosophy, which I first heard from management guru Tom Peters, forces the remaining team members to be creative. That's where you start. Lean and hungry. Fewer than a dozen if you can manage. You can always add later.

GETTING SMALL AND FAST: SAP

Not that long ago, the rap on SAP, the German-headquartered software giant, was that it had fail-safe software, but you had to reengineer your entire company to use it. Perhaps that thinking had some basis, but the SAP of today is a profoundly different company than it was just five years ago. And the most striking change has occurred in the use of product development teams.

Of SAP's 65,000-person worldwide workforce, some 20,000 are product developers. These are the people who design, develop, code, and package enterprise-level software products and services. And those 20,000 people are spread around the globe. They work across borders, cultures, and beliefs. But to stay ahead of today's ever-present competition and disruption, particularly of the cheaper software-as-a-service (SaaS) kind, SAP leaders knew they needed to cut their product development time from 14.8 months to approximately 6 months. And do it within three years. Think about that: cut the product development time by almost 60 percent in a company with a lot of legacy to protect—65,000 employees, 20,000 developers, $16 billion in revenue, and a $90 billion market cap. No easy feat.

"When I thought about where SAP needed to go," Jim Snabe (then co-CEO of SAP) explained to me in 2013, "I didn't look at our main competitors who were our size or bigger. Instead, I looked at the small companies out in Silicon Valley. We visited a number of them, including gaming software companies, where we saw the agile development methodology, which is basically prototyping and fast integration with customers."

Snabe realized that the real challenge, the lethal disruption, to SAP would come from below and not from peers like Oracle and IBM. So he looked at those small, nimble companies and asked himself, "How do we match their speed? How do we get to six months?"

Snabe went radical. He took his management team and all of SAP's heads of development on what he called a "leader's quest." During this time, they visited other large companies in different industries in order to gather new ideas and gain inspiration. "We visited Intel," Snabe said. "We visited Cisco. And we also visited Porsche." Porsche was particularly helpful because it had increased its production volume fourfold and improved profitability by 19 percent. How? "They did it by creating mini-teams that were empowered to constantly improve the way the company was run," Snabe explained.

Subsequently, the SAP leadership combined these two methodologies:

> Methodology number one: Look at small, nimble software start-ups—their (and your) true disruptive competitors—as a way of seeing where they needed to go.

> Methodology number two: Look at other large companies that had transformed themselves as a means of seeing how to get there.

"We came back," Snabe explained, "and said, okay, let's trust our people. We created a strategy which radically changed the way we innovate in order to become much more agile and much, much faster. A lot of that was putting aside our pride as managers and letting people loose. We had to trust that they would be able to find a faster and better way alone than when headquarters tried to help them."

That was the key idea—small teams empowered to make their own decisions.

"It's not important whether it's exactly eight or ten or twelve people," Snabe said. "It's a group of roughly ten people who had the competence to make the decisions necessary to complete the entire cycle, including the quality of the software, the functionality, and architectural blueprint. It's that team of ten. By acting like this, we're basically a bunch of start-ups, but we work under one master plan."

That gave SAP two powerful benefits: the speed of an entrepreneur multiplied by enormous scale in the market. "I've always said," Snabe remarked, "innovation is not turning money into ideas. Innovation is turning ideas into money. That means you have do more than just build a product. You have to get it to market at scale. You need the scale to have something that's a true innovation. Otherwise it's just an invention."

The result: SAP cut product development time from 14.8 months to 7.8 months. "Cut nearly in half in three years," said Snabe. "And the quality of software is significantly up. Now SAP's goal is to get development time to 6 months."

SAP's transformation was extraordinary. In many ways, it's a fundamental corporate model change. Just take a moment to think about some of Snabe's phrasing: "radically changed the way we innovate"; "more agile and much, much faster"; "trusting people"; and "letting people loose."

SAP's story of transformation highlights just a few of the most important practices and benefits associated with small, high-performance teams.

IF SHARING IS GOOD, WHY IS IT SO HARD?

In theory, teams can manage stress more effectively, be more flexible, make better decisions, and be more productive than individuals acting alone. Because of these factors, there's little doubt that today more businesses and industries are *trying* to implement high-performance, team-based systems than ever before.

Did you see the key word in that sentence? *Trying*. We're trying. And trying. But still often failing. Vivek Wadhwa, a former software entrepreneur and now affiliated with Singularity University in Silicon Valley, had an interesting take on the struggles with building and managing great teams. I visited Wadhwa at the Singularity campus near the NASA Ames Research Center in Silicon Valley, where he told me that a big part of the problem stems from traditional education. "When you and I went to school, we were taught to be individuals," he explained. "We sat row after row and the teacher was on the blackboard imparting knowledge. We wrote down our own personal notes. We went back, we studied on our own, in our own textbooks. Then we returned and took tests. If we shared knowledge with each other, it was called cheating."

But sharing is what great teamwork is all about. Successful teams must go through a process of sharing knowledge, opinions, and insights. And not once but continuously. For teams to over-achieve and outperform their rivals—and isn't that the goal of all teams?—those with differing views and divergent perspectives must be seen as valued group members. But like so many things in life, doing so is much easier said than done.

Which leads to a subject that most of us have a hard time talking about—diversity. In fact, diversity is so politically loaded, it's almost dangerous to talk about it.

DIVERSITY WILL FAIL IF IT'S SHALLOW AND LEGALISTIC

It's clear that the workforce, both in the United States and in other countries, is increasingly diverse.[6] That's a good thing. Changing demographics and civil rights gains made by women and minori-ties have created organizations that are far more diverse—or *heterogeneous*, as researchers would say—than in the past.[7]

This, I think, has helped develop a strong belief among researchers and the general population alike that diversity in teams leads directly to increases in synergistic knowledge and information sharing, and therefore, greater creativity. And that, by definition, equates to higher team performance. But—

You knew there had to be a "but," right?

But an examination of the research reveals no consistent, positive effects of racial and gender diversity on team performance. In fact, an award-winning paper by Thomas Kochan, a professor at the MIT Sloan School of Business, concluded that the financial case for diversity remains hard to support. Based on a five-year research effort, Kochan and his team flatly stated, "We found that racial and gender diversity do not have the positive effect on performance purposed by those with a more optimistic view of the role diversity can play in organizations."[8]

Hold on a second. Different perspectives, more skills, and more knowledge: what could possibly be the problem with those qualities?

Well, many studies have found that diversity can have negative effects on team communication. And by extension, this can result in poorer performance and lowered team member satisfaction.[9] Put another way: the different perspectives, behaviors, attitudes, and values diverse team members bring to a task may negatively affect sharing. As a result, this can quickly create disharmony. So leading or working with a diverse team can be difficult. It requires an ability to unlock potential and make the most of individual abilities.

To be clear, this isn't an argument against diversity. I know the glass ceiling is alive and well. Twitter went public in 2013 with an all-white male board of directors. Sad thing is, Twitter is viewed as an enlightened California company. So please understand, I fully support diversity initiatives that reduce discrimination and increase access to opportunity. These types of efforts are both a moral imperative and a critical part of success in a more competitive marketplace.

But I also appreciate efforts to understand how the increased diversity of teams influences work performance. If we don't have a strong handle on the implications of crossing cultural, occupational, and generational boundaries, how can we cultivate the knowledge and expertise of each individual?

We can't. It's that simple.

And, in truth, increasing team diversity without a strong understanding of *how* to mitigate these differences is counterproductive.

The flipside of the argument, of course, is that diversity creates value and improves team outcomes, even when it creates challenges for teams and team leaders. Because diversity includes relationships among people with different information and experiences, diverse teams have an enhanced capacity for creative problem solving. Diverse teams have a broader range of knowledge and skills. Diverse teams produce higher-quality solutions, and they do it faster. Those are tangible benefits; ones that are identified and explored in detail in many of the great resources and books on team performance and leadership.[10]

So what's the best way forward?

It's this: stop thinking of diversity solely in terms of categories like gender and race. That kind of diversity is important for societal reasons, but isn't sufficient for higher performance. From my exploration of teams and team dynamics, I've found the broader and more inclusive designation of *cognitive diversity*—which includes age and experience alongside race and gender—to be a more powerful concept, yet underreported in existing literature. It's not my intention to define and examine every facet of cognitive diversity, but instead to bring the concept to light.

WHY COGNITIVE DIVERSITY WORKS

In its most basic form, cognitive diversity relates to differing forms of generative and relational thinking. Or, put more simply, it refers to how we come up with ideas and tackle problems. This means cognitive diversity includes differences in mental process, perception, and judgment. Do we follow our gut or crunch numbers? Are we analytical and logical, or are we creative, flexible, and intuitive? Are we organized and detail oriented, or empathetic and expressive? Most likely, we're each made up of a wonderfully unique combination of these traits (yes, an engineer can be empathetic, and an artist can be logical).

In essence, all these cognitive characteristics define who we are and what we've learned. And this means they encompass a broad range of variables—generational differences, educational and skill variation, and social and cultural elements, including, of course, race and gender.

In the context of an eight-to-twelve-person team, harnessing the power of these cognitive differences entails combining people with different ways of thinking, feeling, and seeing. Nest Labs' founder and CEO Tony Fadell won his management chops at one of the most argumentative, and successful, companies in history—Apple during the 1997 to 2011 reign of Steve Jobs. Fadell is considered the father of Apple's first noncomputer product, the iPod. In that role, he worked alongside Jobs and saw how Jobs lighted fires of brutally honest creative argument to find the sweet spot between human intuition and machine logic.

I visited Fadell at Nest Labs' Palo Alto headquarters to talk about cognitive diversity in teams. Nest makes a "smart" thermostat that learns from a user until it can manage a house's heating and cooling by itself.

"At team meetings," Fadell said, "we have user-experience people, we have management, we have product management, and we have the algorithms and algorithms-analysis people." When making tough decisions at Nest, Fadell gets all these diverse people together in the same room. Some are women, some are men. The skin tones range from pale to dark. But it's not about gender or racial diversity. Rather, Fadell likes to mash up a room full of the cognitively diverse. Why? "If I left it solely to the algorithm people, they'd write code without considering other factors like design, marketing, or user experience. Each of Nest's customers have different comfort levels, and there are many different types of houses with very different heating and cooling needs."

By combining varied perspectives in Nest meetings, Fadell knows the Nest thermostat algorithms won't be written solely to satisfy the code jockeys at Nest. Instead, they'll be written to deliver a satisfying experience to a wide variety of Nest customers.

So, why cognitive diversity? Easy. Because your customers are cognitively diverse.

My conversations with Fadell and others highlight one effective technique for increasing team performance: it's vitally important for you to have analytical people and intuitive people in the room together on every major issue. You need the complementarities of the design people and execution people, the creative people and discipline people, the math people and sales people.

Before moving ahead, though, I want to correct one possible misconception. It would be very easy to read through the previous example and believe that cognitive diversity equates to different skills and intellectual styles. While it's true those things do play a significant role in cognitive diversity, they're not the only determinants. As I stated at the beginning of this section, cognitive diversity represents a much broader umbrella that includes age and knowledge. It includes race and gender. It includes experience and education. It's not just putting dreamers together with doers or numbers people together with creative types: it's also putting the young with the old, and the old with the older. It's putting together team members with different backgrounds and from different locations.

Now I can return to my opening story, because it illustrates how diversity helped FedEx with a specific challenge. As you recall, a FedEx board member, Phil Greer, and FedEx's chief operating officer, Jim Barksdale, had both worried that FedEx might miss a big transition from mainframe computers to networked computers. If FedEx bungled this transition, it would lose the informational and cost advantages it had enjoyed in its core business of air freight delivery.

Greer, Barksdale, and Smith were smart enough to see that FedEx needed a fresh and knowledgeable perspective. But where would FedEx find that perspective? Why not in Silicon Valley, where young companies were leading a revolution in networked computing? But who, exactly, in Silicon Valley? Well how about a technical genius, inventor, and entrepreneur named Judy Estrin? At age thirty-six she's old enough to be toughened by life, but still young for a large company board. No experience on a company board? Well, that's good. She'll speak her mind. Oh, and she's a she. Better still.

By mixing perspectives, thinking styles, and levels of experience, you can create the type of diversity needed to push performance and drive innovation. This is what FedEx did with Judy Estrin. This is the correct path, but it's not an easy road. It creates a very real and challenging problem—conflict.

SEEK DIFFERENT PERSPECTIVES, COMMON CORE VALUES

For a team to be successful, it's not enough to simply say, "Let's get together, knock heads, and it will all work out in the end."

No matter how much team spirit is created on the surface, conflicting preferences will limit collaboration and even thwart success.

What to do? My recommendation is to avoid generalizing preferences from a specific identity group. Not all members of an identity group have identical preferences. And not all stereotypes of an identity group are true.

Just think, the prevailing wisdom is that older people, say baby boomers like myself, dislike changes in their routines—both at work and at home—while younger people embrace change. Studies have shown that, in fact, resistance to change has little to do with age. Instead, it has more to do with how much a worker has to gain or lose as a result of the change.[11] That's just one example of many cases in which commonly held beliefs about specific groups just don't apply.

Therefore, instead of pigeonholing each identity group within a team, look beyond their differences to discover what they have in common. Beyond any social, cultural, generational, or educational differences, all employees want a chance to be respected, be challenged, and continue to grow. We all need credible leaders: people who encourage us and listen to us. We all want to learn more and receive training that helps us do a better job and get to the next level in our organizations. All the people I interviewed for this book truly believe this. One and all, they consider these cross-identity realities—that we all want to grow, learn more, and be better—as a basic tenet of their companies and true soft-edge excellence.

So take care to emphasize what's similar between team members instead of what's different. Some experts call it "bridging." Most researchers call it a "superordinate identity." My guess is that the rest of us would call it "common ground."

That said, great teams aren't just about finding common ground. Common ground can help create unity and trust, sure. And it can help lubricate collaboration. Those things are true. But common ground can also be a trap. It can reduce our willingness to discuss different perspectives and increase our tendency to focus on commonly held information. It can make us insular. It can cause us to reject good ideas that are not our own, as happened to American car companies in the 1970s and IBM in the early 1990s. IBM was so insular then, it even had a snarky phrase for outside ideas: "Not invented here." Don't laugh too hard at IBM's folly, because it could happen to you. The lure of insularity exists at all companies. It's always easier and safer to discuss commonly held beliefs and information rather than exchange information that could be considered controversial or contrary.

And that circles back to the importance of cognitive diversity and the lessons Tony Fadell learned at Apple. One of those lessons: sometimes it's just better to argue it out. Yes, there will be tension. It may be messy, and there will very likely be misunderstandings. It might even feel dysfunctional. But sometimes you just have to get people together, urge them to speak up, and convince them to face their disagreements. Encourage these difficult conversations. In the end, their differing opinions and interests will sharpen the company and result in better products and services.

So where are we? Diversity is a valuable tool. Check. Cognitive diversity is the best kind of diversity. Check. But it creates the potential for conflict. Understood, but now what? Tamp down the conflict and you get insularity. Bad. Let conflict run its course and you risk becoming so dysfunctional you get nothing done. Bad.

So aim for diversity that creates good conflict—about products and processes, not personalities. But how do you find the right mix and recruit the best individual team members to do so?

THREE ESSENTIALS: CHEMISTRY, PASSION, AND GRIT

Getting team chemistry right is essential to high performance. But that's not news, so let's get to the hard part. How can you tell if someone will make a good team member? What kind of screening can you use? In the corporate world, we haven't seen many meaningful advances since the advent of the Myers-Briggs Type Indicator test—in the middle of the last century!

Sure, there are more recent cognitive or thinking-styles tests like the Herrmann Brain Dominance Instrument, Kirton's Adaption-Innovation Theory, and the Five Factors Personality Test, but the effectiveness of each is debatable. The explosion of big data and analytical tools has not yet produced much good insight on how to staff and manage high-performance teams.

The U.S. military, by contrast, uses training and testing to find out pretty quickly how a person fits in. The military, and especially the Special Forces, used to put a big premium on pedigree. Did you attend one of the three academies? Did you rank in the top quartile? Do you have a high IQ, high test scores, and excellent grades?

But the military found that those types of standards didn't necessarily correlate to strong performance under fire. And that drove the creation of training exercises that mimic the extreme conditions of an operating theater. For example, Bill Owens—a retired Navy admiral and former vice chair of the Joint Chiefs—told me that one of the last things they do in

Navy SEAL Team 6 training is to fly over a body of water at jet altitude, nearly thirty thousand feet, and have candidates throw their inflatable rafts out the door. Then they jump out of the plane, pull the parachute, and, in the dark water, assemble all the pieces they need to get ashore and accomplish their mission. It may seem extreme, but that's the way it really works when stuff hits the fan.

But in the corporate world, we can't ask prospective employees to jump out of a plane, right? Well, maybe some people can, but most of us still need to resort to other techniques. Which puts enormous pressure on team leaders to do an exceptional job recruiting and choosing team members. From my interviews and discussions, I discovered a few things you should look for in a team member.

Eric Edgecumbe, chief operating officer at Specialized Bicycles, a global leader in high-end bicycles and bike gear, looks for commitment and a background in team sports. "To me, it's that selfless committing to the goal of the team. When I interview people I always ask them, 'Did you play any team sports in high school or college?' Tell me what you liked about being on a team; what you didn't like about being on a team."

Mike Sinyard, the founder of Specialized, believes you've got to passionately love your product. So you can't work at Specialized unless you love biking. Period. Is this fair? Why not? It's a bike company! You *should* love bicycles if you want to work there. And don't try to fake it. Specialized employees told me that Sinyard watches to see who does lunchtime group rides. You don't have to be a great cyclist, but you do have to *love* bikes. He doesn't just say that: he absolutely believes it.

"There's love, and then there's love," as Tony Fadell, of Nest Labs, remarked.

Fadell himself actually quizzes people on their passion: "One of the questions I ask when people come in is, 'When did you find your passion for the thing you do every day?' And for me, most of my best hires figured it out when they were in first, second, third, or fourth grade. They had some great story about how they found what they loved to do, and they just continued to learn about it."

In forming teams, you want people who are passionate. Those are the ones who will spend all the extra hours on a project; who will think about that problem or product on the weekends, in the shower, wherever they go. Every great invention, every significant advance in human history began with passion. A passion for change, for making the world a better place. A passion to contribute or discover something new. It might even be a revolutionary passion to kick an old, dysfunctional industry into the grave.

What is your passion?

How did you find your passion?

When did you find your passion?

Those are the questions you need to ask people when putting together a high-performance team. With a team full of passion, you can accomplish nearly anything. Without it, your team is likely to be a gaggle of clock-punching automatons.

But it doesn't just end with passion. In choosing team members, many of the leaders I spoke with brought up an old-fashioned trait—grit. Grit is the ability to overcome adversity. Robert Egger, chief designer at Specialized Bicycles, said: "I want a kid that's had it a little bit rough. I don't want the kid who says, 'Well, you know, my parents sent me to boarding school and then I went to Stanford where I read about your company.'" Similarly, Northwestern Mutual's Jennifer Brase told me: "People who do well at Northwestern have had to overcome something that has been extremely difficult. Sometimes I think to myself, wow, I'm not sure I could have overcome that."

Team orientation, passion, grit: those are the attributes of great team members. Passion and grit often count more than an off-the-charts IQ or an impressive degree when putting together a team. If you keep these factors in mind, you'll get the right people in the right place. But how do you push those chosen few to a higher level of performance?

CULTIVATE THE GIFTS OF HIGH EXPECTATIONS

One common trait I found among all these enduringly success-ful organizations was a demanding culture. This type of culture is built on a clear expectation of high performance, one of con-stant growth and improvement. But it's an expectation that's also built on an optimism about human capability. *Yes, we'll ask a lot of you. We do so because we really do believe you can be better and achieve bigger things*. Todd Schoon, executive vice president of Northwestern Mutual and manager of the firm's field rep force, referred to it as "the gift of high expectations."

Chef and restaurateur David Chang, founder of the acclaimed Momofuku restaurant group, told me the same thing in a slightly different way: "We don't want to hear what we're doing well, because we *should* be doing that well. It's supposed to be great. As a leader, you could be thankful. But never let the criteria for being good get too low."

These types of high expectations serve a number of purposes. They're a reference point for giving meaning to behaviors and actions. They motivate team members because they require more effort and have a much bigger return than vague or eas-ily met goals. Software giant Oracle has a famously tough and demanding company culture. Oracle's co-founder and CEO, Larry Ellison, is happy to defend it. "People don't burn out from hard work," he once told me. "They burn out from futile work."

A team leader who has high expectations is paying the team members a compliment. And when the team members then meet those expectations, the feeling of success not only becomes normative, it begins to grow and multiply. A virtuous cycle begins. That hard-to-define "winner's attitude" begins to take form. By creating high expectations and building a culture where, as Specialized Bicycles founder Mike Sinyard put it, "good isn't good enough," you institute a natural deterrent against the inertia that dooms so many companies and careers to mediocrity.

A big part of creating this atmosphere of achievement is being directive: demanding it. Let team members know your expectations. Don't screw around. Don't be a passive-aggressive wimp about it. Don't be afraid to drive people, cajole them, and push them to find that last 1 percent of team performance.

But do it with love.

As Tony Fadell reminded me, the true soft skill in raising team performance is being able to simultaneously drive and reassure your team members. "I've said this before," Fadell told me. "I said 'If you're not slightly scared or slightly worried, you're not pushing hard enough.'"

How does a leader maintain this vital balance? Fadell continued: "The leader needs somebody on the outside to help balance that scariness and kind of go 'Okay, look, everything's okay.' You're really pushing hard and you need that. You need the assurance that says, 'It's going to be really good.'" Fadell himself seeks the counsel of Bill Campbell, a board member of Apple and Intuit and an advisor to Nest. Campbell is often referred to in Silicon Valley as "the coach." Indeed, Campbell once coached football at Columbia University.

Ask big. Push hard. Fight complacency. Then use love and reassurance to get the balance right. A chronically scared team won't produce the best results. You want a slightly scared team—bold enough to stretch but scared just enough to remain alert. Find a coach like Bill Campbell to help you keep that balance.

Don't underestimate the power of reassurance. It is based on the genuine belief that good things—whether a new client, a groundbreaking product, or a championship—will come from working hard and following a system. This kind of real-world optimism is more than hope: it's the ability to approach your task as an opportunity. It's letting your team know that if they stay positive but alert and a touch paranoid—just a touch!—they'll have a shot at achieving something bigger and better.

Tara VanDerveer, head coach of the Stanford women's basketball team, summed it up perfectly: "To win, I strongly believe you need to have very high expectations of people's behavior and performance. But you also want to be really optimistic and positive."

And now we come to a subject that trips up a lot of managers: the need to control.

CREATE SPACE FOR PERSONAL AUTONOMY (WITH BOUNDARIES)

Team members worth a fig, by definition, will want some control over their own environment. Old-school managers fight that. But according to a 2008 study by Harvard University, there's a direct correlation between employees who have the ability to call their own shots and the value of their creative output.[12] So take notice:

a team member who has to run every detail by you will quickly lose initiative.

Remember the earlier SAP story, with its "bunch of start-ups" working "under one master plan"? Look at what people can accomplish when given the chance to make their own decisions. Look at how much faster individuals and teams can innovate when unencumbered by bureaucracy. But keep in mind, these highly autonomous "teams of ten" needed to check in every two to four weeks to show progress. They had support. They had to work within a system. They had accountability. And that's the secret of innovative teams: this ability to have autonomy, to have freedom, but within a strong, well-defined support system and with clear accountability.

Back to my Memphis meeting with FedEx's Fred Smith: "This is how we operate," he said, pointing to the thinner of two spiral-bound books, the FedEx Corporate Operating Manual. "These are the rules," Smith said. "They are to be followed."

This doesn't sound like much autonomy, I replied.

But Smith corrected me: "If the operating manual doesn't specifically tell the CEOs they have to do it this way, then everything is delegated to them and their operating teams." Smith compares his operating manual to the U.S. Constitution. Some of the rules of the FedEx Corporate Operating Manual are clear. An example includes: "The President/CEO of each core company will deliver before 8:30 Central time, each Friday, a summary of the key developments of the week . . . to the FedEx Corporate CEO." To Smith, in other words.

Were I working at FedEx, I wouldn't want to test an ex-Marine like Smith on that. No, sir!

But other FedEx rules leave more room for interpretation. Take business meetings, for example: "All business meetings will be scheduled judiciously to make efficient use of the participant's time, and should be conducted with agendas and statements of purpose. When appropriate, a summary with conclusions and follow-up assignments should be provided to participants, and other interested parties, as soon as possible. When feasible, the participants should be polled to assess the effectiveness of the meeting."

See the difference? The first example includes words like "will deliver." Don't test Smith on these. In the second example, there are qualifiers like "when appropriate" and "when feasible." Here Smith is saying don't sacrifice productivity for bureaucracy.

That's how FedEx's Smith balances tight organization and entrepreneurial autonomy in his four companies. While autonomy is good, how does FedEx prevent any one of its four CEOs or their employees from going rogue and damaging what Smith calls his "Purple Promise" brand?

Smith points again, this time to the other, fatter manual. It's 158 pages thick and is called The Global Manager's Guide. It speaks to leadership ethics and standards of performance. These fall under chapter headings such as Corporate Philosophy, Corporate Mission and Strategy, Mechanics of People Philosophy, and Being a Leader at FedEx. It's nothing more, really, than common sense and common decency.

But how many companies bother codifying it as FedEx has done?

Not enough. And it really goes beyond merely telling people what they can't do. Instead, it's a matter of being clear about rules and boundaries from the start, which immediately establishes an atmosphere of accountability.

This type of accountability helps articulate the expectations that team members adhere to high standards and pursue challenging goals. When team leaders are as clear as possible in setting boundaries, people actually feel freer to express thoughts or make mistakes than when boundaries are vague. The take-away: always establish and clarify boundaries at the outset of establishing a team.

So far, this chapter on teams has been mostly human driven, focusing on issues like leadership, conflict, expectations, and accountability. I grant the skeptic's point that the human aspects of team building are all easier said than done. That's been one of the big obstacles to good teamwork: so many of the concepts seem obvious and easy, yet they're very hard to implement consistently. But we all learn by studying the great leaders and successful models of the kind discussed in these pages. Therefore, my primary hope is that you'll take the lessons I've offered to heart, including the following:

- Embrace the power of small teams.
- Foster diversity in thinking styles, including in race, gender, age, and experience.
- Identify team spirit, passion, and grit when picking team members.
- Be explicit with your high expectations, but temper them with sincere sense of optimism, even love.
- Provide the autonomy needed to be creative and innovative, but set explicit boundaries.

All these tips are clear enough and basic enough to provide a powerful framework for building and managing the types of small, high-performance teams that ensure improvement and increase innovation. Now, let's change things up a bit and take a look at what technology and big data are contributing to the development of both bigger teams and better teams.

HOW TO USE CROWDSOURCING
TO MAGNIFY YOUR TEAM

In the preceding sections, I've focused on eight-to-twelve-person teams. Through my discussions with great organizations and great leaders, I've found this is the size and configuration that seems most conducive to team cohesion and performance. But to understand the real reach of technology, to comprehend how growing digital networks and increased data gathering are changing our perceptions of teamwork, you need to look beyond the idea of static, carefully composed teams and examine a new kind of team that's taking shape beyond their stable boundaries.

Earlier in the chapter, I introduced Singularity University's Vivek Wadhwa. In his association with Singularity, Stanford, and Duke, he's doing some very cool things with teams and team structures. One project with Stanford, in particular, involved the issue of discrimination against women. Wadhwa's research had shown him that the best way to solve the problem of discrimination is to get the victims involved in the solution. Or, in essence, to get people to help themselves. The question then was how do you inspire and motivate women to help each other overcome discrimination? His answer was to create a book that would include the voices of hundreds of women from all over the world.

In tackling the project, the critical skill for Wadhwa turned out to be managing teams and teamwork. And he wasn't dealing with a "two-pizza rule" team of eight or ten people: he was dealing with a team of nearly five hundred people. To handle teamwork on this scale, Wadhwa used social media, one of today's largest conduits of big data and digital networking. In particular, he used a crowdsourcing and crowdfunding campaign to aggregate the hundreds of stories and ideas needed for the whole book. And not only did these five hundred women provide stories, answer questions, and exchange ideas, they also became ambassadors and sales agents for the resulting book.

These new teams, as Wadhwa sees them, aren't just virtual. They're massive. "My role as a manager," he said, "has been to facilitate, to understand, how people work and think, to carve up the work into meaningful segments, and to inspire and motivate people to do it."

Great team leaders have always known how to take advantage of new technologies. But as a leader of teams on this scale, your value goes beyond understanding new tools like social media and crowdsourcing. You must also provide people with new ideas and motivate them. As Wadhwa put it, his job was to "throw this idea out there and say, 'Look, use your crowd, the untapped knowledge of your people.'"

Wadhwa's crowd-sourcing approach to writing a book probably won't knock great investigative reporting out of the box, but it's an interesting approach to creating massive, fluid teams. It also may be a significant part of our future. We may not like it. We may feel uncomfortable with it because, as team leaders and team members, it requires new skills and a different mindset. But, at the end of the day, failing to consider the future of teams and teamwork will only leave leaders and their organizations at a disadvantage.

Keeping that in mind, can science and technology also help us construct better teams? It's worth a look.

SOCIOMETRICS: THE HARD SCIENCE OF TEAMWORK

What makes a team click? That's an elusive question. We've all seen it and felt it. But without meaningful data there's simply no way to understand the dynamics that drive successful teams.

All we really have is an anecdotal sense of the behaviors—good leadership; shared commitment; a sense of trust, passion, and grit—that define great teams.

That may change. Through new data gathering and analytics technology, big data offers promising insights into the social patterns that define effective teamwork. Once invisible, the newly revealed data can uncover valuable models of how thousands of different people work and communicate within their own departments and teams.

Alex Pentland, a professor at the MIT Human Dynamics Laboratory, is the inventor of data-gathering badges that record a new type of human statistics called "sociometrics." This is a measure of how people interact, including things like their tone of voice, gesturing behavior, and even their levels of empathy.

With the help of a group of students, Pentland has been equipping people in banks, universities, call centers, and other businesses with sensor-packed badges. As these people collaborate, the sensors measure the timing and energy of their speech. The badges also measure, as Pentland put it, the "unconscious face-to-face signaling behavior" that suggests things like whether people are engaged listeners or enthusiastic followers. He contends these unconscious signals are often as important in communication as the actual words and their underlying logic.[13]

The badge-based studies have allowed Pentland's team at MIT to identify the communication patterns that make for successful teamwork. "We capture how people communicate in real time," Pentland explained. "And not only can we determine the characteristics that make up great teams, but we can also describe those characteristics mathematically."[14]

It turns out that productive teams have certain "data signatures" that are so consistent, Pentland can predict a team's success simply by looking at the data and without ever meeting its members. Now we're getting into *Moneyball* territory!

The data reveal other interesting facts, too. For example, individual talent contributes far less to team success than you might expect. This means the best way to build a great team may not be to select individuals for their talents or accomplishments, but instead to learn how they communicate. "The sociometric stuff told us what the facts really are, independent of the sociology and cultural clutter," said Pentland. "And some of the facts are surprising, like the fact that gossip improves productivity."[15] Dish for dollars—who would have guessed?

As a result of these experiments, the MIT team has identified a group of social signals that predicts the outcomes of sales pitches, the success of negotiations, and even the formation of trust—the foundation of all five of the soft-edge advantages and the topic of a previous chapter. These signals include the amount of time a person speaks, how much a person steers the conversation, and the impact of mirroring, which occurs when one participant subconsciously mimics another person's expressions and gestures during an interaction.

This additional channel of communication acts in parallel with verbal communication and is surprisingly powerful. For example, if one member of a team is happy and excited, others will tend to become more positive, an effect termed "mood contagion." This helps to lower feelings of risk within groups.[16]

And often team decision making doesn't even require language. In a sense, everyone assesses each suggested action and signals a level of interest, say with a quick nod. Then, while making a final decision, group members add up the various gestures to choose the option with the most positive signaling.

Moreover, negotiations with lots of mirroring tend to be more successful, regardless of which party starts copying the other's gestures. Mirroring with regular nods or short acknowledgments like "Right" or "Ah" may help build empathy between speaker and listener. Each of these signals, Pentland suggested, is likely to have roots in the evolution of the human nervous system.

In much the same way that sociometrics can quantify team dynamics, it can also measure individuals against an ideal. In nearly all types of teams, Pentland and his colleagues have discovered the "data signature" of what they consider the ideal team member. These people circulate actively, involving people in short, high-energy conversations. They talk to employees high and low and actively engage customers to seek ideas from outside the team. These ideal team members aren't necessarily extroverts—thankfully for many of us—although they do typically feel comfortable talking with other people.

Considering these results, Pentland envisions a time when sociometric badges and analysis can give leaders and managers more reliable ways to assemble the best possible teams. By analyzing the data, they'll be able to choose complementary team members, as well as avoid unnecessary conflicts, based on communication style. And, if deployed over an entire department or organization, leaders can actually create a digital dashboard that tracks idea flow and communication effectiveness among employees. Are people talking enough? Are the right people connecting? Is an organization harvesting internal expertise effectively? With this information, leaders can make adjustments that help shape and optimize communication behavior.

Similarly, for individuals who want to improve their communication skills, software programs may soon be able to analyze the tone, listening behavior, and other aspects of a conversation. The programs could then tell participants whether they tend to interrupt others or appear inattentive when colleagues speak.

These are exploratory days for the role of analytics in team building. But if Professor Pentland is on the right track, then the possibility exists that data and tools can close the gap between the Fred Smiths, Tony Fadells, and Tara VanDerveers—intuitive team-building geniuses—and the rest of us. This should offer great hope. Intense competition and growing disruption are giving rise to an increased need for collaboration and communication. This means the best leaders and managers must be able to motivate people to work harder, think smarter, and meet ever-rising goals. That ability has traditionally been disparaged as a "soft skill," but it's very quickly becoming one of the most important skills of all.

GAINING THE EDGE

- Teams are old, but the idea of teamwork in business is surprisingly recent.
- Teams, even in large companies, tend to perform best when they're at their leanest—eight to twelve people.
- Teams, when small, can move faster. Team members will sacrifice for other team members at a smaller size, but not at a larger size.
- Teams do their best when they encourage cognitive diversity—that is, diversity in thinking styles as well as in race, gender, and age.

- Teams should borrow an idea from sports and the U.S. military—use real-world stress tests to see how team members respond under pressure.
- Teams are best built from people who have overcome difficulty in their lives.
- Team leaders should cultivate the gift of high expectations. Demand great performance from team members. There is no higher compliment.

6

▲

Taste

Beauty Made Practical, Magic Made Profitable

Two miles west of Stanford University's divinely spectacular 180-acre campus in Northern California lie two geographical markers whose names imply something more like hell. One is the San Andreas Fault. When the big earthquake comes and again smashes the San Francisco Bay Area, it's a good bet it will happen along the San Andreas.

The other place of anguish is a twisty 3.2-mile road that rises 1,290 feet through the redwood trees. It is named Old La Honda Road, and it is so well known by local bicyclists that they call it simply OLH. In the cycling hotbed of the San Francisco Peninsula, OLH is the gut test of a cyclist's ability to grind up a steep hill (7.8 percent average gradient) and endure pain in legs and lungs. There's really no escaping the gruesome test of OLH. If you ride a bike in these parts, you will climb OLH at some point and you will time yourself. "It's the hill on which everyone knows their best time," according to a local blogger. A local cycling club called Western Wheelers even sorts its A- to E-level group rides based on how fast a cyclist can climb OLH.

For years, the rumored all-time OLH climber was Eric Heiden, the Olympic speed skater who won five gold medals at the 1980 Winter Olympics. Heiden then deployed his famous thunder thighs to bicycling and won the 1985 U.S. professional road race championship. He also rode in the 1986 Tour de France. Like many American speed skaters, Heiden hailed from Wisconsin. He had started college at the University of Wisconsin in Madison but then transferred to Stanford, graduating in 1984. He dabbled in pro cycling for a few years, then returned to Stanford to start medical school. He rented a house on Old La Honda Road. One day word got out that Heiden had climbed up OLH in just under fifteen minutes, the equivalent of a four-minute mile, the barrier everyone said couldn't be broken. But Heiden had done it.

So the legend said.

But since 2009, a social website designed for hikers, runners, and cyclists called Strava has put an end to guesses, rumors, and legends. If you have a watch, a cyclometer, or a smartphone with a GPS chip in it, Strava will map your walks, runs, and rides and record your times along segments to the last second. Since 2009, more than four thousand cyclists have recorded more than twenty thousand rides up OLH. The best time up OLH is 14:42 by a rider named Ryan Sherlock.

My best time is 25:18.

Or it was my best. In July 2013, I climbed OLH in 11:42. I shattered my own personal record and beat Sherlock's record by an even three minutes. In Strava terms, I was the new King of the Mountain with a gold crown next to my time.

How big of a difference is three minutes on a climb like OLH? Think of Secretariat's thirty-three-length destruction of the field at the 1971 Belmont Stakes. Or imagine outsprinting the world's fastest man, Usain Bolt, by 20 meters in the 100 meter dash.

Sorry, Mr. Sherlock.

It turns out Lance Armstrong's first book title was wrong; for me, it *was* about the bike. My new bike, the Turbo, made by Specialized Bicycles, had turned me from weekend grinder into Superman. The Turbo is indeed one of those magical products that reflects you not just at your best but even better—*you at your self-actualized best.* It gives you power; it makes you feel in control. What kind of company is capable of consistently making products or services that touch the highest reaches of our self-actualized hopes? And can you do it, too? Those are the subjects of this chapter. My hope is to capture, even if just obliquely, how a spark of innovation is made into something physical: how a synaptic inflection becomes a tangible object that surprises and delights.

But first, let me begin defining taste and answering why some products and services, to use my friend Guy Kawasaki's perfect word, *enchant* us.

WHAT IS TASTE AND WHY IS IT SO VALUABLE?

Initially, the focus of this chapter was on the theories and principles of great product design. And if you think about it, during the last few decades, design has become an increasingly valuable competitive asset in nearly every industry that touches our lives. This emphasis on design has pushed theories like Design Thinking into the mainstream consciousness and helped launch niche companies like IDEO—which has been featured in books, Harvard Business School case studies, and even on the CBS News program *60 Minutes*—into the public consciousness.

To be sure, this attention to design has stimulated market growth in many areas by making new products more desirable to consumers. And not just by putting a pretty wrapper around an idea but by imbuing objects with meaning and emotion, something vital to commercial success in today's crowded marketplace. As Daniel Pink wrote in his 2006 best seller, *A Whole New Mind*, "Abundance has satisfied, and even over-satisfied, the material needs of millions—boosting the significance of beauty and emotion and accelerating individuals' search for meaning."

Designers like Tom Kelley and Mario Bellini and writers like Donald Norman, Bruce Nussbaum, and Virginia Postrel have brought the importance of design, aesthetics, and glamor to the forefront. In debating ideas like object language, creative cognition, and total product design, they've made our world more intelligible and more habitable. That's something that can't be denied.

But on its own, the term *design* didn't seem to encompass all the aspects of why some products work and others fade away: why some creations endure, while others vanish.

This is especially true now. With so many competing theories and definitions of design, the term itself feels too restricting, too mechanical and bereft of emotion. With design, the focus often seems to fall too heavily on creativity and not enough on discernment. Design has become a process, a group of steps codified by a few experts, but taste is much more. It's a universal sensibility—one that appeals to the deepest part of ourselves.

My thought: maybe we've become too enamored with the process and forgotten about the sensibility.

So what exactly is taste? It includes an aesthetic, of course, but goes beyond the merely aesthetic. It's giving people a glow. It's delight and wonderment. It was the word Steve Jobs used to explain what was right with Apple and wrong with others. Something tasteful may be new, even radical, but somehow it's still deeply familiar. Triggering fascination and desire, true taste kindles a product's emotional touch points.

Often the emotional connection to a product is what engages us in the first place. Time and again, we see successful products that were not necessarily the first to market but were the first to appeal to us emotionally—a Coca-Cola bottle, *Star Wars*, the Sony Walkman. I remember as if it were yesterday walking into a sporting goods store in 1970 and seeing a blue shoebox with three diagonal white stripes containing a pair of Adidas running shoes. This blue box from West Germany—it was magic to me. To hold this blue box, in a basement store in a town in North Dakota, was to feel invited into the international brotherhood of track athletes. The great sprinter Bob Hayes and miler Jim Ryun had held such a blue box!

So taste goes beyond function and form into meaning. But, beware, you cannot skip function and form and go straight to meaning. The road to taste is a long journey.

THE BIG THREE: FUNCTION, FORM, MEANING

Over the last couple of decades, dissecting when and how consumers are affected by things like product aesthetics and design has become a trendy area of research. During that time, consumer researchers have convincingly claimed that products that excite customers will be more successful than those that don't.[1] No less of an expert than designer Bruce Nussbaum has touted "superior product design" as a sustainable advantage for firms operating in competitive environments.

But what is "superior product design"? That's not easily answered. Most research, however, has zeroed in on three critical elements that affect our judgment of any product: function, form, and meaning.

Function

A better-looking mousetrap had still better catch the mouse, right? When new products miss the mark, it's often because they try to be a better design rather than a better product. This is especially true of me-too products. Try a pair of cheap knockoff designer sunglasses and see for yourself. Or, rather, don't see, because the knockoff optics will be terrible.

But form over function also can afflict successful product lines when managers lose their focus, usually blinded or bullied by the hard-edge demands of financial performance. American cars fell into this trap by the 1970s. Successful software companies have a tendency to bloat up versions 2.0 through 8.0 with needless features. A successful long-running television series can crash when cleverness replaces story, a tendency popularly known as "jumping the shark."

I put function first for a reason. It's the cornerstone of any successful product or service. A number of studies back this up, including research that concludes that most consumers feel they must meet their functional needs before trying to fulfill their pleasurable needs.[2]

But let's be real. We don't buy products purely for utilitarian reasons. At least not anymore. Magazines like to print pictures of the most glamorous gadgets, cars, clothes, and hotels for a reason: they sell. So functionality by itself isn't sufficient for successful differentiation in today's market. Instead, when a threshold is met on the functional attributes, we apply a greater weight to a product's *hedonic*—or cool, fun, and pleasurable— features like form and aesthetics. This phenomenon is called the "principle of hedonic dominance."[3]

Form

Since George Santayana's 1896 book, *The Sense of Beauty*, researchers and theorists have argued that beauty is an inherent property of objects and that certain proportions, shapes, and colors are universally attractive. Likewise, we know that aesthetics arise from a product's sensorial characteristics; things like its appearance, sound, touch, smell, and feel.

At the same time, we know that sociocultural factors, as well as individual characteristics such as age, gender, and personality, also influence perceptions of a product's aesthetics.[4] Coke's original diet drink was called Tab and came in a pink and white can. But even though young men like to shed excess pounds, too, they didn't want to be caught with a pink can. Instead, men would pour Tab into glasses. So in 1982 Coke began to emphasize its new drink, Diet Coke, with a can of unisex design. But Coke didn't stop there. In 2005 it introduced Coke Zero with an aggressive black and red can, essentially for men. Coke fiddled slightly with the artificial sweetener to make Coke Zero seem like an original formula. But really, it was just a repackaging of Diet Coke (nee Tab) for a young male market. And it worked.

All this is to say that any true understanding of beauty and aesthetics must acknowledge the relationship between the product and the perceiver.

Meaning

Meaning refers to the significance and associations customers experience with a product. This experience is a result of the interaction between a company, through its product and marketing, and its customers, through their interpretations of the product. This means a product's meaning is not necessarily universal. Instead, its meaning is based on a broad range of outside influences and biases that we each bring to the product. For some, a Hummer is the greatest car ever built, reflecting masculine ruggedness. It can go anywhere and tow almost anything. It's the car, and I use that term loosely, you'd want to own during the apocalypse. But for others, it's the world's most wasteful and irresponsible manifestation of masculine insecurity. I mean, the body-part jokes almost write themselves.

So there it is: a product that's well-designed and well-executed must have functionality, a pleasing form, and a sense of meaning. That's a start. But it only just begins to tell us why the iPod crushed the Zune. Or why a chef knife made by Global cuts so much better than one from Miracle Blade. Or why I feel and ride like Superman on my new Specialized bike.

Okay, okay, time to fess up. There's a little more to my Specialized story.

Within twenty-four hours, my new record up OLH was red-flagged as suspicious by the Strava community. That's another way of saying that some cyclist in the Strava community doubted—gee, why?—that a twice-weekly rider and magazine publisher could crush Ryan Sherlock's record by three minutes.

I was asked to explain myself.

The reason I was able to beat Ryan Sherlock's 14:42 by three full minutes and Eric Heiden's legendary 14:58 by still more is that I was cheating. Okay, not really cheating, per se, since I had plainly disclosed my secret on the Strava website. My new Specialized Turbo, if you haven't figured it out by now, has a motor.

But the Specialized Turbo is subtly different from any electric-assisted bike that has come before it. Most e-bikes are ugly contraptions, featuring a large battery block positioned somewhere behind the saddle. In China, cheap e-bikes even use car batteries.

The Specialized Turbo uses smart-phone battery technology, scaled up to an 18-inch cylinder that slides, almost unnoticed, into the bicycle's down-tube. For you non–bike geeks, that's the tube that starts at the bottom of the handlebars and slants back to the pedals. But in addition to a battery, you need a motor, and the Turbo's motor is positioned at the rear-wheel hub of the bike. Like the battery, the motor's presence was stealthily integrated into the bike's form by Specialized's designer Ian Hamilton. A typical cyclist on a normal bike will stare at the Turbo's fat rear hub and wonder: Is that a new kind of gearing? Disc brakes, perhaps? Oh—it's a *motor*?

What I have just described is the Turbo's distinguishing hardware, and very elegant it is. But the bike's software is truly magical. It's so good it convinces me that I am Superman. Surely it's my own legs, not the motor, that are responsible for my incredible climb times up OLH. How did Specialized trick me into thinking this way? Why does this bike make me feel so good about myself? To find out, I decided to visit the Turbo's designers at Specialized's headquarters in Morgan Hill, California.

There I asked designers Amber Lucas and Ian Hamilton how they did it. Hamilton is the hardware guy who gave the Turbo its dashing looks and perfect weight balance. Lucas is the software expert. Lucas looked startled at my question, then leaned in and said, "We are all cyclists, and we *know* what a bike should feel like. We *know* what a bike should sound like. We *know* that it shouldn't make some electronic noise. We *know* the rider shouldn't feel the motor kick in or out."

Lucas leaned back and added, "Personally, I wanted a bike that would let me kick Tony Martin's butt on a hill." Martin is one of pro-cycling's best time trial riders.

The Turbo's magic subtlety is that one rides with the speed of a Tour de France rider like Martin, or even faster when going up hills like OLH, but the motor's contribution is so silent and so smoothly reactive to your own pedaling power that you quickly become convinced it *is* you, not the bike. In a sense, it is you in your dreams, living out your highest aspirations, on your best day ever.

But how do you produce such Maslovian satisfaction from technology? Lucas explained, "You shouldn't have to think about a throttle or pushing buttons. So we designed the torque sensor inside of the rear hub so that it reads torque off of the cassette. The sensor knows what gear you're in. When you're in that lower gear, which is a bigger ring—it has a longer torque arm, and so you get a little bit more power helping you to accelerate in that gear. Then when you shift into a smaller ring, which is a higher gear, you get a little bit less. So it's really about the way that your foot—*your power*—is transferred through the chain, to the cassette. The bike's software can read it and give you that beautiful, smooth acceleration."

How long did it take you to get it right, I asked her.

"Well, the trick was being able to build an algorithm that makes it so that you don't have to pedal a full stroke before the motor kicks in, or suffer any delays that would throw off your cadence," she said. "And so, really, it was a long process. This is biggest reason why the Turbo was a multiyear project.

It was really a struggle. Ian kept coming up with great hardware improvements and I had to constantly write revisions to the software to get it all smoothed out."

Next, I asked, "When did you know that you were close to getting it right?"

"When one of our employees, not a fast cyclist, won the Friday group ride on a Turbo while wearing flip flops," Lucas said, laughing. "There were a lot of red faces that day."

Specialized Bicycles is not the only company to create magical products, of course. Disney excels at it. Virgin America transports the air traveler to a different place, psychologically, than does Delta or American. The highest-grossing film of all time, at $2.8 billion revenue, is *Avatar*. The imagined world of the planet Pandora, apparently free of Earth's original sin and soul-destroying technology, created a sense of longing in many viewers. So much so, that CNN reported an outbreak of *Avatar* blues soon after the movie's release: "James Cameron's completely immersive spectacle Avatar may have been a little too real for some fans who say they have experienced depression and suicidal thoughts after seeing the film because they long to enjoy the beauty of the alien world Pandora."[5]

A new and better world. Completely immersive. Longing. Beauty.

I chose Specialized as the star of this chapter for this reason: if it's possible to inject magic and taste into a product as common as a bicycle, then maybe it's possible to do so with any product or service. So how are some companies able to imbue their products and services with powerful emotions such as I experienced on the Specialized Turbo?

There's no easy answer for that. But one thing is sure: these next-step, next-generation products that set new trends and build sustainable margins won't be simple products. As design and all its corresponding theories become more widespread, a pretty product alone won't be enough to create a sustainable edge. Instead, the new must-have gadgets and uber-cool machines will be complex and well-integrated combinations of products, services, and information.

INTEGRATION AND INTELLIGENCE: NEST LABS

I asked Nest's Tony Fadell, who worked alongside Steve Jobs to launch the iPod back in the early 2000s: What did you learn from Jobs? What lessons are you applying at Nest so that you stand out and command premium prices?

Design, right?

Fadell quickly corrected me. "Design is just one facet. The more important thing is total experience. It starts with anticipation of the product. If you want to own the customer experience—and we do—then you want to own the anticipation. You need to also own the package the product comes in. Then how the customer opens the package. See, it's all about integrated experience."

Fadell had worked at Apple through the launch of the iPod. Following that breakout success, Fadell and his wife, who also worked at Apple, left to spend more time with their young children and finish building their dream home. When it came time to purchase the home's thermostats, Fadell was struck by how little these devices had evolved. Cheap, plastic, ugly—and not very smart—they controlled half the energy in the home. So that's what led Fadell to start Nest, whose first product is a thermostat.

A thermostat? Well, Fadell decided, why not? The more he thought about it, the more Fadell figured he could develop home products, starting with a humble thermostat, that created desire and commanded premium prices, just like Apple products. Part of that formula was great design. But a greater part was integration of the total customer experience.

Another important factor, however, was doing things that made no sense but were consistent with the company's point of view. "Sometimes you need to do things that don't seem very sensible to provide that total experience," he told me. "Your point of view can't always be rational. If it is, you will be too predictable. And if you are always predictable, others can clone you."

And some of things Nest has done really do seem irrational and weird. Such actions would likely get you fired if you were a product manager at Philips Electronics or Johnson Controls.

Weird thing number one: shape the thermostat like a hockey puck, with no buttons or levers.

Weird thing number two: ship it in a bamboo box, to evoke green feelings.

Weird thing number three: include a custom-made screwdriver and screws in the bamboo box. The screwdriver costs Nest about ten times more to make than simply buying standard screwdrivers in volume. The screw economics are worse: Nest custom screws cost about a hundred times the average commodity screw.

Way to screw your company, Tony!

As Fadell admitted, "Every business school in the world would flunk you if you came out with a business plan that said, 'Oh, and we're going to design and fabricate our own screws at an exponentially higher cost than it would cost to buy them.'"

But these aren't just screws. Like the thermostat itself, they're better screws, epic screws, screws with, dare I say it, deeper meaning. Functionally, they utilize a specific thread pattern that allows them to go into nearly any surface, from wood to plaster to thin sheet metal. And the screwdriver, it feels balanced in the hand. It has the Nest logo on it and looks "Nest-y," just like everything from Apple looks "Apple-y."

This notion of creating and selling the entire experience flies in the face of classic business ideas like economy of scale. As Fadell said, "I mean, there are already millions of screws out there for sale. You don't need to make screws; you can buy them for fractions of a cent. A board member lectured me on that. 'But they wouldn't be ours,' I said. The Nest experience, you see, is feeling smart about your smart thermostat. The custom screws are designed to let anyone put them into any surface." You don't have to be a carpenter. You feel competent. You feel in control. You feel smart.

Laugh at his screwy philosophy, but Fadell is onto something big, very big, with the idea of smart.

Clever product design and integration are, as Apple board director and Nest Labs advisor Bill Campbell told me, "proxies for intelligence." Customers want to feel smart. Intelligence is a huge advantage in an information economy. If your product is seen as smart, you're far along the road to lasting success.

In a busy world, this makes sense. Nobody has the time and energy to evaluate every product they buy on a strict cost-benefit basis. So instead, we look for proxies. The best proxy of all is smarts—the assurance of deep intelligence in the product and service.

Smart, of course, has many ways of expressing itself. Smart can be healthy, responsible, durable, eco-friendly, strong, or rich.

But reaching this level of integrative meaning isn't easy. It takes passion, of course. But it also takes courage. It takes a willingness, like Tony Fadell, to stand your ground against the bean counters and hard-edge people, against important stakeholders like board members or investors. As hard as that is, though, it's even harder to maintain that passion and courage over the long haul. That's because the founders or aesthetic leaders who have that strong point of view leave or retire at some point.

And if you look at the difference between a founder-led company and a corporate-led company, "It's the same as a babysitter versus a parent," as Fadell so aptly put it. "When you're a parent with your kid, you can go bungee jumping. You'll be smart about it, sure, but you'll take risks with your kid because you want them to have a learning experience. You want to have fun with them. You understand what can and can't be done. But a babysitter, they would never take the kid bungee jumping."

So when the founder is gone, companies often lose their appetite for risk taking. Don't harm the child. Make sure it stays safe—and profitable. And that means not doing the weird or irrational things necessary to create great products and integrated experiences. It's a valid point, absolutely.

But you know what? Sometimes even parents can lose their way.

HOW SPECIALIZED LOST ITS TASTE

No company rode the mountain bike boom better than Specialized. With the huge success of its Stumpjumper in the mid-1980s, Specialized was off and rolling as a real bicycle company, not just a parts supplier. After Greg LeMond won the Tour de France in 1986, 1989, and 1990, founder Mike Sinyard perceived the rise of carbon fiber road racing bicycles. Specialized made a carbon fiber bike called the Epic Allez that sold for $2,995 (about $6,000 today). In the LeMond-inspired road cycling boom, the Epic Allez sold well.[6]

Then Sinyard made a mistake that nearly cost him his company. He listened to the data. Well, he overlistened to the data. He literally took leave of his own soft-edge senses, his fine intuitive sense of the bike market built on beauty and quality—a taste honed by transformative love and salvation.

Ah, we're getting too rhapsodical. What happened to Sinyard was just this: he went down market. He started building bikes for the masses and distributing them through outlets like Costco.

There is honor in doing that, of course, but in Sinyard's case it was false to his own truth. Building and selling utilitarian bikes, absent love and passion and design and taste, was not who Mike Sinyard was. A family shopping for bikes at Costco was looking for good old utilitarian value, not magic, not mojo, certainly not salvation. They were looking for ways Johnny and Jill could get themselves to soccer practice. Sinyard's magic margins evaporated.

But it was worse than simply enduring low margins. Sinyard now had to carry unsold inventory on his balance sheet. The data analysis showed Sinyard how he could grow Specialized to become a multibillion-dollar company. But somebody forgot to mention the cash flow part.

Between 1999 and 2002, Specialized, having compromised its taste and now operating from its weakness and not its strength, struggled with inventory costs, brand erosion, and dealer confusion. The company almost died. Death looming, Sinyard and Specialized finally awoke from their mid-life identity crisis. Sinyard fired his consultants. He empowered his chief designer, Robert Egger.

From now on, Specialized would design bikes so good it would help save the world, or at least itself.

HOW TO RECLAIM YOUR MOJO

As Specialized proved, it's possible for mature companies to get their taste back. Disney is another great example of a company that lost its way but later refound its magic. In recent years, the entertainment conglomerate has been reinvigorated and is at the top of its game. Disney is now trying more digital media than ever. And Disney is doing this after publicly championing hand-drawn animation over digital animation for years, even in the face of successes like *Toy Story* and *Shrek*.

Disney, of course is a business-to-consumer brand. But this kind of rebirth is possible for a business-to-business brand, as well. Consider German software giant SAP, a company discussed in depth in Chapter Five. A lot of people in Silicon Valley wrote off SAP as the ultimate rigid enterprise software company. But to refresh its product line, SAP did two really intriguing things.

First, SAP embraced Design Thinking, the innovative methodology pioneered by IDEO and currently advocated by the Stanford School of Design. In essence, this is an iterative, creative way of understanding and solving problems. With Design Thinking, SAP can now generate a solution that excels in three dimensions: viability (it has to make business sense); feasibility (it has to be technically possible); and, most important, desirability (people have to *want* it).

To make its products more desirable—and this is the second intriguing step SAP took—the company has started to move enterprise software in the direction of consumer and gaming software. In the old days, SAP would benchmark one of its enterprise systems against someone else's enterprise system. But now, SAP benchmarks against products made by companies like Electronic Arts, the popular video game maker. You see, a successful game tends to elicit signs of visible joy in seven minutes. If it doesn't, the game will probably be a flop. This type of visible reaction creates what's known as "emotional momentum."

"That's how we need to rethink desirability in business software," Jim Snabe, former co-CEO of SAP, said. "It's a soft skill but an extremely important one. And if you come back to your hard skills, it's viability and feasibility. Those two things are easy to measure. You can make a business case that it's viable and you can check feasibility from a technical point of view. But I would argue more and more that if it's not desirable, it will never succeed."

With this in mind, Snabe asked the engineers at SAP how long it takes before a financial accountant expresses visible joy when using new SAP software. "To be honest," he told me, "right now, it's a little bit over seven minutes." My guess is, that's based on the false presumption that accountants ever show visible joy.

Jokes aside, it's possible for any company to rediscover its taste. It's just a matter of will and time. Typically, most companies are born out of the passion of one or more founders. Which means most companies start with a taste-driven, point-of-view-driven culture, one in which teams work together to come up with new and innovative products or services. So the cultural DNA is already there. And sooner or later that DNA will start being expressed as products. Sometimes it takes a little soul-searching, a close call with failure, or a completely new way of thinking in order to dredge it up.

But it's there.

UNLOCKING THE SECRETS OF TASTE

Why do we celebrate creativity? I'll share my own opinion, which has a religious angle to it. Do you believe humans are created in

God's image? I do. Now unpack this thought: if people have been created in God's image, by God, then logic says people are created by a Creator to go forth and create. As divinely inspired creatures, it is practically our duty to create. If that is so—and I believe it—then why would God deny us the capability to do so?

Okay, let's say you reject my belief-based rationale. Does evolution select for creativity? That's the question. Do humans, as winners (thus far) of the evolutionary sweepstakes, have inborn creativity? Is that a survival mechanism? Or have some of us, alas, evolved only to be order-taking drudges?

I'll make the argument, in this chapter and throughout the book, that everyone is creative—latently or obviously—and far more than we think. The problem, for most of us, is that we don't know how to *unlock* our creativity. And while creativity isn't the only factor in taste, as much of this chapter has worked to suggest, it's still a pretty good start. It's the launching point toward cultivating our own point of view, as Tony Fadell calls it. Creativity drives the generation of novel approaches or ideas, which is essentially the basis for innovation, as well as our humanity.

And just as creativity isn't the singular realm of artists and designers, people with taste and aesthetic discrimination aren't created only by design schools. In other words, don't sweat it: taste, creativity, and design sensibility can be learned. You don't need to be a natural. If everyone understood more about the mechanics of attraction and affection, they could begin developing an aesthetic vocabulary.

You see, technology changes rapidly, but people don't. That means certain aesthetic principles remain constant through eras: we've developed very clear visceral likes and dislikes through millions of years of neurological evolution. Now let's look at a few of those principles.

Simple Geometry

For thousands of years, philosophers, mathematicians, and artists have admired the unique properties of the "golden rectangle." This so-called magical shape, based on the "golden ratio" of 1.618, or approximately five by eight, is common in the shapes of books, flat-screen TVs, and hand-held electronic devices. It also provides the basis for the aspect ratios of both Pulitzer Prize–winning photographs and blockbuster films. And many great artists—ranging from Leonardo da Vinci to Mondrian and Salvador Dali—used it as their primary geometric proportion in many of their greatest masterpieces. Why?

In 2009, a Duke University professor named Adrian Bejan discovered that human vision and cognition developed together, resulting in the ability to scan an image fastest when its shape is a golden rectangle. For example, it's the perfect layout of a paragraph of text, the one most conducive to reading, interpreting, and retaining information. How many golden rectangles are in this book? Maybe not as many as there should be, but probably more than you'd ever have realized. Why? Because this simple shape accelerates our ability to absorb information.[7]

As much as we may love these magic rectangles, though, we don't actually like their sharp corners. Harvard Medical School's Moshe Bar and Maital Neta, in neuroimaging studies published in 2006 and 2007, found a strong preference for designs that are rounded rather than angular. This is true of the product itself, its packaging, and even the design on the package. This preference was attributed to an adaptive fear response to sharp shapes and contours. Bar and Neta hypothesized that this probably relates to a greater likelihood of sharp objects inflicting physical harm to a person.[8]

This isn't a new concept. Many studies—dating all the way back to the 1920s—demonstrate the negative effects of angularity and the association of fear with angular shapes.[9]

The appeal of rounded corners led Apple to patent the idea and then sue Samsung for using them. Fortunately, a judge threw out this aspect of Apple's lawsuit. In a sense, Apple would need to own the human brain and the thousands of millennia of brain evolution in order to patent a golden rectangle with rounded corners.

Beyond the Visual

Touch seems to provide a direct and more intimate connection with the product. We feel more confident about buying something that we've touched before rather than something that we've only seen. As such, touch might appeal to more basic needs and perhaps automatically generate a like or dislike response at both a conscious and subconscious level.[10]

Indeed, to actively explore a given product, we need to touch it. Therefore, the perception of acting on an object—deciding when, where, and how to explore it, and not merely being a passive spectator—might provide an important dimension to the pleasure-creating experience of those products. Over the last few years, researchers have started to address just how important tactile content can be to our evaluation of items and products.

Neuroscience researchers have distinguished between the contributions of several different independent submodalities—or building blocks—to the perception of touch, such as pressure, temperature, vibration, pleasure, and pain.[11] This means the final feeling of a product is not determined by the sum of its individual sensory attributes. Instead, the tactile experience represents the synergistic activation of different combinations of receptors in what are known as "touch blends."[12] So, for example, it's been shown that what we think of as the feeling of wetness doesn't come from a single receptor for detecting the presence of moisture, but instead through the combination of receptors coding for temperature and pressure. Similarly, feelings like greasy and spongy reflect touch blends. So when we talk about a product feeling rough, or smooth, or even cheap, we're really talking about very complicated touch blends that involve multiple sensory inputs.

Speaking of multiple sensory inputs, I once interviewed Helmut Panke, who was CEO of the German automaker BMW. I asked Panke what distinguished the BMW brand. He sat back in his chair, closed his eyes, and said, "I want to be able to blindfold someone, put them in the right seat of a BMW, drive them around, and have them know by *all* their other senses that they are in a BMW."

Familiarity Breeds . . . Love?

Don't reinvent the wheel, just make it better. Words of wisdom if ever there were any. This is one of most prevalent pieces of advice from design experts, as well as one of the most-researched topics in marketing. Even when a product is new or novel to the point of being revolutionary, people still need to associate with it. They need to connect with it and understand it at first glance. In many cases, a successful product is an iterative design that evolved from an earlier, innovative icon. Which means that if you keep an archetype elegant as it evolves, you can keep it iconic.

Specialized's Turbo combines the look of a vintage Stumpjumper mountain bike—the world's best-selling mountain bike, the one that put Specialized on the map; it's the only bicycle in the Smithsonian—along with the slight hint of motorcycle menace. The Turbo's hardware designer, Ian Hamilton, and his boss, Robert Egger, are Italian motorsport fans as well as hardcore cyclists. The Turbo comes in one color—a familiar blood red. "It's Ferrari racing red, if you want to know the truth," said Egger.

And so it goes. The first Apple Macintosh was designed to look vaguely like a human, with the high forehead of a presumed genius. It also included a handle in the back, because Steve Jobs wanted you to be able to take your genius friend with you. The wildly successful Tesla S Model eschews the nerdy look an electric car, and instead looks like an Aston Martin, the uber-upscale sports car most closely associated with James Bond. Walt Disney's original vision for Disneyland was designed to replicate the feelings Walt had enjoyed in the Swiss Alps, a place he felt looked the most magical on earth. And Howard Schultz of Starbucks wanted to bring the Italian coffeehouse experience to America: the décor, the barista, the cappuccino, the whole ambiance, even to the point of confusing us with "grande," "venti," and "trenta" size designations. Comprehensible, no; beguilingly romantic, yes.

Why? Research on aesthetic preferences shows that familiar objects—ones we've been exposed to, heard about, or seen—are preferred over objects that we've never come across before. This is known as "exposure effect."[13] Even the brain's wiring is changed, as repeated exposure to an object results in the development of internalized rules or algorithms, often without our awareness, that play a role in assessing beauty and desirability.[14] In other words, patterns, relations, and designs that we've encountered in the past play a huge role in forming our preferences.

You've probably heard or read the name Jony Ive. If not, he leads the design team at Apple. Even if you are familiar with Ive's work, you're probably not familiar with his primary inspiration: a designer named Dieter Rams, a true legend, who worked for the German consumer company Braun during the 1950s and 1960s. If you feed "Rams Apple" to Google, you'll find many Internet sites comparing Braun and Apple products. Give it a try right now, if you can.

What do you think? Yeah, the Apple products—particularly the iPod and iPhone—look like dead-on knockoffs of Braun products. Now, this isn't meant to be a slight of Jony Ive or his talent. He just reimagined new products in a familiar skin. And it wasn't like Rams's designs were pulled from some preternatural mystic ether. Much of the inspiration for his designs came from the earlier Bauhaus design movement based in Weimar, Germany. As Specialized designer Ian Hamilton explained, "That design school and that type of minimalist design were the roots of modernism. So Dieter Rams, as a product designer, really approached design from very much a modernist, Bauhaus-influenced perspective. And Jony Ive, he's just keeping that philosophy alive."

Understand Your Customer, but Be Selfish

Margit Wennmachers, a partner in the successful venture capital firm Andreessen Horowitz, told me: "I think taste is a matter of really understanding your customer on a very, very fundamental level." That's true. Whether it's a theory like Design Thinking or human-centered design, one the most important tenets is always knowing and understanding your customers. What do they like? What do they want? What do they need? Those questions are important, yes.

But Tony Fadell of Nest Labs looks at it a bit differently: "Is it really about, what does a customer want? Or is it about, what do I want? I design it all, get it done exactly the way I want it. Then I ship it to people." In other words, Fadell approaches product creation from the perspective of, "Hey, I want that product and I'm going to design it for me, and I hope everybody else will like it as well." Those are his words, not mine.

And if you look at many of the products that I've mentioned—from *Star Wars* to the Apple iPod to six-figure sports cars—these taste makers are designing their product for themselves, or for a very small set of people whom they trust.

Robert Egger, the design chief at Specialized, put it a little more bluntly: "Some of it is based on our selfishness. The other day, I designed a lot of stuff for myself, because I want to have the most beautiful bike. I want to have the fastest bike. I want to have the most aerodynamic helmet. I want to have the stiffest shoes. So a lot of the best products come from our selfishness of wanting better stuff."

Know Your Brand and Keep It Consistent

Mike Sinyard knows and loves bikes. He didn't start Specialized to make money, he did it to spread salvation. He truly believes bikes can save the world. So Sinyard knows a thing or two about what drives his product, his company, and his brand. "One of our designers will present a new product and we'll say, 'Well, why is that Specialized?'" Robert Egger added, "We use this mental test. Take the logo off our bikes or products. Does it still say Specialized? If not, we've haven't done our jobs."

You see, at Specialized, they design, engineer, and build bikes according to a few paired principles: Is it functional *and* innovative? Is it timeless *and* exciting? Is there value *and* quality? In other words, when they look at a Specialized bike ten years from now, they want to still be proud of it. Cool is good, but it isn't enough. Will it stand up? Is it authentic? Those are principles they wrestled with while birthing their electric bike, the Turbo. Some designers asked, "Are e-bikes really for us?" But then somebody else said, "Well, let's not make it pedestrian. Let's make it like a Ducati motorcycle. Let's make it something really exciting. Let's make it Specialized."

Sinyard, Egger, and the leadership at Specialized has drilled this approach all the way down to the level of color schemes. Specialized has always been a company steeped in racing, so red is the color it has wanted to own. Red is aggressive; it gets people fired up. It's not a coincidence that red has had such a long history in the world of motorsports with Ferrari's F1 cars and Ducati's MotoGP motorcycles. Other bicycle companies have tried to own red. But as Egger pointed out, "We pushed hard and were consistent year after year, you know, using red packaging, making red bikes, having our red S, arguably the best symbol in the bike industry."

Maybe this type of consistency is easy, as well as applicable, if you only make one product or work in a niche market, right? But take a look at a company as large and varied as Virgin, a multinational conglomerate made up of more than four hundred separate companies. While dealing in products and services as varied as banking, air travel, video games, cosmetics, and mobile phones, everything Richard Branson does still has that unified look. All of his Virgin properties use the same red and everything is branded with the slashing Virgin logo, the checkmark "V" cleverly signifying Branson's seal of approval. You always know that with anything that Branson does, there'll be a sense of excitement and delight.

Just Say No

When it comes to spending money, we all have a lot of choices in today's marketplace. So, as mentioned earlier, a new product or service needs to make you feel smart. Which, more specifically, means it needs to be intuitive. It needs to be simple. And when I say simple, I don't mean simplistic. Instead, I mean your new device or machine needs to be uncluttered and purposeful.

If it needs a manual, forget it. Many young people today wouldn't even recognize a manual. If you give them a binder full of instructions, they're likely to throw it away. Even IKEA's two-page instructions are too much of a burden for most people, much less a whole book of coded directions. It may be a cultural thing that comes partly from an abundance of choice and partly from an expectation that well-designed, taste-driven products will be natural, instinctual, innate.

This means the hardware and the software, the communication, the customer service, the whole experience: it needs to make sense and be clear. In explaining the design process of the Specialized Turbo, Ian Hamilton said, "I was pretty insistent on the fact that it had to be self-guided, that the 'on' button is very easily recognizable. And even in the LCD user interface, the modes are laid out in a vertical way, with easily recognized icons. This helps get a lot of information onto a compact screen, but it also means no one has to explain it to you."

Simple, clean, clear—that should be easy, right? Well, no. It's actually the opposite. Taking stuff out, limiting the buttons and features, keeping things off the package, those are the hard decisions. "I always say some of the simplest things are some of the hardest to do," Egger remarked. "Some of the simplest designs in the world really are the most tedious and tenuous to make." This reflects what Amber Lucas said about the Specialized Turbo's algorithms. They took a long time to "smooth out."

One paradox, among many, about Steve Jobs is that while being famous for his love of form, he felt so strongly about function that he would ruthlessly eliminate all but the absolutely essential functions until he arrived at the purest expression of a product. "Steve said no far, far more than he said yes," Tony Fadell revealed.

This attitude has carried over to Fadell's own company, Nest Labs. Like many start-ups, it has extensive customer support and an active customer community. Through those touch points, it's able to gain insights, like its customers' top ten issues. And, of course, its people take the time to go through these issues one by one and fix them—or say no. For example, some customers believed Nest should incorporate a weather indicator and a clock in their thermostat. Nest's answer: "It's a thermostat. We're not doing it."

Clearly, that's a point-of-view, taste-driven issue. Even though Nest has feedback indicating a set of users want those extra functions, it's not doing it. "It's very simple to use," Fadell said. "So we had to say no to some customers who wanted additional features. We had to be very clear: we're not going to screw up a simple, elegant experience for the rest of our customers."

So, if you think about it, saying no in that case is very Apple-like. It also flies in the face of the traditional market research, make-your-customer-happy-at-all-costs route. But the world is going the opposite way. Less is better. And sometimes to get less, you just have to say no.

While a deep understanding of creativity and strong sensing skills are important to taste, it's also essential to understand that any long-term design success will have a data component. This includes analyzing data to improve ideas, find new customers, and show measurable business outcomes. This is where the soft stuff of taste, opinion, and point of view intersect with the hard stuff of data and analytics.

WHERE TASTE MEETS DATA

On a late May day, a block away from Specialized's main building, Mike Sinyard and I were looking through a glass wall at a black time trial bike called the Shiv. This latest model, designed to be ridden by top pros, costs $12,000 when equipped with the aero wheels and tires. As befits its royal status, the Shiv was sitting on a white pedestal on the other side of the glass. Sinyard and a group of younger men, all dressed in black T-shirts and blue jeans, were all looking at the Shiv and pointing. At the wall in front of the Shiv, ten large fans were stacked in two rows. The fans were wired to blow air at up to sixty miles an hour in precise one-mile-per-hour increments, while the Shiv could be rotated right or left to mimic quartering and cross winds. Controlling the fans and wind speeds and angles were two Specialized aerodynamic technicians. They sat in front of three large computer monitors on the other side of the glass, along with the spectators.

The purpose of the wind tunnel, of course, was to measure the Shiv's drag coefficient at simulated race speeds and winds. The lower the drag, the better, but professional racing bikes—much like Formula One race cars or airplanes—are by necessity exercises in compromise. The theoretically perfect aero design, the one with the lowest drag coefficient, might not provide the torsional strength and rigidity necessary to transfer pedal power to speed. What, then, is the ideal balance of tricks and innovations to a bicycle that must cut through the air, stay on the ground, transfer power on the pedals to rotational speed in the wheels, and be light enough to go uphill fast but strong enough to support a rider who weighs ten times as much as the bike?

Sinyard's Italian mentor, Cino Cinelli, racer and artisan, could only guess at these answers. As a professional rider, Cinelli had special insights. But he had little data to go by. Thus, intuition—the "golden guts" of legendary designers like Cinelli and Ernesto Colnago—would rule the day.

Hard data began to transform bike design and racing strategy in the 1990s for three reasons. One driver was Greg LeMond's shocking come-from-behind win at the 1989 Tour de France. LeMond used then-revolutionary "aero bars" to tuck into an aerodynamic position and win the last day's time trial. LeMond beat a Frenchman, Laurent Fignon, to whom American aero bars were an assault to tradition. The second driver was affordable computer power to collect and analyze data. And a third was money. By the 1990s, the world's top cyclists could make multiple millions of dollars per year. That meant they had every incentive to seek not only a doping edge but also a data edge.

Now it was 2013, and we stood in a Specialized wind tunnel spectator gallery, watching a bank of finely calibrated fans blowing air at the new black Specialized Shiv on its white pedestal. The bike itself was festooned with sensors. With us on the other side of the glass wall was a bank of computers, noting the drag coefficients of tiny changes in wind speed and wind angles on the bike.

It was hard to imagine a more perfectly optimized wind-cheating time trial aero bike than the new Shiv. Every drag-producing edge was as slippery as it could be made given the conflict of other requirements. Chief among those conflicting requirements was frame strength and rigidity. It wouldn't do the rider any good to be maximally cheating the wind while a softly flexing frame sapped his power. Watch a watt-producing, monster rider like Germany's Tony Martin on a bike, in hyper slow motion, and you'll be shocked by how much the frame flexes like a noodle in response to his pedal strokes. Flexibility is bad, rigidity is good. Aerodynamics has to work with this fact.

And then there's the rider. In 2004 Lance Armstrong's team spent more than $2 million trying to design a bike that could cheat the wind and give Armstrong an edge. Nothing was overlooked in Armstrong's quest for the perfect time trial bike. After a while, the bike's designer determined, from testing, that Armstrong could shave time if his knees and lower legs were as narrow as possible. The data was indisputable about this. The idea was to move the pedals in a few millimeters closer to the front gear wheel, which would keep the lower legs and knees closer together. Do that, and you could cut wind resistance. So said the data. But that's where Armstrong got into trouble. The narrow legs and knees sapped his power. Armstrong gave up, wrote off the $2 million investment, and got back on his old time trial bike.[15]

I asked one of the Specialized Shiv designers, Mark Cote, what progress had been made since 2004. Cote has a masters in aerodynamic engineering from MIT, and he's not the only one at Specialized with such a pedigree. Cote described two changes. One was the plummeting price of NASA-level wind tunnel testing, which cost $20,000 per hour in 2004 and was now available for a tenth of that cost at places like Specialized's wind tunnel because of cheaper sensors and computers and software. The other change from 2004 was the increased knowledge of the human body.

"It's possible, with physical therapy, strength training, yoga, and Pilates-type dynamic stretching, to get a rider into a more aero position without loss of power," Cote said. "But for every rider, the optimal position will be different. Two riders that are six feet tall and 160 pounds may differ significantly in things like torso-to-leg-length ratios, hip width, upper-leg-to-lower-leg ratios, foot size, foot shape, and so on. And that's just the structural stuff. Even two riders with identical structures might differ significantly in strength and flexibility and the ability to improve strength and flexibility."

I asked Cote whether it's possible to find a perfect match of rider to bike so as to generate the most speed for a given distance.

"That's my job. It's to find that elusive sweet spot between data truth and human truth." Specialized designer Robert Egger had used the same phrase: "the sweet spot between data truth and human truth."

FINDING THE SWEET SPOT

Soft skills like design and creativity have always been seen as the province of intuitive geniuses. An exquisite sense of taste, the ability to invent both the object and purpose: those are talents bestowed on a few lucky people. The real question for the rest of us then becomes, is data going to democratize this intuitive genius?

The awkward answer: well, sort of. It's always a balancing act, weighing something that's beautiful with something that functions perfectly. And this comes down to making specific decisions: When is taste an opinion-based, point-of-view decision? When is it a data-driven decision? What's the fine line between those two? And how do you find that sweet spot between what the data is telling you and what your gut is telling you? With the help of some people who have both the sensing skills needed to hear what the world wants and the databases required to build for the long haul, it's possible to pick the lock on a few of these mysteries.

There's little doubt that data is good for many things. Since the Specialized product team is fanatical about both innovation and function, data allows them to extensively test new products. Often, they go through twenty or thirty iterations, testing helmet safety, bike frame stiffness and handling, human fatigue, and aerodynamics. "Data drives a lot of that," Mike Sinyard told me. "I would say virtually everything goes through those data filters. These are great new tools. And really, it makes me cringe to think we ever made stuff just because it was cool, but it didn't have that proven functionality."

This has been a big change. Previously, this sort of assurance was based more on intuition and experience. Product designers had a gut feeling that something worked. As Robert Egger explained about those pre-data days: "You were a little nervous when you put a bike out there or a helmet or a shoe. And when it worked, you're like 'Wow, we were pretty spot-on,' or, 'Hey, we missed it and we've got to start over.'" But now all the data-driven testing confirms things that were once the realm of intuition or rule of thumb. Moreover, data also provides designers and product developers with new insights. "It tells us secrets about things that we didn't realize," Egger added. "And sometimes what you think you knew, you didn't know."

That's a real benefit—one that directly affects the bottom line—but data isn't the answer to everything. You still have to understand the taste-driven, opinion-based perspective. What's the point of view? Who is this product being made for? What are the true goals you're trying to achieve? Data won't answer those questions. Which means that a large measure of beyond-the-numbers insight is required to move past the bits and bytes so easily gathered with today's technology.

In this sense, taste and design are still skills that need to be learned over time and influenced by experience. "Sure, there's data that can inform the opinion," Tony Fadell offered, "but at the end of the day, when you create new designs, you're still sitting in the mind of the customer."

Yes, the customers. There's no doubt that they play a significant part in the equation. But you still need to use a little caution when applying a customer-centric approach to taste and design. As discussed earlier, customers offer an abundance of helpful information, but they can't do the inventing part for you: they can't create your idea or define your point of view. "When you're looking for taste, you can't find it by doing focus groups," Margit Wennmachers, the venture capital partner, told me. "I attend a lot of focus groups, and customers can't tell you what they need unless it already exists."

Don't misunderstand this point: if you have a very well-defined and well-understood product such as Intuit's accounting software, Quicken, then data and focus groups can be useful. But the hard reality is you can't use a focus group to find your product. Would a focus group have ever come up with something like Pinterest? Not likely.

So you have to have a strong point of view, a spot of judgment, and a bit of inspiration. There's just no way to get around that fact. Even Singularity's Vivek Wadhwa, a true technology evangelist, conceded, "I don't see technology as taking over the human side of designing new products." There are just too many decisions data can't inform, too many choices data can't guide. The human ability to factor in behavior, needs, and preferences can't be reduced to an algorithm.

Instead, you need to get your initial product done and marketed. Then you can start the data-gathering and iteration process. Borrowing an idea from Nest Labs' Tony Fadell, here's the important distinction: new products are 90+ percent point of view or taste driven, and maybe 5 to 10 percent data. Version 2.0

is approximately 80 percent point of view and 20 percent data. Version 3.0 is 70:30. Version 4.0, 60:40. And each generation of your product inches along toward a data-driven perspective—and, yes, every product inches along at a different pace.

The really great thing about this process is that data, and especially big data, provides early indications of the surprising, unplanned ways customers are actually using a product. For the Nest Labs, data lets Tony Fadell and his team know how people are really using their thermostat to heat, cool, and control their home environment. What's a real-world comfort level? Do they need to tweak the algorithm? Just as Amazon or iTunes uses your purchasing data—what do you like, what don't you like, what new products are recommended—this information allows Nest to personalize the thermostat, its software, and the entire product experience. Additionally, it helps Nest understand how its product or service could reach a fringe set of customers that didn't fit the initial point of view.

So, as a product develops and grows, you face a whole set of data-driven decisions. But you also face a whole set of opinion-based decisions. That's where the two worlds run into each other. And, even today, the outcome is dominated by human insight and ingenuity. It has to be.

It's now so easy and cheap to collect, sort, and analyze data that it's just too tempting to let it overwhelm human truth. In that case, we'll all be like Lance Armstrong's $2 million dollar bike team; we'll design the perfect machine, but the machine will fail at what it's designed to do—make the rider faster. Why? Because the machine forced the human to conform to the data. The sweet spot of taste was lost.

"There's no computer that can do something as beautiful as a sculptor can do with his hands," Robert Egger told me. "It's not there yet. We use 3D printers and 3D programs a lot, but then we always put in the hand labor. The auto industry does the same thing. They do a lot of digital work, but at the end of the day, the best cars are still done with clay. It's that last little 5 percent—it's done with clay and a person who has a good eye."

GAINING THE EDGE

- Taste is more than design. It's a sensibility that appeals to the deepest part of ourselves.
- Taste starts with the big three—function, form, and meaning—and smoothly integrates them.
- Taste is uncluttered and purposeful. Taste-driven products will be natural, instinctual, innate.
- Taste need not be original. It often borrows from successful products and services of the past.
- Taste always has a touch of irrationality, a hint of an idealized world.
- Taste is not the result of random genius. It takes hard work, discipline, and patience.
- Taste signals the deep intelligence of a product or service. Most customers will pay more to feel smart.

7

▲

Story

The Power of Story, Ancient and New

On January 12, 2010, a 7.0 earthquake rocked the poorest nation in the Western Hemisphere, Haiti. The death toll was so large it was never exactly determined, but somewhere around 150,000 people died. A half million more were injured, tens of thousands permanently. Haiti's fragile water, sanitation, and health care infrastructure was ripped apart. Epidemic disease threatened to kill off the whole country and spill into Haiti's island neighbor, the Dominican Republic.

An Alabama gastroenterologist named Richard McGlaughlin could stand it no more. Watching the devastation on TV, hearing pleas for help at his church, McGlaughlin overwhelmingly felt, he said, "an itch to do something. Money and prayers and good thoughts weren't going to scratch it." So McGlaughlin decided put his own skin in the game and help Haitians he didn't know. He flew his single-engine-and-propeller four-seat airplane, a Cirrus SR22, from Birmingham to Ft. Lauderdale, Florida, where he loaded the plane up with supplies—antibiotics, IV fluids, tubing and casting materials, crutches, needles, syringes, scalpels, and scrubs from local hospitals—and flew them to the Saint Damiens Hospital in Port Au Prince, Haiti. While making flights to Haiti, McGlaughlin saw the need to set up a GI Lab and donate more of his time. Thus, by late 2010, McGlaughlin was all in for the Haitians. He was making a monthly flight in his Cirrus from the States to Haiti and spending a week on the island with each trip.

McGlaughlin liked to educate others about the urgent problems in Haiti, and the best way to do that, he thought, was to bring them along and let them see. On separate flights in the Cirrus SR22 he had brought his airplane buddies, his wife, and his daughters. Now on January 7, 2012, he was bringing his daughter Elaine for the first time.

The flight from Tamiami, Florida, to Port au Prince went fine for the first hour. The Cirrus was cruising along nicely, making close to two hundred miles per hour, 9,500 feet above the water. But sixty minutes into the flight McGlaughlin noticed that the oil pressure gauge had started to act funny. The needle started a slow fade from the normal value of 50psi down to 40psi. Always careful, McGlaughlin didn't like the trend. He called air traffic control and asked for a diversion to Andros Island, the largest of the Bahamian islands. The Cirrus, with McGlaughlin and his daughter Elaine, was still about forty-five miles offshore.

But the oil pressure kept dropping—30psi, 20psi, 10psi, 0psi—and then, said McGlaughlin, "the engine seized, the propeller stopped."

Instinctively, McGlaughlin glanced at a mysterious red handle on the ceiling of the plane. A last resort? As if deciding better of it, McGlaughlin trimmed the Cirrus for the best rate of glide.

But he and his daughter would not make it to Andros Island. At best, they would glide into the ocean two miles offshore.

What's it like when you know you are going to land in the ocean in a small airplane, with your daughter aboard?

"Your throat tightens, your voice goes up, your vision narrows, and you're aware that you aren't very competent," Dr. McGlaughlin said. He thought about ditching into the ocean, the safest way of which is landing the plane parallel to the waves. But in his panicked brain he remembered a crucial fact: while only 10 percent of ditching attempts result in immediate fatality, another 10 percent of the survivors die from their injuries. "That's an 80 percent chance of doing okay. Not good enough." McGlaughlin also knew that his Cirrus, with fixed landing gear, had a greater risk. "The wheels hit the water, you might flip. You might break the windshield and now you're underwater with your daughter next to you."

So McGlaughlin quickly rejected the ditching option.

Instead, he reached up with his right hand and pulled the mysterious red handle on the ceiling of the Cirrus.

The red handle activated a little rocket which broke through the roof of his plane. Following the rocket came a big parachute. Not for the pilot and passenger, but for the whole airplane. The Cirrus and its two occupants floated downward, descending at seventeen miles an hour, and hit the ocean. "When you hit the water, you feel it in your back. You feel it in your neck. Not a soft landing. But we were alive."

Still shaking with adrenaline and overcome with relief, the doctor and his daughter unhooked their safety belts. They opened the door, stood on the wing, inflated a rubber raft they had brought, and waited for the Coast Guard to pick them up.[1]

This is an amazing story, but it is only partly due to a pioneering airplane company, Cirrus Aircraft, and its revolutionary whole-airframe parachute. The truly amazing thing—that McGlaughlin had actually pulled the red handle—has another reason.

McGlaughlin, in fact, had made the decision to pull the parachute several years before he actually needed to do it. What persuaded him to pull the chute if ever over water with a failed engine was not anything Cirrus had said in its marketing literature or its operating manual. No, the impetus to pull came from the Cirrus Owners and Pilots Association (COPA), the loudest, smartest, and most opinionated owners group in all of aviation.

The irony is that the airplane's manufacturer, Cirrus Aircraft, and its owner's group, COPA, are both revolutionary organizations—and often at each other's throats. Like America and China, they are sometimes friends, sometimes enemies. The relationship once got so bad that Cirrus even tried a secret program to kill COPA.

Welcome to the new world of company branding. What shapes a brand is no longer exclusively about the story the company wants to tell. It's the stories the customers want to share.

STORY IS NARRATIVE WITH CONFLICT

Story has many definitions: some overly technical, some mind-bendingly complex, and some even contradictory. But in its broadest sense, story is the narration, or telling, of a sequence of events. These events are usually connected or causally linked. The story itself can be true or fictitious.

Individually and collectively, stories help us make sense of our past and understand possible futures. In its very essence, a story expresses how and why life changes. Therefore, most stories follow a dramatic arc that begins with a life that's in balance, followed by an event that upsets that balance and creates conflict, which is followed by actions and decisions aimed at restoring balance, which then result in a new state of balance or a new reality. Consider the classic western: the bad guys ride into town on horseback. Crime and fear ensue, until a hero emerges to restore balance.

Since stories are inherently human-centered, we're naturally drawn to them. In a speech at the Centre for Contemporary Cultural Studies at the University of Birmingham, philosopher and influential critic Roland Barthes expressed the centrality of stories throughout culture: "The narratives of the world are without number. The narrative is present at all times, in all places, in all societies; the history of narrative begins with the history of mankind; there does not exist, and never has existed, a people without narratives."[2]

Some of the earliest evidence of storytelling comes from the Lascaux Caves in southern France. Created between 15,000 and 13,000 BC, more than two thousand figures, mostly animals, were painted by Upper Paleolithic hunters. Using iconographic methods of analysis, anthropologists who've reviewed these paintings believe that one particular composition appears to be our earliest example of an illustrated myth. As story expert, executive consultant, and best-selling author Nancy Duarte told me, "For thousands of years, story has been used to transfer insights, transfer morals, keeping entire cultures knit together. And this is pre-literacy—thousands of years of pre-literate people."

As should be clear, the creation, telling, and retelling of stories is a universal human activity. And even today, the ancient art of storytelling is far from lost. Stop to look around, and you'll see that stories saturate our lives. In TV, movies, online, in the news, and even in sports. The Olympics is as much about the stories of the athletes as it is about the athletic events. The same is true with the Tour de France, the World Cup, the Masters, the Kentucky Derby, and every other major sporting event in the world.

Likewise, in our personal lives, we think in stories, talk in stories, communicate in stories, and even dream in stories. We all continuously share stories of what happened, why, and what might happen next. When we're asked about our dinner out last night or our most recent vacation, we don't provide a pie chart or an analytical abstraction. We tell a story. And these stories are replete with a cast of characters, multiple plots, and plenty of drama.

No matter the form, a good storyteller describes a conflict, calling on the main character, also known as the protagonist or hero, to make decisions, take action, and ultimately discover a new truth. "With storytelling, in particular, the thing that we love is watching someone transform," said Nancy Duarte. "The classic three-part story structure is that there is this likable person who encounters these roadblocks and emerges transformed. I think that storytelling creates that tension and release that is so important to create change."

The key is that stories affirm who we are, that our lives have meaning. We're naturally compelled to make reason out of chaos and assign causality to all the random events that make up our lives. Stories help us do that. Stories shape our world: who we are and how we should behave. So if you want to understand what's going on in an organization, you just need to listen to the stories. Moreover, if you want to get anything done in an organization, you need to know how to use story to motivate people.

WHY STORIES IN BUSINESS?

In the business world, stories are used to launch new brands and enhance the image of existing brands. They're used to train new hires and invigorate seasoned employees. Stories help CEOs position themselves with investors, while also building trust and unlocking passion, two soft-edge requirements discussed in earlier chapters.

In fact, stories are so functional and malleable, so effective and ubiquitous, it's almost impossible to list all their uses and benefits. But I'll try anyway. Stories help with employee recruitment, morale building, sales and marketing, outside investment development, and change initiative support—*a quick breath, and*—stories capture and communicate knowledge, drive innovation, build community, strengthen organizational culture, and promote individual growth.

"In terms of story," venture capitalist Margit Wennmachers told me, "I actually think it's a fundamental thing that goes across *everything* in business." That's a very strong statement. But it's also a true statement.

Why, in the land of spreadsheets and pie charts, are stories so valuable? Because stories are how we remember. Simple, right? By contrast, we tend to forget lists and bullet points, spreadsheets and data dumps. But stories have an impact not so much through transferring large amounts of information as through synthesizing understanding. They enable us to grasp broad ideas very quickly. Stories can change the way we think, act, and feel—and they do it in a nonthreatening way. Which, by extension, means storytelling plays an important role in our own reasoning processes, as well as in our ability to convince others. In truth, making employees smile or laugh with a story is a better way to teach them something than by reciting a long list of bullet points.

Some businesspeople distrust stories because they fear exaggeration and manipulation. Nancy Duarte said she often sees the misconception "that business isn't a place for story, that story isn't true or factual, that we therefore discount their value or dismiss them completely."

But leaders, especially, can use the power of a good story to influence and motivate their teams to new heights. In Chapter Three, I recounted how insurance leader Northwestern Mutual invites its ten thousand financial reps to an annual meeting at Milwaukee's BMO Harris Bradley Center—the largest arena in town. For two days, stories are told and shared of Northwestern Mutual reps overcoming challenges or going the extra mile to serve policyholders. The leadership at Northwestern Mutual understands that stories can inspire everything from understanding to action. Stories can create legends for an entire workplace culture to build upon, and they have the power to break down barriers or turn a bad situation into a good one.

You see, the most powerful way to persuade others, to overcome resistance, is by linking an idea with an emotion. And the best way to do that is with a good story. If you can stimulate imagination through a good story, it causes people to suspend analytic thought.

Now, this is a very important lesson on the power of story. When we read or hear factual arguments, we tend to evaluate them intellectually. We're skeptical: we're ready to deflect or rebut any arguments. But when we're entranced by a good story, we willingly drop our guard and suspend our disbelief. In *Tell to Win*, Mandalay Entertainment Group CEO Peter Guber likens a well-told story to the Trojan Horse. To the listener, the story seems like a gift. But, in the end, the story is just a conduit, a container for the teller's agenda. It's a trick for slipping a message into the synaptic fortress of our minds.

"We have to push and prod our people along," said Duarte, "so that we're at the right place in the future, and story is the best way to do that." Call it narrative magic or verbal judo, but human minds yield to the pull of a good story. Storytelling can be used to affect both employees and customers. In that way, it's both an internal and external tool. And while it has many uses, two areas where I believe storytelling is particularly important are in creating purpose and in building brand.

Story and the Importance of Purpose

In the end, a leader's job is to articulate and help people cohere around a shared purpose that embraces the company's past and outlines its future. And when it comes to communicating a purpose for your organization—Why does it exist? What value does it offer to employees, customers, or society?—few vehicles serve to deliver your message as effectively as the art of storytelling.

Right here and now, let me just say *purpose* is a hugely important soft-edge factor. It is the thing that leads you to create authentic products and heroic customer experiences, even if that isn't the right ROI thing to do in the short term. And at any given point, but particularly the larger you get—and especially if your company is publicly traded—words like faith, authenticity, durability, and how your great efforts will be rewarded two years from now, instead of next quarter, can be a harder and harder sell. Yes, it takes soft-edge traits like courage and passion. But as soon as you lose that real belief in your greater purpose and fail to sell it, you begin compromising whatever it was that made your brand great.

In Chapter One, I wrote about Hewlett-Packard. HP is an example of a company that lost its purpose—the HP Way—during the reign of CEOs that optimized the company for scale and profit. The short-term profit emerged, right on schedule, and the CEOs were lauded. But the purpose was lost—and so eventually were the profits. Current HP chief Meg Whitman now is laboring mightily to reestablish the HP Way, as defined by founders David Packard and Bill Hewlett.

I discuss the importance of purpose in Chapter Three, but let me just add that communicating a strong purpose involves creating meaning beyond things like career bumps or pay raises. A purpose needs to include aspirational goals that energize people and encourage collective responsibility.

And how do we get those aspirational goals across? With a story. It's not through graphs and charts, statistics and dry-as-toast policy notices that employees identify with a company's goals and help embed them within the organizational DNA, but instead through the experience of story. "Stories are the things that can knit culture together," Nancy Duarte explained. "When you think about it, a hundred years ago, the biggest gathering place was at a church, and they shared norms and beliefs. They rallied around these very ancient stories. And today, people don't do that as much anymore; their big gathering place is work. So we're having to create meaning in a place that sometimes is just, you know, about putting widgets together."

While stories can play a big role in shaping culture and attitudes internally—in both catalyzing and galvanizing a company's purpose—they can also be a powerful force outside of your organization.

Story and Brand Building

There have never been more ways to reach consumers than there are today. That's a fact. But it's also never been harder to connect deeply with consumers. Transactions happen only once and are more fleeting than before. Repeat business requires relationships. For almost any business to work, we need customers to come back. Again. And again. And, yes, again. We need them to be fans. We need them to tell their friends.

This relationship depends on storytelling. If you really want to create fans of your business, the people who'll become apostles and advocates, you need to use narrative. We consumers are hardwired to receive a good story.

If we look at the research on branding, and there's a lot of it out there, brand stories really do help shape our culture. How so? Well, just consider the rhetorical and metaphorical devices used by researchers, psychologists, social scientists, and anthropologists to describe brands: brands have personalities; brands are icons; brands represent reference groups, represent "the self," and mark ethnic boundaries. Brands anchor nostalgia and are romantic partners. Brands can be the basis for both community and individualization. Brands tell stories about us and, likewise, we tell stories about them.[3]

Considering these conceptualizations, it's not surprising that brands represent the emotional relationship, the touch point, between a consumer and a product. And let's be honest, there's a lot of stuff to choose from out there. For nearly any product type, we might have five or ten or more manufacturers to pick between. As they say in real estate, it's a buyer's market. Therefore, at its very core, marketing is storytelling. Or, I should say, good marketing *must* be storytelling. In a sense, storytelling de-commoditizes a commodity and wraps meaning around your product.

Really great branding is the ability to apply an entire world of meanings and imaginations to a product, service, or corporation. This means not simply showing a product but also communicating on a much deeper level what the product means within a wider culture. In this sense, story transcends the product. Nike isn't just shoes; it's stories of iconic athletes. Aston Martin isn't just a car; it's the car the world's greatest spy drives.

In this way, brands communicate and reinforce particular qualities to us through popular culture, inviting us to embrace certain identities, lifestyles, or ideals. They do so because brands help us to achieve pleasure through enacting a specific archetype—the cowboy, the spy, the astronaut, the athlete—and essentially retelling that brand story every time we use and reuse that product.

You see, you want your story to become your customer's story. As your audience sees their own values, hopes, and dreams in the story you create, they'll deepen their emotional connection to your brand. They'll begin to use your brand to describe themselves: I'm a "Mac User," a "Chevy Guy," a "Bud Drinker." Consider Harley-Davidson: the fact that people will tattoo a company name and logo on their bodies shows an extreme level of engagement with a brand story.

STORY GONE WRONG: DELL

For every well-spun story, countless others are poorly told. Margit Wennmachers provided some thoughts on how a seemingly great story can quickly go bad. Wennmachers is a gifted entrepreneur, having founded Silicon Valley's leading public relations firm, The OutCast Agency, in 1997. What makes Wennmachers unique is that she left OutCast to become a general partner in one of Silicon Valley's hottest venture capital firms, Andreessen Horowitz. No PR person had ever become a general partner at a major VC firm. But firm co-founder Marc Andreessen wanted Wennmachers to join for this reason: tech start-ups, in the age of cheap technology, ready financing, and global markets, have become so crowded that they need a good story to stick out. "I think in technology the big trap," Wennmachers said, "is the company positions itself around financial success or financial numbers."

When I asked her for an example, she told me about working with Dell back in the go-go 1990s while she was at her PR firm. "It's probably okay to share by now," she began. "When we had our first big sit-down meeting, I asked them, 'So what does success look like? What do you want out of this?' And they basically said, 'Look, we're a $30 billion company today. We're planning and staffing up and building offices and an international footprint to become a $60 billion company. Our stock price is at x dollars and you just basically need to help us scale up.'"

And why wouldn't a company want to scale? Scaling isn't the problem. The problem is that scaling isn't a story. Wennmachers continued, "If your story is about money and about the stock price, that always changes. And you've essentially told your employees and your customers to look at those two things. And when the stock price goes south or the revenue flattens or the growth rates flatten, it's all about the failing numbers. There's nothing else of substance to make an employee stay longer or a customer stick with you when those numbers change."

For Dell, the story made the company disposable. It locked itself into a single wave of growth, instead of creating a story that endures through good times and bad, through the inevitable stumble or misstep. As Wennmachers said, "Luck always runs out on the stock price."

Though intangible, stories have something solid that helps maintain a sense of normalcy, calm, and purpose during times of crisis as well as times of plenty. "A good story is the most important foundation for all of your employees," Wennmachers pointed out. Now Dell is a private company. As such, it has a second shot at greatness, without shareholders second-guessing its every wiggle. The early signs are encouraging. Dell's new story strategy is to celebrate other entrepreneurs and startups.

Financial performance isn't the only story trap to avoid. "The other big one in technology, in particular, is product," Wennmachers explained. "Say, your story is only the list of the features of your current product. And, as you know, product cycles change, feature sets change, right? Your new competitors will come up with twenty more features that get them on the front pages of tech sites. Look at what's been happening in mobile. You've got iOS and you've got Android. Every cycle, they one-up each other. If you walk into our office at Andreessen Horowitz and your story is 'We're an iPhone app that does x,' that's not a business. That's not something you can recruit people for, and that's not something that can withstand change."

In some ways, you could say that having a compelling story can buy you grace when you hit a rough patch. "Grace, and it provides inspiration beyond the current state of being," said Wennmachers. There's no doubt that stories can change the way we think, act, and feel. Leaders, especially, can use the power of a good story to influence and motivate their teams to new heights.

LEADERSHIP AND STORYTELLING

Make no mistake, story can be a very powerful leadership tool. Great leaders know this, and many top CEOs today use stories to illustrate points and sell their ideas. Persuasion is at the very core of business activity. Why, then, do most high-level executives struggle to communicate, let alone inspire? Too often, they get lost in the muddle of corporate communication; things like sterile messages from internal PR departments and warnings of what *not* to say from legal departments. In these cases, even the most thoughtful efforts are routinely greeted with cynicism or apathy.

Instead, to motivate people, leaders must engage their emotions. And the key to people's hearts is story. "The story—leaders often relegate it to marketing or a PR function," Wennmachers remarked. "It's really something that the founder or the CEO needs to own. You can't outsource the narrative of your company. . . . Essentially, the story is the company and the company is the story, and they can't be divorced from each other." To sum it up, she said, the foundational story really is "the encapsulation of what the company does."

This means storytelling could be the *key* leadership competency for the twenty-first century. Knowing the right story to tell combined with knowing how to deliver it effectively can inspire everything from understanding to action. It can be used to connect employees to a strategy by providing understanding, belief, and motivation. Story can give a workplace something for people to lean on through rough economic times.

In the end, CEOs are responsible for navigating their companies through the storms of down economies and tough competition. In those types of situations, story can be the steady hand that steers the plane when the typical measures of company health experience turbulence. And speaking of turbulence, let me return to the story of Cirrus Aircraft and its cantankerous customers.

WHY CIRRUS PIONEERED THE WHOLE-AIRFRAME PARACHUTE

On a lovely April evening in 1985 a twenty-seven-year-old Wisconsin man, Alan Klapmeier, was on an instrument flying lesson near the Sauk Prairie airport. The trick of instrument flying is to possess both the skill and the calm nerves to operate the airplane when you can't see out the window because of clouds or darkness.

When John F. Kennedy Jr. crashed in 1999, the probable cause was the loss of visual reference. Kennedy, his wife, and his wife's sister had departed the small Essex County, New Jersey, airport in the early evening. As the sky darkened, Kennedy followed a course along the Connecticut coast on his way to Martha's Vineyard. But in the twilight and haze over the Atlantic Ocean, Kennedy lost his visual references and likely suffered a spatial disorientation. He was not a certified instrument pilot. He wasn't trained to deal with this circumstance. He lost control of the airplane and he and his passengers died.

But young Klapmeier was practicing instrument flying with his instructor in clear conditions. Klapmeier was wearing a hood that allowed him to see only the instruments on the airplane's panel and nothing outside. This is how instrument training is done in clear conditions.

Klapmeier's hood kept him from looking out the windows, and his instructor (who was free to do so) was not looking outside, either. He was watching Klapmeier, who had the plane in a climbing right turn. Neither of them saw another airplane headed in their direction. The pilot of this plane was looking straight into the setting sun. That pilot didn't see Klapmeier's plane—until it was too late.

The midair collision sheared three feet off the left wing of Klapmeier's Cessna 182. The plane was barely flyable, but Klapmeier and his instructor managed to land it safely despite the damage.

The other pilot wasn't so lucky. That plane was damaged beyond control. From 1,600 feet above the Wisconsin countryside, it began an uncontrolled descent into the earth, killing the pilot.

A year before the accident, Alan Klapmeier and his younger brother, Dale, aviation nuts since they were boys, had started a company to build do-it-yourself planes out of their parents' barn near Baraboo, Wisconsin. After the accident, Alan Klapmeier decided that small airplanes needed something to make them safer. This aim took form in a radical idea. Why not have a parachute for the whole airframe? Great idea, right? But in the world of aviation, every new idea is much easier said, or thought, than done.

Nothing happens fast in aviation. It's capital intensive, and it obeys locked-in aerodynamic laws instead of the rapidly evolving Moore's Law that governs computers, phones, and the Internet. Aviation is also highly regulated—in the United States, by the Federal Aviation Administration. But by 1999, fourteen years after Alan Klapmeier's crash, he and his brother Dale had successfully run the gauntlet of high costs and regulatory certification. They unveiled the most radical advance in small airplane manufacturing since the 1940s. It was called the Cirrus SR20, a single-engine, four-seat, composite material airplane with an airframe parachute.

Cirrus, the company, was off and flying. In 2000, the Klapmeiers' company announced a plane with a larger engine called the SR22 that could fly two hundred miles an hour for more than four hours on full fuel tanks. The plane was such a success it was back-ordered for up to two years. In 2003 Cirrus built the first FAA-certified small airplane to replace the traditional instrument gauges with two flat-panel computer screens, at the time a feature only offered in big jets. Among their many modern wonders, the glass panels had a large moving map, to show the plane's location, altitude, and speed. The glass panel system would soon connect to XM satellite weather, so the pilot could see and avoid any dangerous weather along the route.

The parachute, the situational awareness provided by the glass panel displays, and real-time weather depiction made quite a package. With these, Cirrus appeared to fulfill Alan Klapmeier's hope of making small airplanes as safe as automobiles. Klapmeier had been right to worry about safety, and not just because of his own mid-air accident. Industry statistics for small planes were sobering. On a per-mile basis, small planes were about ten times likelier to kill the occupants than were cars. Small planes were about as safe as motorcycles, which is to say, not all that safe.

With its host of safety features, Cirrus looked to close the gap. But a curious thing happened. From 1999 to 2005, the Cirrus accident and fatality rate did not do better than the overall small plane safety statistics. In fact, the Cirrus statistics were, if anything, slightly *worse* than the small airplane industry average. Pilots were still killing themselves and their passengers. They were flying into mountainsides. They were losing control in the clouds. They were futilely trying to land the planes after engine failures over hostile terrain. And oddly, Cirrus, the company founded to improve safety, wasn't doing much about it. It had its own problems.

That's when the Cirrus plane owners themselves decided to take matters into their own hands. More on this story later in the chapter.

GOOD STORIES AND STORYTELLING

So what makes a good storyteller? The good news is we're all natural storytellers. We've simply been browbeaten into thinking that storytelling is some kind of arcane skill that only a few gifted people have. As I mentioned earlier in the chapter, we all use stories and storytelling in everyday conversations and as a regular part of our lives. We frequently tell stories to our friends, our kids, other family members, and our closest colleagues. And believe it or not, those stories are often funny, gripping, engaging, and memorable. So how do we translate that natural ability to meetings and presentations?

Storytelling involves an array of tools and methods. While there is no one right way to tell a story, the greatest commandment of good storytelling is, "Make me care." Fulfill that requirement, and you're in pretty good shape. But I've picked up a few more tips from story experts like Nancy Duarte and Margit Wennmachers. These aren't rules, but instead just a few helpful guidelines:

- Keep it simple.
- Know your audience.
- Avoid Chicken Little.
- Make it real.
- Don't forget the pain and suffering.
- Practice, practice, practice, then practice some more.

Keep It Simple

Many people make the mistake of believing that more is better: more visuals, more flash, more sparkle. People believe these elements will add excitement to their stories rather than draw away from the emotional or thematic spine.

Instead, simplification is a key to any creative process. Whether you're a novelist, painter, or designer, innovation cuts with Occam's razor: the simpler solution is the better solution. As story expert Nancy Duarte explained, "The greatest speeches of all time didn't have visuals, because the verbal was so beautifully written that it painted the pictures, it painted the scenes that we wanted to see—that we want people to see." As much as Hollywood labors to prove otherwise, good stories aren't built on clever plot points and huge explosions. Simple words and plain language can create new places and spark feelings as authentic and meaningful as any real, tangible event.

Know Your Audience

One trait good storytellers share is the ability to read a room. "If you're talking to an analytical audience," Nancy Duarte commented, "you need to pull back on emotional appeal and keep your credibility intact. If you're talking to a highly emotional audience, you pull back on the analytical appeal." Odds are, you won't want to give the same speech in a conference room as you would in a locker room, right?

One notable example is a TED talk given by a well-known venture capitalist. While talking about climate change, he said earth wouldn't make it and he began to choke up. Yes, people bring their own biases into a story or presentation. So if you're an environmentalist and already strongly pro-green technology, you'd probably give the speaker the benefit of the doubt. Wow, he really cares.

But if you're on the fence, you're likely to wonder if the speaker—who had raised a billion-dollar green fund—is trying to manipulate you emotionally. That was some people's initial reaction: he's great salesman and *maybe* he can make himself cry on demand.

In all fairness, for some people the speech worked very well. And I don't think the speaker was faking it—I think he believed in what he was funding and selling so strongly that it became emotional. But I do think he hurt himself when he broke down and cried. "His credibility dropped because he overused emotion," Nancy Duarte observed. "He tried too hard to appeal to our emotion." And in doing so, he crossed a line in storytelling. If you're speaking to a broad audience, if your goal is broad appeal, you have to be more cautious. And that takes me to my next tip.

Avoid Chicken Little

When I asked Nancy Duarte for an example of storytelling gone wrong, she said, "You know, 'The sky is falling' doesn't work; I've tried it at my own company. My biggest failure of a presentation was this very beautiful and compelling, 'The sky is falling' story. It was 2007. I knew there would be a crash in 2008. 'Wah-aah-ahh! The sky is falling! The sky is falling!' And it completely bombed. It *bombed*. I completely lost my credibility until the economy actually crashed."

When telling a story, avoid guessing at the future. Yes, maybe things will be bad. Maybe they'll get worse. That may be true, but try to temper your message. I'm not saying be dishonest or avoid a candid conversation. Be honest and forthcoming. But don't make wild prognostications that could easily be dismissed as fraudulent or manipulative. And don't go overboard for drama's sake, like the teared-up venture capitalist in the "Know Your Audience" section.

Make It Real

Verisimilitude is always important in storytelling. When I say *verisimilitude*, I'm talking about adding realism to a story, not necessarily making it realistic. Making it realistic would mean sticking to the facts, the cold, hard numbers and data that often preoccupy the business world. By adding realism, I'm referring to small details that help set the scene and transport readers or listeners to a new place. When telling a story, share what you see, smell, feel, taste, and hear. Share the emotion; describe the moments. There's great power in nostalgia and remembrance. When you trigger these senses in someone, you draw them into the story with you.

But this isn't just about adding details or flowery touches. You also need to include the background, the genesis, of your product or business. Guy Kawasaki, former chief evangelist at Apple and author of *Enchantment*, recommends weaving an "origination story" into your company's cultural history. You started out building your product in your garage or you created the next great social network in your dorm room. Brian Maxwell created PowerBar, the first energy bar, in the tiny kitchen of a home he shared with his future wife. Then personalize your story even more—you began with your grandma's recipe or your father's old soldering iron.

Similarly, many products are created out of a real-world need. Outdoor apparel companies Patagonia and Northface were founded because Yvon Chouniard and Douglas Tompkins couldn't find quality mountaineering equipment, so they made it themselves. Mike Sinyard started Specialized Bicycles because he couldn't get quality biking equipment in the United States, and instead imported it from Italy. Filson Clothing was founded because miners and loggers in the Pacific Northwest needed better, more rugged clothes than could be found through regular outlets.

Regardless of how you choose to do it, a certain level of realism helps listeners and audience members suspend disbelief. It helps draw them into your world and your product's world. Sometimes it's a carefully chosen detail; sometimes it's a cultural reference; sometimes it's just being honest about why you took a flyer on starting a company to begin with. Stories can capture the imagination and make things real in a way that cold, hard facts can't, but only if they contain at least the seeds of authenticity.

Don't Forget the Pain and Suffering

Self-disclosure through storytelling is a powerful method of engaging and inspiring others. Nancy Duarte told me, "I would follow a leader that has tried and failed (and he's willing to talk about it) much sooner than I would follow a leader who pretends he's never failed. It requires a vulnerability. There's no transformation if you haven't gone through hardship."

Therefore, you absolutely do not want to tell a beginning-to-end story describing how your results effortlessly met your expectations. They're what I call the Immaculate Conception stories—Company A adopted a product, everything went perfectly, and now it's tearing up the world. Wow! The implementation must have been *so easy*. It's boring. And it's probably untrue. Instead, you want to display the struggle between expectations and reality.

Which means that as a storyteller, you want to be up-front about problems and show how you've overcome them. The antagonists, or villains, can be a competitor, a creditor, or any force offering resistance and providing conflict. This creates some suspense: it was a struggle, a battle. Then raise the idea that the story might not have a happy ending: hey, this could all blow up. It's not that the sky is falling, but the stakes are real. And they're high. Then reveal the choices you made, the hard decisions you reached in the face of adversity. Our true spirit is revealed in the choices we make under pressure. When you tell the story of your struggles against real challenges, your audience sees you as an exciting, dynamic, and even heroic person.

But how do you get there? How do you find the hard, gritty, heroic story of struggle? Just be honest.

"When people ask me to help them turn their presentations into stories," Nancy Duarte said, "I begin by asking questions. Most companies and executives sweep the dirty laundry, the difficulties, the antagonists, and the struggle under the carpet. They prefer to present a rosy—and boring—picture to the world. Everything is analytical: get stuff done; measure this; meet this objective." All so easy and so easily predicted.

But what's wrong with staying persistently positive? I mean, most public relations professionals would tell you to never utter a negative word, no matter how difficult the challenge or dire the crisis. Well, the problem is, it doesn't ring true. Your audience knows it's never that easy. And self-disclosure, warts and all, through storytelling is a powerful method of engaging and inspiring others.

Practice, Practice, Practice, Then Practice Some More

Another fact about good storytellers is they practice. Not a little but a lot. Somewhere along the line, many of us seem to swallow the idea that storytelling is a God-given talent and fool ourselves into thinking that the great speakers just have a knack for spinning a good yarn. "The better stories are more planned than we think in the sense that these people have thought through them," Nancy Duarte revealed.

While there's some truth to the idea that a small portion of us may be more comfortable and confident in crafting a narrative than others, the idea that it comes naturally, even for gifted speakers, is patently false. I asked Nest Labs' Tony Fadell about Steve Jobs's legendary speaking ability, and he said, "Are you kidding? By the time Steve got up at MacWorld, he'd given that talk five thousand times."

So maybe there's a little more artifice behind a natural like Jobs than we think. Nancy Duarte mapped his entire 2007 iPhone launch and discovered there were physical reactions to his content—the audience laughed, ooh'd or ahh'd, or clapped—every thirty seconds, on the dot. That's why he could talk for ninety minutes and still keep people engaged. Not only did he master the right storytelling rhythm, he showed incredible enthusiasm, almost wonderment, at his own product. "I actually tracked how much he marveled at his own product," Duarte said. "You can see how many times he was exclaiming how glorious the work his team had done was. So I think his passion played a very significant role, and his passion to get things right."

But we can't all be Steve Jobs, right?

So what do you do if you have a lot to offer but just can't get up in front of a crowd and knock them dead? Practice. Then practice some more. It takes some grit—that ever-present underpinning of the soft edge. Most people, in their first ten, twenty, or even thirty talks, go from bad to mediocre. But everyone, when talking about a subject on which they're authoritative and passionate, can be very good, as TED proves, if they work through those early bad repetitions. "Oh, yeah. Every single person on TED at one time was not ready to get in front of a huge audience," Duarte confided. "They work them. They work them hard. They work them all year long. Not everyone gets dramatic. But if you have a clear structure, clear content, a big idea, you know something worth spreading, the people at TED will work you all year."

So if you want to tell stories like your favorite speaker on TED, work at it.

WHEN YOUR CUSTOMERS TELL A BETTER STORY THAN YOU CAN

Alan Klapmeier's technologically advanced Cirrus airplane, with its whole-frame parachute, was at first met with skepticism by aviation's old guard. Many of these older pilots were trained to fly by the U.S. military, in World War II and later during conflicts in Korea and Vietnam. When these pilots retired as civilians, found careers and accumulated some wealth, they often bought airplanes for their own use. They bought aluminum airplanes designed in the 1940s and 1950s, and these old designs were okay, because they were familiar.

What Cirrus discovered was a market of younger people who had never flown their own planes, or even flown at all. Many of them, like Curt Sanford and Rick Beach—two men intimately involved with COPA—had made enough money from technology careers that they could afford to take up flying for the first time.

Beach, a former Xerox executive and university professor, said, "Cirrus had cleverness and technology. After reading about it, I endeavored to get a private pilot's license and buy one." Sanford had made a boatload of stock compensation as a group president at Lucent during the go-go 1990s. He was looking for a hobby and felt the same desire as Beach. He wanted an airplane! But he wanted a technologically advanced one.

That these rich, tech-savvy first-time pilots were attracted to Cirrus was a fulfillment of Alan Klapmeier's dream and more. But it came with a hitch—a big hitch.

As Sanford explained, "At Ascend and Lucent, we had one of the very first online user groups on the Internet. Our customers immediately banded together and started talking about our products. I quickly saw how powerful user groups could be in terms of what they do to a company. Cirrus had a user group that was just getting going. I thought: This is a force that is going to change Cirrus whether it knows it or not."

COPA was a natural home for Cirrus owners like Beach and Sanford—affluent, tech-savvy, data-driven, opinionated, and independent. The COPA website was soon brimming with shared experiences about training, good and bad maintenance shops, cool places to fly, best ways to use the plane, and so forth.

When praise for the Cirrus airplane was earned, COPA members dished it out lavishly. When criticism was merited—over misaligned doors, for example, or parts that appeared to be poorly engineered or made—COPA members again dished it out, much to the chagrin of Cirrus management.

In particular, though, Beach, Sanford, and many COPA members were becoming alarmed at the Cirrus safety record, which was no better than the average for small airplanes. Which is to say, it was bad. Cirrus pilots were dying in accidents that the safety technology should have prevented. It was a mystery—and a very dangerous one.

"It was so bad that insurers would not touch Cirrus. We looked into the future and saw that our planes might not be insurable," said Beach. But Cirrus was curiously passive about promoting the use of its most innovative safety feature—its whole-airframe parachute. "What happened is that Cirrus was advocating using the chute only under certain circumstances—after a mid-air collision, or a structural failure such as a damaged wing," said Beach. But in fact, most pilots die, as John F. Kennedy Jr. did, as a result of spatial disorientation in a perfectly good airplane.

Why wasn't Cirrus openly advocating a chute pull when disorientation occurred? Beach says Cirrus was cowed by its lawyers. No complicated mechanical system involving rockets and parachutes will work 100 percent of the time. So Cirrus felt legally obligated to say that use of the parachute could result in death. This legal wording led to a very unfortunate result. Some Cirrus pilots who should have pulled the chute after a failed engine or spatial disorientation were not doing so. And they were dying in preventable crashes.

"It was heartbreaking," says Beach.

So COPA took matters into its own hands, and Rick Beach took it upon himself to spread the gospel to Cirrus pilots. "Pull early, pull often" became his and COPA's mantra. If Cirrus wouldn't say it, COPA would. "You might kill yourself if you pull the parachute after becoming disoriented," Beach said. "Odds are very slim, but you might. No guarantee. But there is a far, far, greater chance that you will die if you don't pull the chute."

Many lives—including those of Dr. McGlaughlin and his daughter, Elaine—have been saved since COPA began its campaign to pull the parachute at the first sign of loss of control. There have been forty parachute pulls, which have saved more than ninety lives, including those of a seventy-four-year-old pilot and his three grandchildren. The older pilot lost control of his Cirrus in mountain turbulence over the Canadian Rockies. He pulled the chute. All four occupants survived with only minor injuries.

Thanks to COPA, the safety record of the Cirrus has improved astonishingly. But there is a caveat. It has improved only for active COPA members who post frequently on the COPA website. The accident statistics have not improved much for Cirrus pilots who won't use this resource. Beach's statistics say that COPA members who post regularly are four times less likely to be involved in a fatal accident as is the general Cirrus pilot population.

Yes, it's a new world of storytelling. The Cirrus-COPA relationship is a glimpse into the future. No longer does a company control its own story. Customers want to share their stories, too, especially when it's a matter of life and death.

TECHNOLOGY CHANGES BUT STORIES ENDURE

Today, you have to master many different new forms of communication. And to do that, you really need a deep sense of where technology is taking each one, so you won't be surprised by new opportunities. You won't overlook them and you won't dismiss them. Who knows what television will look like tomorrow? Or what about the future of the book? Social media will surely be around, but it will continue to morph.

If all these are in flux, what do we know? If past is prologue, we know stories and storytelling will remain. And the heart of storytelling is creating a connection through shared experience and emotion. Social media brings with it exciting and new opportunities for this type of interpersonal connection. In essence, social media forges a social contract, one fostering sharing and mutual contribution. Just to be clear, by social media I mean the usual suspects like Facebook, LinkedIn, Twitter, and Pinterest, as well as blogs, forums, and self-directed user groups like COPA. With these types of forums, empowered users assume ownership of their communities and transform brand narrative into a collective experience.

Because social media is receiver-oriented and involves two-way conversations, it's a dramatic change from the traditional one-way, sender-oriented concept of advertising and marketing. As Vivek Wadhwa, of Singularity University, said, "Knowledge has been democratized, ideas have been democratized." So how do you build on this new freedom to strengthen your culture and the perception of your brand?

Let people talk.

Get them online and challenge them with some questions, tell them what you're looking for. This is where company leaders have to be active: they have to start communicating one-on-one within their organization. This type of management and leadership is top-down, at least at the start. You set up the forums and say, "Look, I'm looking to achieve this, this, and this. Help me." And you let everyone in the company participate equally. You let the truck driver, the mailroom clerk, the junior clerical assistant express ideas just like the senior executives and strategy consultants do. One of the big problems with corporate hierarchies is that people at the bottom struggle to air their opinions or ideas. So much so, they usually quit trying. Next stop, company-wide apathy. Then your organizational culture begins to crumble at its foundation.

But social media flattens this hierarchy. You don't just allow everyone to express opinions, you give them the tools, the forum, the proverbial soap box to do it with. Through this active engagement, you have the internal storytelling ability needed to organically disperse your purpose and your cultural touch points. You're now sharing knowledge equally and creating meaning, even if it's in a place, as Nancy Duarte said, that's just "about putting widgets together."

But beware: currently, there's a tremendous amount of enthusiasm for networks on the web and the wisdom of crowds. Is there a more popular catchphrase than "crowdsourcing"? Possibly. But these days, we're crowdsourcing money, we're crowdsourcing knowledge, we're crowdsourcing labor, and, as I described in Chapter Five, we're even crowdsourcing stories for books. So this enthusiasm is justifiable in some cases—it works really well when you have a large crowd. "But inside the enterprise," as Keith Collins, chief technology officer of SAS Institute, told me, "it really has been about understanding who the true influencers are, and you have to be really careful. When the population gets smaller, one whiner can distort things."

So that's the internal aspect of storytelling, but what about technology's effects on external brand building?

When we talk about brand storytelling through media channels, it isn't a new concept. But with the explosive growth of social media, the ability to tell stories as part of direct and indirect brand marketing has become a strategic priority. John Earnhardt of Cisco, who manages the company's award-winning blogs, says storytelling in social media is a distinct "fourth space" not previously occupied by corporate marketing, PR, or investor relations.

Advances in technology are transforming the nature, reach, speed, and focus of human influence. According to many experts, we've moved from the "knowledge economy" to the "conversation economy," which means having meaningful dialogue with customers is now crucial to the success of most businesses. So with the proliferation of media like Twitter and Facebook, where outsiders can weigh in and sometimes have a greater voice on your brand than you from the inside do, narrative is more important than ever. What is your company about? What are the values that it stands for? If it had a voice, what would that voice sound like?

Don't know? Your competitors surely do.

Social media demands that brands be able to provoke conversations and inspire meaningful stories. In this space, brands communicate and engage alongside trusted members of an individual's social network, whether they're private pilots like the ones in COPA or Harley enthusiasts or scrapbooking buffs. To help ensure engagement, be sure that your brand is consistently creating content, whether it's Facebook posts, tweets, an e-mail newsletter, or videos. We've all heard the message "Keep your audience engaged" time and time again, but it's imperative for your brand's ongoing narrative in this age of electron-fast attention spans and total media saturation. When your content ends, so does your brand's story.

Clearly, social media's growth and popularity have changed the game for companies, for marketers and advertisers. You aren't required to embrace every new channel, but don't limit yourself to traditional media just because that's all you know. So many tools out there now are more effective and less expensive than the traditional branding and storytelling channels, and inevitably even newer tools will come along, tools that we haven't yet even imagined. Just think of it this way: all this new technology should inspire us, it should challenge us to think of new and better ways to create stories that provoke thought and arouse emotion.

DATA STORYTELLING

In my experience, many people on the hard edge of business—in technology, operations, and finance—are, let's just say, not the best storytellers. Why? Because they live and breathe data. It's the language they speak. But the rest of us can't absorb data so easily. We don't think in data. We don't think in rows and columns, in numbers and statistics. We think in stories. Which means if you give us a story, we can rapidly absorb the meaning of large amounts of data.

The worlds of data, IT, and finance are populated by people who have natural analytic skills. But when you get into fields like marketing or human resources or sales, you're dealing with people likely to have different skill sets, and the other side of their brain may be dominant. These types, and I'm one of them myself, have always wrestled with deeper statistical concepts. But the great promise of data visualization is that we now have a lingua franca—a common working language—that spans the organization.

Fittingly, this idea circles back to the soft-edge pillar of trust. In Chapter Three, I discuss the power of data visualization and explain how the plain language of images, story, and context are a driver of consensus. With data visualization, you can tell a data-driven story to a wider group of people, get faster penetration, and elicit a much more inclusive response. There really is an internal advantage to being able to say, "Hey, this is the situation we're in," or, "This is the problem the customer faces," and then being able to look at the data, comprehend the underlying story, and agree on a path forward.

This means a data scientist's real job is, or soon will be, story-telling. Which, in turn, means the most important part of that job is—surprise!—qualitative. Things like asking questions, creating directives from data, and telling its story. The data scientist of the future will be a new kind of professional who combines the skills of a statistician, an anthropologist, and an artist to extract the nuggets of insight hidden under the mountains of data. This is why Keith Collins, the CTO at SAS Institute, looks for artistic or musical talents in the data scientists he hires. He told me this as we sat next to an artistic sculpture of the pi sign on the lawn of SAS's campus in Cary, North Carolina.

Without a human frame, such as images or words that make the underlying emotion salient, data will only confuse most people. Raw data or information on its own has no meaning, but story adds meaning and context. Data gives you the what; humans know the why. Which means data and story are inexorably connected.

Don't get me wrong: storytelling doesn't replace analytical thinking. It supplements it by enabling us to imagine new perspectives and new worlds. It proposes marrying the communicative and imaginative strengths of storytelling with the advantages of statistical analysis. In essence, we humanize the data and make it much more powerful by turning the raw numbers into a story. Yes, there will always be someone who uses a spreadsheet, but I think what we're finding in the business community is that when it comes to things like data and advanced analytics, the story will truly be the endpoint.

And just to add a little personal context to *this* story—I was one of the people who came into the computing world through the Macintosh. I remember the first time I saw one in a department store in 1984. All of a sudden, I could see the whole world unfolding in front of me and I had this vision of desktop publishing. It really was, as Steve Jobs portrayed it, the computer for the rest of us. And it seems to me that the promise of data storytelling and visual analytics is similar. It's the analytics for the rest of us. It's doing for data and data analytics what graphical user interfaces and desktop publishing and all of those visual tools did for an earlier generation of computing.

I can hardly wait!

GAINING THE EDGE

- Stories are a universal human activity. They express how and why life changes. They affirm who we are, that our lives have meaning.
- Stories are a powerful leadership tool. Persuasion is at the very core of business.
- Stories go across everything we do in business. They're the key to a strong culture. They stick in the memory in a way that bullet points and spreadsheets do not.
- Stories can turn customers into apostles and advocates.
- Stories need to be fought for. The best company stories ironically have to run the longest gauntlet of corporate communications and legal departments.
- Stories are often better told by your customers, and sometimes your critics, than by your own employees. Embrace these outsider stories.
- Stories in the age of data will require statisticians with the skills of an anthropologist or artist.

Conclusion
The Sweet Spot of High Performance

A few days after I turned in *The Soft Edge* manuscript first draft, I participated in a delightfully strange discussion—strange in a business setting, that is—at a conference in Napa, California. Billed as a CIO-CMO Forum, it was organized by Forrester Research of Cambridge, Massachusetts. The audience consisted of two executive roles—chief information technology officers (CIOs) and chief marketing officers (CMOs)—who evidently fight and squabble in all too many companies. The reason seems obvious, at least on the surface. In the age of web commerce, mobile devices, and social media—all of them new channels for marketing messages—CMOs now command a growing share of company investment in technology. In most companies this growing investment comes straight out of the pockets of CIOs, who are not all that happy about it.

In Napa, I sat on the stage with Sheryl Pattek, who runs Forrester's CMO-related research. She had worked with a

Forbes colleague to write a study that revealed a stark Venus-Mars-like divide between CMOs and CIOs. Pattek, who has a perpetual sardonic smile, explained that most CMOs secretly think their CIOs are nerds who speak in tech jargon, have no sense of urgency—about sales and marketing especially—and lack even a basic understanding of how their company gets its revenue. For their part, CIOs secretly think CMOs are smooth-talking fakers when it comes to technology more complex than a PowerPoint slide show.

From the stage, I tossed a question to the audience. Are these stereotypes true in your company? Hands shot up. A woman in the front row said, "I asked my CIO to attend this meeting. He was disdainful. He said he had better things to do."

Such as what, I asked?

"He said he had to be at a board meeting," she said.

That's pretty important, I offered. Most CIOs are required to give a presentation to the board of directors.

"Why is that not required for my job?" she shouted back. I noticed that the women CMOs in the audience murmured their approval. The men stared at their shoelaces.

Thus it was impossible to know whether the CMO-CIO divide in the conference room was mostly about the fight for technology budgets or more deeply about the roles of men and women in business. As of 2014, more CIOs are men and more CMOs are women. This difference has no inherent reason but reflects traditional gender roles, I suppose. Things are starting to change, but the fact remains that CIOs are still dispropor-tionately men and CMOs are more often women. The women's anger at not being included at their company's board meeting was raw. Women are grossly underrepresented at the corporate board level.

A budget fight? War of the sexes? Believe it or not, there is a third plausible explanation for the CMO-CIO crack. This one goes back to 1959, when a jowly middle-aged Englishman, bearing a passing resemblance to filmmaker Alfred Hitchcock, took the lectern at the Senate House at Cambridge University and began to speak. His name was Charles Percy Snow, and he was a chemist by training and a novelist for fun. With a foot in both the scientific and literary worlds, C. P. Snow had a unique perspective. His Cambridge lecture was called "The Two Cultures and the Scientific Revolution."

"Many times I have been present at gatherings of people who, by the standards of the traditional culture, are thought highly educated and who have with considerable gusto been expressing their incredulity at the illiteracy of scientists," Snow began. "Once or twice I have asked the company how many of them could describe the Second Law of Thermodynamics. The response was cold: it was also negative. Yet I was asking something which is the scientific equivalent of: Have you read a work of Shakespeare's?

"I now believe that if I had asked an even simpler question—such as, What do you mean by mass, or acceleration, which is the scientific equivalent of saying, Can you read?—not more than one in ten of the highly educated would have felt that I was speaking the same language. So the great edifice of modern physics goes up, and the majority of the cleverest people in the western world have about as much insight into it as their Neolithic ancestors would have had."[1]

Snow mocked the pretentions of his literary friends, who believed that people of science were only narrowly educated. Snow flipped the argument on its head. It was the liberal arts crowd that knew nothing of the way the world worked.

And so our CMO-CIO crack, which exists in more companies than not, could signify at least three fractures in broken company culture: one, a fight over budgets; two, a battle between the sexes; and, three, a long-standing mutual disdain between technologists and liberal artists.

Whatever the reason, the larger truth is that companies exhibiting these broken C-suite relationships are those that have neglected to invest in the soft edge of their companies. Put another way, you are far less likely to see a public CMO-CIO fight break out at FedEx, Specialized, Northwestern Mutual, Mayo Clinic, or any of the soft-edge stars mentioned in this book.

A strong soft-edge culture won't end budget fights. It can't stop the eternal battle between the sexes. It won't entirely reverse the mutual disdain of C. P. Snow's two cultures. But a strong soft edge will establish priorities in your company. It will give you the right language to discuss these differences. It will give you strong values to bridge them. It will keep ego-driven conflicts from damaging your company's performance.

Let's imagine what a CMO-CIO relationship might look like in a soft-edge excellent company.

Trust. In a healthy CMO-CIO relationship—I'll use NetApp as an example—trust would reveal itself in many ways. The CIO would trust that the CMO's requests for greater technology budgets were not a power grab but a reflection of reality. The share of marketing that goes through digital channels—through the web and social media, on smartphones and tablets—is growing like crazy. Social media in particular is always tossing up market opportunities that are fleeting in nature. These must be grabbed or they're lost, and CIOs need to realize this. Conversely, the

CMO might acknowledge that too much of what NetApp CMO Julie Parrish calls "shadow IT" tends to sprout like weeds within marketing. This creates a mess for the IT department. Trust, says NetApp's CIO Cynthia Stoddard, comes from showing that you have the other person's best interest in mind, working hard to achieve common language and transparency, and doing what you say you'll do.

Smarts. To stay ahead of the curve, NetApp's Parrish and Stoddard regularly get together to discuss trends in predictive analytics, sentiment analysis, and other valuable information. This requires a healthy CMO-CIO relationship. To stay smart, Parrish likes to remind everyone, "What are the questions we should be asking? If you don't ask the right questions, you can quickly build up a lot of technology in marketing without any coherence." Stoddard added that proper governance facilitates faster learning. "We use an enterprise executive architecture committee, with all the leaders of every company function— marketing, sales, HR, operations, finance, and so on. That's how we can come up with a road map for the whole company."

Teams. In a healthy CMO-CIO relationship, members of the marketing team and the IT team do regular "tours of duty" on the other side. Embedded marketers get to learn from their IT counterparts about data and analytics; embedded IT people get to learn about key marketing programs and metrics. At NetApp, both sides are open and honest about their cost structures. CMO Parrish established a foundation of good teamwork with CIO Stoddard when she admitted that marketing owned too many projects. "I raised my hand for an IT audit," Parrish said. From that day, Stoddard knew Parrish wasn't trying to build an empire.

Taste. In a soft-edge excellent company, CMOs teach CIOs how marketing platforms are crafted and how to fine-tune messages for any given audience. CIOs show where complexity will slow down deployment, and therefore suggest areas to simplify the platform for maximum rapid deployment. Sometimes there is disagreement. Don't try to bury it! Shine light on it! Recall how Nest Labs' CEO, Tony Fadell, likes to put analytics people and marketing people in the same room to discuss which algorithms will create customer enchantment and loyalty in Nest's products.

Story. NetApp has a deep story that is both rare, hence valuable, and a harbinger of things to come. It is one of the few companies in the world, along with Google, Singapore Airlines, Starbucks, and very few others, that regularly makes two annual lists: the world's best places to work and the world's most innovative companies. NetApp takes huge pride in making both lists, and it should. But aside from pride, the real value of making both lists is that it creates a consistent story for employees, suppliers, and customers. Whenever NetApp CMO Julie Parrish and CIO Cynthia Stoddard disagree on anything, they can call a time out, step back and ask: What would a top innovative company do? What would a best place work company do? Thus NetApp's story—its belief about itself—drives the right behavior and, more often than not, good decisions at every turn. It is a beautiful thing.

INNOVATION AT TWO HUNDRED MILES PER HOUR

I conclude with one more story, from an intensely competitive, high-stakes, life-and-death sport: Formula One Racing. It's a most unusual story, but it shines a light on how a strong soft edge can bridge completely different cultures.

In 1971, in the foothills of the Himalayas in northern India, was born a girl named Monisha Narang. Her parents moved the family to Vienna, Austria, when Monisha was young. Like so many Indian immigrants around the world, Monisha assimilated, worked extremely hard at her studies. She became a lawyer, with a specialty in international trade law. She interned at the United Nations and a law firm in Stuttgart, Germany, where she met her future husband, Jens Kaltenborn. She finally went to work for the Fritz Kaiser Group, a wealth management firm in Lichtenstein.

When Monisha Kaltenborn joined the Kaiser Group, the firm happened to be a one-third owner in an auto racing team based in Switzerland, Sauber Formula One. The team's other main owners were founder Peter Sauber and Dietrich Mateschitz, the founder of Red Bull. The young lawyer was put in charge of the racing team's legal affairs.

As a child, little Monisha often stared at the sky and dreamed of being an astronaut. The idea of moving fast and precisely had sparked her imagination long before she moved to Europe or fell into professional motorsports. Now as Sauber's lawyer, Monisha Kaltenborn soaked up everything she could about F1 racing. She attended races, managed driver contracts and relationships with suppliers like BMW and Pirelli, the whole works. In 2010, rewarded for her enthusiasm and hard work, she was named CEO of Sauber Motorsports, the first and still only female CEO in F1 racing. In 2013 Kaltenborn acquired 33.3 percent ownership in Sauber.

I met Kaltenborn in late 2013 at the Formula One Grand Prix race in Austin, Texas. After a Saturday of qualifying rounds at the track, we drove to a resort hotel in the West Austin hills and lake country, where I interviewed her onstage before an audience of CEOs and technologists.

Beyond Kaltenborn's gripping personal story, I was interested in how a Formula One team uses technology to design its cars—a new, multimillion-dollar car is designed for each season. And what about the role of data in making midrace adjustments? Sauber's F1 race cars generate up to 18,000 rpm with a tiny 2.4 liter eight-cylinder engine. The engines are constantly on the edge of self-destruction, so having data in real time is crucial. The same goes for tire selection, temperature, and inflation pressure, suspension adjustments, airfoil adjustments, and for every inch of the car that generates power, touches the road, or cuts through the wind. Each Grand Prix race course and type of weather present more variables. There is a right combination of adjustments for every track and every kind of weather, but the sheer number of variables and combinations are beyond anyone's ability to get right.

Thus sensors, computers, and analytics have become a crucial part of a Formula One team. Sauber uses a "mobile data center" configured by NetApp. Kaltenborn likes the rig because it's easy to set up before the race, disassemble afterward, and ship to the next race. For example, one week after the Austin Grand Prix was another race in Brazil. A portable, durable data center is crucial.

But then there is the driver. Ah, the driver! Think of a slim young man who can double as a Hollywood actor or fashion model, who is impetuous, courageous, cocky, and never lacks for a sexy bedmate. He has more money than good sense. The top F1 driver often ranks among the highest-paid athletes in the world. This year, Germany's Sebastian Vettel will compete with LeBron James and Tiger Woods to be ranked as the world's best-paid athlete.

What makes a great F1 driver? I asked a former driver, who told me it is about "the feel in your fingertips, the tips of your toes, the seat of your pants, about where is the absolute limit in any given second." Go over your limit, and you crash. Go under your limit, and drivers will pass you.

Can you see where this story is going? A huge conflict—between F1 ownership and F1 driver—is absolutely guaranteed in every Formula One race. The former F1 driver explained it: "Suppose the data shows that I am losing two-tenths of a second on the fourth turn on each lap. The pit team will radio this information to my earpiece. Everyone knows it. But what's the right response? Should I attempt to take the fourth turn two-tenths of a second faster? I can't do that, because my fingertips, the tips of my toes, and the seat of my pants are all telling me that I'm already at the limit."

Who or what, then, is responsible for those lost two-tenths of a second on each lap?

I asked Monisha Kaltenborn this question. In cases like this, do you believe the driver or the data? "Oh, the data!" she said. The audience of fellow CEOs and technologists, left brainers all of them, laughed in agreement. Of course you can't trust that right-brained driver, that impetuous, cocky, overpaid kid, to give reliable information!

But then Kaltenborn became serious. "The answer is not easy. It requires you trust the driver, get the most detailed explanation of the problem that you can get from him, even though he's under stress circling the track at two hundred miles per hour. Then you work with the team to find a deeper level of data. Perhaps the car needs a tiny asymmetric suspension adjustment. Maybe the temperature on the track is going up, affecting the tires or the airfoil. Everyone has to trust each other. You have to speak in a common language. You have to work as a team. Or you will keep losing those two-tenths per laps. Or worse, overcompensate and crash."

It all comes down to is this: Sauber must innovate in real time. It must innovate at two hundred miles per hour, to be precise. To do so, Sauber relies on best-of-class technology to capture and analyze the data. But after Sauber does all that, it still has to contend with the human driver, that flawed guy behind the wheel who remains the indispensable part of the performance equation.

The driver, you see, is really us.

No company can get around the fact that imperfect humans are still in charge, and imperfect humans are not exactly rational and consistent in the way that sensors, computers, and analytics software are rational and consistent. Most of us tend to do our best work when we are "in the zone." But what does that mean in a data-driven world? It means that we must find "that elusive sweet spot between human truth and data truth," as Specialized Bicycle's chief designer, Robert Egger, put it in Chapter Six.

Finding that zone, that sweet spot, and operating within it are the keys to high performance in today's economy. But as Specialized's Egger said, this search can be maddeningly elusive. The good news is that our chances of finding and operating in the sweet spot are vastly improved when we have that soft edge of deep values:

- We trust our colleagues, even when their race, gender, age, and thinking styles are different from ours.
- We apply grit to constantly test ourselves and learn.
- We keep our teams lean and organize them around the elusive sweet spot.
- We get truly excited by the products and services we deliver.
- We tell a compelling, purposeful, and authentic story.

Technology and competition are constantly raising the bar of high performance in our companies. But funnily enough, as the bar goes up, it's the ancient values of trust and smarts, teamwork and taste and storytelling that become even more important.

We can't afford to ignore our company's soft edge.

Afterword

Clayton M. Christensen

*Kim B. Clark Professor of Business Administration,
Harvard Business School*

Hundreds of years ago things like earthquakes, famines and floods, thunder and lightning, and disease and healing seemed unfathomable. The explanation often was, "Stuff happens— and deal with it when it does." Opinionated individuals occasionally opined about what things were and why they occurred, but the will of God often was blamed.

Thank goodness for Francis Bacon and others who conceived and followed what came to be known as the scientific method. They brought a view that almost everything in the physical world has a cause. When something appears to be random it is because we don't know the cause. This mindset motivated researchers to identify what causes things to occur. As they then learned how to control those causal mechanisms, the natural world became quite predictable.

The scientific method entails six steps. First you observe and describe phenomena, and then you sort what you see into categories according to their characteristics. Third, you measure correlations and probabilities between the attributes of things in each category and the outcomes of interest. Fourth, by studying a single event, a single organism, or a single company at deep depth, you can learn what causes things to happen, and why. Then with this understanding of causality, you (and other researchers) can then study the different situations in which things must be done differently in order to achieve the desired result. Finally, try to find anomalies—phenomena that the theory cannot explain. Resolving these anomalies is the way that theories improve. Over the last four hundred years the laws of the universe have not changed. But thanks to the scientific method, our understanding of the physical world has changed remarkably.

As yet, however, researchers of business rarely follow the scientific method to understand how business works. Rather, the belief of most is the same that people had four hundred years ago about the physical world: "Stuff happens—and deal with it when it does." Gurus often opine about why things have occurred, but "the market" (rather than God) often is blamed. Venture capitalists believe, for example, that for every ten companies they invest in, one or two will succeed—but they can't predict which will and will not. This is not true. The creation of successful companies appears to the venture capitalists to be unpredictable because they do not yet understand what causes the phenomenon of success.

A small team of us are becoming increasingly convinced that the world of business is not inherently unpredictable and unfathomable—and as such it might be amenable to the scientific method. I am grateful that Rich Karlgaard is one of this group.

As publisher of *Forbes* for these many years, Rich has become one the most astute observers of the phenomena of business. Every so often, Rich steps back to assess where our attempts to understand business have been and what we need to do next. That is what this book is about. Rich starts by describing the phenomena—building his narratives around stories of companies that have prospered by doing the things that comprise the three categories: strategy, the hard edge, and the soft edge.

Rich's purpose is not to establish causality but to show through stories what is possible. Rich describes phenomena, suggests how to characterize these phenomena to make them make sense, and poses relationships that merit more study. Rich is a navigator for the rest of us.

Rich leaves a lot for the rest of us to do. Can we succeed by doing one piece of the soft edge, or do we need to do all of them well? How does a manager create these abilities? Will these characteristics and capabilities endure, or can we expect every company's abilities to regress to the mean? These are the jobs that I and a few others of the team shoulder.

I am grateful for this team, for Rich's key role as a team member, and for the guidance that this book gives us about the issues that we as researchers need to explore next.

Notes

Chapter One: A Wellspring of Enduring Innovation

1. This description of Tim Cook and his work habits is based on the following article: Adam Lashinsky, "The Genius Behind Steve: Could Operations Whiz Tim Cook Run the Company Someday?" CNNMoney, last modified November 10, 2008, http://money.cnn.com/2008/11/09/technology/cook_apple.fortune.

2. Norman Schwarzkopf, who was commander-in-chief of the U.S. Central Forces Command in the Persian Gulf War, said this in a TV interview during the invasion of Iraq in 2003. But while researching the quote, I found that it's actually an old military saying. In fact, most writers and journalists introduce the saying with "As they say," or "As the old military saying goes."

3. Thomas J. Peters and Robert H. Waterman, *In Search of Excellence: Lessons from America's Best-Run Companies* (New York: HarperCollins, 2004).

Chapter Two: Hard Versus Soft

1. Richard Foster and Sarah Kaplan, *Creative Destruction: Why Companies That Are Built to Last Underperform the Market—and How to Successfully Transform Them* (New York: Random House Digital, 2011).

Chapter Three: Trust

1. Warren G. Bennis and Burt Nanus, *Leaders: Strategies for Taking Charge* (New York: HarperCollins, 2003), 43.

2. C. Ashley Fulmer and Michele J. Gelfand, "At What Level (and in Whom) We Trust: Trust Across Multiple Organizational Levels," *Journal of Management* 38, no. 4 (2012): 1167–1230.

3. Fulmer and Gelfand, "At What Level (and in Whom) We Trust."

4. "2013 Edelman Trust Barometer," Edelman, accessed December 8, 2013, http://www.edelman.com/insights/intellectual-property/trust-2013; and John Wood and Paul Berg, "Rebuilding Trust in Banks," Gallup Business Journal, last modified August 8, 2011, http://businessjournal.gallup.com /content/148049/rebuilding-trust-banks.aspx.

5. Fulmer and Gelfand, "At What Level (and in Whom) We Trust"; Amy L. Pablo, Trish Reay, James R. Dewald, and Ann L. Casebeer, "Identifying, Enabling and Managing Dynamic Capabilities in the Public Sector," *Journal of Management Studies* 44, no. 5 (2007): 687–708.

6. Pamela S. Shockley-Zalabak and Sherwyn P. Morreale, "Building High-Trust Organizations," *Leader to Leader* no. 60 (2011): 39–45.

7. "2013 Edelman Trust Barometer."

8. Many studies have established the connection between trust and increased customer loyalty, including the ability to charge higher prices. These include the following: Elena Delgado-Ballester and Jose Luis Munuera-Aleman, "Brand Trust in the Context of Consumer Loyalty," *European Journal of Marketing* 35, no. 11/12 (2001): 1238–1258; Frederick F. Reichheld and Phil Schefter, "E-Loyalty," *Harvard Business Review* 78, no. 4 (2000): 105–113; Sulin Ba and Paul A. Pavlou, "Evidence of the Effect of Trust Building Technology in Electronic Markets: Price Premiums and Buyer Behavior," *MIS Quarterly* (2002): 243–268; Hean Tat Keh and Yi Xie, "Corporate Reputation and Customer Behavioral Intentions: The Roles of Trust, Identification and Commitment," *Industrial Marketing Management* 38, no. 7 (2009): 732–742; Walfried Lassar, Banwari Mittal, and Arun Sharma, "Measuring Customer-Based Brand Equity," *Journal of Consumer Marketing* 12, no. 4 (1995): 11–19; and Johan Anselmsson, Ulf Johansson, and Niklas Persson, "Understanding Price Premium for Grocery Products: A Conceptual Model of Customer-Based Brand Equity," *Journal of Product & Brand Management* 16, no. 6 (2007): 401–414.

9. Richard Branson, "Give People the Freedom of Where to Work," Virgin Corporation, last modified February 25, 2013, http://www.virgin.com /richard-branson/give-people-the-freedom-of-where-to-work.

10. Tom Clarke, "Students Prove Trust Begets Trust," *Nature*, last modified March 13, 2003, http://www.nature.com/news/2003/030310/full /news030310-8.html.

11. This quote by Jennifer Aaker, professor of marketing at Stanford Graduate School of Business, has been reported through numerous outlets, including the following: Lydia Dishman, "Secrets of America's Happiest Companies," *Fast Company*, last modified January 10, 2013, http://www.fastcompany .com/3004595/secrets-americas-happiest-companies; and Jon Stein, "The Culture of a Successful Company Mirrors Its Mission," *Forbes*, last modified February 11, 2013, http://www.forbes.com/sites/jonstein/2013/02/11 /the-culture-of-a-successful-company-mirrors-its-mission. To gain a deeper understanding of Professor Aaker's work, see Cassie Mogilner, Sepandar D. Kamvar, and Jennifer Aaker, "The Shifting Meaning of Happiness," *Social Psychological and Personality Science* 2, no. 4 (2011): 395–402.

12. W. Edwards Deming, *Out of the Crisis* (Cambridge, MA: MIT Press, 1986).

13. See, for example, Amy Edmondson, "Psychological Safety and Learning Behavior in Work Teams," *Administrative Science Quarterly* 44, no. 2 (1999): 350–383; Markus Baer and Michael Frese, "Innovation Is Not Enough: Climates for Initiative and Psychological Safety, Process Innovations, and Firm Performance," *Journal of Organizational Behavior* 24, no. 1 (2003): 45–68; Ingrid M. Nembhard and Amy C. Edmondson, "Making It Safe: The Effects of Leader Inclusiveness and Professional Status on Psychological Safety and Improvement Efforts in Health Care Teams," *Journal of Organizational Behavior* 27, no. 7 (2006): 941–966; and Amy C. Edmondson, "Psychological Safety, Trust, and Learning in Organizations: A Group-Level Lens," *Trust in Organizations: Dilemmas and Approaches* (2004): 239–274.

Chapter Four: Smarts

1. Filip Lievens and Charlie L. Reeve, "Where I–O Psychology Should Really (Re) Start Its Investigation of Intelligence Constructs and Their Measurement," *Industrial and Organizational Psychology* 5, no. 2 (2012): 153–158.

2. Ian J. Deary, Lars Penke, and Wendy Johnson, "The Neuroscience of Human Intelligence Differences," *Nature Reviews Neuroscience* 11, no. 3 (2010): 201–211.

3. Ingrid M. Nembhard and Amy C. Edmondson, "Making It Safe: The Effects of Leader Inclusiveness and Professional Status on Psychological Safety and Improvement Efforts in Health Care Teams," *Journal of Organizational Behavior* 27, no. 7 (2006): 941–966.

4. Kenneth M. Steele, "Arousal and Mood Factors in the 'Mozart Effect,'" *Perceptual and Motor Skills* 91, no. 1 (2000): 188–190; and Sylvain Moreno, Carlos Marques, Andreia Santos, Manuela Santos, and Mireille Besson, "Musical Training Influences Linguistic Abilities in 8-Year-Old Children: More Evidence for Brain Plasticity," *Cerebral Cortex* 19, no. 3 (2009): 712–723.

5. Gerd Kempermann, Klaus Fabel, Dan Ehninger, Harish Babu, Perla Leal-Galicia, Alexander Garthe, and Susanne A. Wolf, "Why and How Physical Activity Promotes Experience-Induced Brain Plasticity," *Frontiers in Neuroscience* 4 (2010); and Kristel Knaepen, Maaike Goekint, Elsa Marie Heyman, and Romain Meeusen, "Neuroplasticity—Exercise-Induced Response of Peripheral Brain-Derived Neurotrophic Factor," *Sports Medicine* 40, no. 9 (2010): 765–801.

6. Amy Edmondson and L. Feldman, "Phase Zero: Introducing New Services at IDEO (A)," Case study—Harvard Business School (2006).

Chapter Five: Teams

1. Natalie Sebanz, Harold Bekkering, and Günther Knoblich, "Joint Action: Bodies and Minds Moving Together," *Trends in Cognitive Sciences* 10, no. 2 (2006): 70–76.

2. Robin I. M. Dunbar, "The Social Brain: Mind, Language, and Society in Evolutionary Perspective," *Annual Review of Anthropology* (2003): 163–181.

3. Nicolai J. Foss and Siegwart Lindenberg, "Teams, Team Motivation, and the Theory of the Firm," *Managerial and Decision Economics* 33, no. 5–6 (2012): 369–383.

4. See, for example, Chris Argyris, *Knowledge for Action: A Guide to Overcoming Barriers to Organizational Change* (San Francisco: Jossey-Bass, 1993); Chris Argyris, "Today's Problems with Tomorrow's Organizations," *Journal of*

Management Studies 4, no. 1 (1967): 31–55; Deborah G. Ancona and David F. Caldwell, "Bridging the Boundary: External Activity and Performance in Organizational Teams," *Administrative Science Quarterly* (1992): 634–665; Deborah Gladstein Ancona, "Outward Bound: Strategies for Team Survival in an Organization," *Academy of Management Journal* 33, no. 2 (1990): 334–365; Deborah Ancona, Henrik Bresman, and David Caldwell, "The X-Factor: Six Steps to Leading High-Performing X-Teams," *Organizational Dynamics* 38, no. 3 (2009): 217–224; Amy Edmondson, "Psychological Safety and Learning Behavior in Work Teams," *Administrative Science Quarterly* 44, no. 2 (1999): 350–383; and Amy C. Edmondson, Richard M. Bohmer, and Gary P. Pisano, "Disrupted Routines: Team Learning and New Technology Implementation in Hospitals," *Administrative Science Quarterly* 46, no. 4 (2001): 685–716.

5. Jeffrey F. Rayport, "The Miracle of Memphis," *MIT Technology Review*, December 20, 2010, http://www.technologyreview.com/news/422081 /the-miracle-of-memphis.

6. Elizabeth Mannix and Margaret A. Neale, "What Differences Make a Difference? The Promise and Reality of Diverse Teams in Organizations," *Psychological Science in the Public Interest* 6, no. 2 (2005): 31–55.

7. Daphna Oyserman, Larry Gant, and Joel Ager, "A Socially Contextualized Model of African American Identity: Possible Selves and School Persistence," *Journal of Personality and Social Psychology* 69, no. 6 (1995): 1216.

8. Thomas Kochan, Katerina Bezrukova, Robin Ely, Susan Jackson, Aparna Joshi, Karen Jehn, Jonathan Leonard, David Levine, and David Thomas, "The Effects of Diversity on Business Performance: Report of the Diversity Research Network," *Human Resource Management* 42, no. 1 (2003): 3–21.

9. Mannix and Neale, "What Differences Make a Difference?"

10. A tremendous number of great books on teams and teamwork are currently available. A few of the best: Patrick Lencioni, *The Five Dysfunctions of a Team: A Leadership Fable* (New York: Wiley, 2002); J. Richard Hackman, *Leading Teams: Setting the Stage for Great Performances* (Boston: Harvard Business Press, 2002); Jon R. Katzenbach and Douglas K. Smith, *The Wisdom of Teams: Creating the High-Performance Organization* (Boston: Harvard Business Press, 1992); and Joe Frontiera and Daniel Leidl, *Team*

Turnarounds: A Playbook for Transforming Underperforming Teams (New York: Wiley, 2012).

11. Many research studies explore the stereotypes associated with age, particularly in relation to the idea of change, including the following: Warren CK Chiu, Andy W. Chan, Ed Snape, and Tom Redman, "Age Stereotypes and Discriminatory Attitudes Towards Older Workers: An East-West Comparison," *Human Relations* 54, no. 5 (2001): 629–661; Barbara L. Hassell and Pamela L. Perrewe, "An Examination of Beliefs About Older Workers: Do Stereotypes Still Exist?," *Journal of Organizational Behavior* 16, no. 5 (1995): 457–468; and Philip Taylor and Alan Walker, "Employers and Older Workers: Attitudes and Employment Practices," *Ageing and Society* 18, no. 6 (1998): 641–658.

12. Teresa A. Amabile and Mukti Khaire, *Creativity and the Role of the Leader* (Boston: Harvard Business Press, 2008).

13. Because I was unable to interview Professor Pentland for this section of the book—but felt that his research is both brilliant and timely—I relied on a number of great articles, papers, and blogs for much of the content in this section. These include the following: Mark Buchanan, "Secret Signals: Does a Primitive, Non-Linguistic Type of Communication Drive People's Interactions?," *Nature* 457, no. 7229 (2009): 528–530; Mark Buchanan, "The Science of Subtle Signals: The Most Successful Telephone Call Center Operators Have the Same Kind of Rhythm in Their Voices as a Mother Speaking Singsong to a Baby. That's One of Many New Insights Emerging from the Use of Sensors and Tracking Devices Within Corporate Walls," *Strategy and Business* 48 (2007): 68. And the quote in this paragraph came from Anne Eisenberg, "You May Soon Know If You're Hogging the Discussion," *New York Times*, October 25, 2008, http://www.nytimes.com/2008/10/26/business/26novelties.html?_r=2&.

14. Alex "Sandy" Pentland, "The Hard Science of Teamwork," HBR Blog Network (blog), *Harvard Business Review*, March 20, 2012, http://blogs.hbr.org/2012/03/the-new-science-of-building-gr.

15. Andy Greenberg, "Mining Human Behavior at MIT," *Forbes*, August 12, 2010, http://www.forbes.com/forbes/2010/0830/e-gang-mit-sandy-pentland-darpa-sociometers-mining-reality.html.

16. Alex Pentland, "To Signal Is Human: Real-Time Data Mining Unmasks the Power of Imitation, Kith and Charisma in Our Face-to-Face Social Networks," *American Scientist* 98 (2010).

Chapter Six: Taste

1. N. Millard, "Learning from the 'Wow' Factor—How to Engage Customers Through the Design of Effective Affective Customer Experiences," *BT Technology Journal* 24, no. 1 (2006): 11–16.

2. See, especially, Ravindra Chitturi, Rajagopal Raghunathan, and Vijay Mahajan, "Form Versus Function: How the Intensities of Specific Emotions Evoked in Functional Versus Hedonic Trade-Offs Mediate Product Preferences," *Journal of Marketing Research* (2007): 702–714.

3. Chitturi, Raghunathan, and Mahajan, "Form Versus Function."

4. This fact has been established through a number of studies, including Daniel E. Berlyne, "Ends and Means of Experimental Aesthetics," *Canadian Journal of Psychology/Revue canadienne de psychologie* 26, no. 4 (1972): 303; Raji Srinivasan, Gary L. Lilien, Arvind Rangaswamy, Gina M. Pingitore, and Daniel Seldin, "The Total Product Design Concept and an Application to the Auto Market," *Journal of Product Innovation Management* 29, no. S1 (2012): 3–20; and Robert W. Veryzer, "A Nonconscious Processing Explanation of Consumer Response to Product Design," *Psychology & Marketing* 16, no. 6 (1999): 497–522.

5. Jo Piazza, "Audiences Experience 'Avatar' Blues," *CNN Entertainment*, January 11, 2010, http://www.cnn.com/2010/SHOWBIZ/Movies/01/11/avatar.movie.blues.

6. This story is based on the following article: John Bryant, "Sinyard the Obsessed," *Bicycling*, accessed December 8, 2013, http://www.bicycling.com/news/featured-stories/sinyard-obsessed.

7. See Karen McVeigh, "Why Golden Ratio Pleases the Eye: US Academic Says He Knows Art Secret," *Guardian*, December 28, 2009, http://www.guardian.co.uk/artanddesign/2009/dec/28/golden-ratio-us-academic; Lance Hosey, "Why We Love Beautiful Things," *New York Times*, February 15, 2013, http://www.nytimes.com/2013/02/17/opinion/sunday/why-we-love-beautiful-things.html?_r=0; and Adrian Bejan and Sylvie Lorente,

"The Constructal Law and the Evolution of Design in Nature," *Physics of Life Reviews* 8, no. 3 (2011): 209–240.

8. Moshe Bar and Maital Neta, "Humans Prefer Curved Visual Objects," *Psychological Science* 17, no. 8 (2006): 645–648; and Moshe Bar and Maital Neta, "Visual Elements of Subjective Preference Modulate Amygdala Activation," *Neuropsychologia* 45, no. 10 (2007): 2191–2200.

9. See, for example, Albert T. Poffenberger and B. E. Barrows, "The Feeling Value of Lines," *Journal of Applied Psychology* 8, no. 2 (1924): 187; and Kate Hevner, "Experimental Studies of the Affective Value of Colors and Lines," *Journal of Applied Psychology* 19, no. 4 (1935): 385.

10. Bianca Grohmann, Eric R. Spangenberg, and David E. Sprott, "The Influence of Tactile Input on the Evaluation of Retail Product Offerings," *Journal of Retailing* 83, no. 2 (2007): 237–245; and Lawrence E. Williams and John A. Bargh, "Experiencing Physical Warmth Promotes Interpersonal Warmth," *Science* 322, no. 5901 (2008): 606–607.

11. Marieke H. Sonneveld and Hendrik N. J. Schifferstein, "The Tactual Experience of Objects," *Product Experience* (2008): 41–67; and Charles Spence and Alberto Gallace, "Multisensory Design: Reaching Out to Touch the Consumer," *Psychology & Marketing* 28, no. 3 (2011): 267–308.

12. D. Katz, *The World of Touch* (L. E. Krueger, Trans.) (Mahwah, NJ: Erlbaum, 1989). (Original work published 1925.)

13. Albert A. Harrison, "Mere Exposure," *Advances in Experimental Social Psychology* 10 (1977): 39–83; and John G. Seamon, Nathan Brody, and David M. Kauff, "Affective Discrimination of Stimuli That Are Not Recognized: Effects of Shadowing, Masking, and Cerebral Laterality," *Journal of Experimental Psychology: Learning, Memory, and Cognition* 9, no. 3 (1983): 544.

14. Pawel Lewicki, "Processing Information About Covariations That Cannot Be Articulated," *Journal of Experimental Psychology: Learning, Memory, and Cognition* 12, no. 1 (1986): 135; Pawel Lewicki, Thomas Hill, and Maria Czyzewska, "Nonconscious Acquisition of Information," *American Psychologist* 47, no. 6 (1992): 796; and Pawel Lewicki, *Nonconscious Social Information Processing* (Orlando, FL: Academic Press, 1986).

15. Daniel Coyle, *Lance Armstrong's War: One Man's Battle Against Fate, Fame, Love, Death, Scandal, and a Few Other Rivals on the Road to the Tour de France* (New York: HarperCollins, 2009).

Chapter Seven: Story

1. Dr. Richard McGlaughlin recounted his own story in a speech at the Florida Air Museum's 38th Annual Sun 'n Fun International Fly-In & Expo: "BRS, BRS Ballistic Recovery Aircraft Parachute Saves Pilot and Daughter Over Open Water," YouTube video, 20:59, posted by "Light Sport and Ultralight Flyer," April 16, 2012, http://www.youtube.com/watch?v=d9FCmfaV0yY.

2. Roland Barthes, *Introduction to the Structural Analysis of the Narrative* (Birmingham, UK: University of Birmingham, Centre for Contemporary Cultural Studies, 1966).

3. Elizabeth C. Hirschman, "Evolutionary Branding," *Psychology & Marketing* 27, no. 6 (2010): 568–583.

Conclusion

1. Charles Percy Snow, *The Two Cultures* (Cambridge, UK: Cambridge University Press, 2012). (Original work published 1959.)

Acknowledgments

I had a terrific amount of help in producing *The Soft Edge*, and would like to begin with Jeff Leeson of Benson-Collister, who deserves coauthor status for his tireless research, writing, editing, organizing, and negotiating labors. Annalisa Camarillo, who introduced me to Jeff, was a steadfast friend of *The Soft Edge*, as were her NetApp colleagues Anjali Acharya, Richard Bliss, and Matthew Butter. Jennie Grimes deserves a special doff of the cap.

Susan Williams was the top editor at Jossey-Bass, and we were lucky to be chosen by Susan as her final project before she launched her own consulting service. Susan's colleague Karen Murphy listened to our first book pitch and declared it sweeping and mushy. On Karen's astute advice, we came back and focused. I would also like to thank Michael Friedberg, Mary Garrett, Hilary Powers, and John Maas of Jossey-Bass, and superstar book consultant Carolyn Monaco.

Next are the many people I interviewed for this book.

From Cirrus Aircraft, thanks to Dale Klapmeier, Pat Waddick, and Todd Simmons, and from the Cirrus Owners and Pilots Association, Rick Beach and Curtis Sanford. I would additionally like to thank Dr. Richard McGlaughlin, a saint and a sage who candidly spoke of his parachute pull in a speech at the Sun 'n Fun airshow in 2012.

Numerous folks at FedEx talked to me, including Fred Smith, the legendary founder, CEO, and chairman, David Bronczek, Rob Carter, Patrick Fitzgerald, Jim Barksdale, and dozens of others, one of whom taught me to land a Boeing 777 in a FedEx simulator. Special kudos to Virginia Wester, Fred Smith's longtime executive assistant, and to Johnny Pitts, the Memphis businessman who gets everyone in town to answer his phone, and who introduced me to Fred Smith.

Karl Oestreich opened doors at Mayo Clinic, where I spent healthy hours interviewing Matt Dacy, Chuck Rosen, David Farley, Doug Wood, Jim Rogers, Lisa Clark, Mark Warner, Pam Johnson, Siobhan Pittock, Kelly Luckstein, and others whose IQ could boil water.

At Northwestern Mutual I was helped by John Schlifske, Todd Schoon, Conrad York, Jennifer Ryan, Marie Squire, Juan Baron, Scott Theodore, Jennifer Brase, Michael Pritzl, Delynn Alexander, and Jimbo Huckabee. I also learned much about the insurance company's devoted and astonishing sales force from conversations with financial reps in St. Louis, Omaha, Seattle, and Portland.

The cycling nuts at Specialized were immensely helpful. Founder and CEO Mike Sinyard is known to be press shy, but he was terrifically helpful to me, as were Robert Egger, Ian Hamilton, Amber Lucas, Eric Edgecumbe, Mark Cote, and Katie

Sue Gruener. Certainly my time at Specialized was the most fun. I will always cherish the day we zoomed past pro cyclist Andy Schleck on our electric Turbos. The great Schleck turned his head and gave us a double take.

Others I would like to thank are Howard Price, Robyn Albarran, Julie Parrish, Cynthia Stoddard, Amy Love, Jessica Rose, Jodi Baumann, Dave Hitz, Jay Kidd, Tom Mendoza, Tom Georgens, Judy Estrin, Tony Fadell, David Chang, Margit Wennmachers, Nancy Duarte, Chris Wicher, Peter High, Jim Snabe, Vivek Wadhwa, Tara VanDerveer, Maynard Webb, Greg Becker, Danny Stern, Emily Snyder, and Karen Tucker.

I'm grateful to the point of embarrassment for *The Soft Edge*'s early draft readers, Tom Peters, Clayton Christensen, Randy Komisar, John Kennedy, Guy Kawasaki, Greg Welch, Jerry Bowyer, Rick Segal, and Pastor John Ortberg.

I'd also like to thank Pamela Berkman, Nic Albert, Eveline Chao, and Kathleen Dolan Davies for all their help and their willingness to share their deep knowledge of publishing. And a special thanks to Patrick Chisholm and all the people at Accentance for their great work in transcribing my many interviews.

Venturing a bit further afield, I would like to thank my Forbes Media colleagues. All of them are the smartest and bravest warriors I have known, but these fine souls deserve special mention: chairman and editor-in-chief, Steve Forbes, CEO Mike Perlis, Mike Federle, Jack Laschever, Mark Howard, Tom Davis, Bruce Rogers, Carol Nelson, Paul Noglows, Janett Hass, Ann Marinovich, Lisa Bentley, Taryn Moy, Lisa Carden, Moira Forbes, Miguel Forbes, Tara Michaels, Brian McLeod, Michael Monroe, Leann Bonanno, Adam Wallitt, Mary Baru, Michael Peck, Jen Cooke,

Sherry Phillips, Menia Poulios, Gheeva Chung, Lewis D'Vorkin, Randall Lane, Andrea Spiegel, Michael Noer, Tom Post, Dan Bigman, Bruce Upbin, Tim Ferguson, John Tamny, David Asman, Elizabeth MacDonald, Sabrina Schaeffer, Rick Ungar, Mike Ozanian, John Huber, Merrill Vaughn, Glen Davis, Elizabeth Gravitt, Mia Carbonell, Margy Loftus, Nina LaFrance, Michael Dugan, Tom Callahan, MariaRosa Cartolano, Elaine Fry, Charles Yardley, and our Asian superstars Will Adamopoulos, Tina Wee, and Cecillia Ma Zecha. I would also like to thank my former colleague, Mike Woods.

A grateful thanks goes to my friends at the Washington Speakers Bureau: Harry Rhoads, Christine Farrell, Ronda Estridge, Anne Thalman, Bob Parsons, Christine Lansman, Georgene Savickas, Ivy Gustafson, Julie Westendorff, Kevin Jeske, Kristin Downey, Kristy Kalo, Liz Chappell, Maggie Molpus, Marissa Williams, Meredith Kennedy, Monica Abangan, Sheldon Bream, Will Lee, and Nika Spencer. Thanks, also, to sage advice from Steve Sobel, Barrett Cordero, and Ken Sterling.

A final thanks goes to those closest to me: my wife, Marji, daughter Kaite, son Peter, mother Pat, sister Mary, and brother Joe. And to those departed but who are still a source of inspiration and mirth: father Dick and sister Liz.

About the Author

Rich Karlgaard is the publisher of *Forbes* magazine, where he also writes a column, "Innovation Rules," known for its witty assessment of business and leadership issues. He has been a regular panelist on television's *Forbes on FOX* since the show's inception in 2001. Karlgaard is also a serial entrepreneur, having co-founded *Upside* magazine, Garage Technology Partners, and Silicon Valley's premier public business forum, the 7,500-member Churchill Club. He is a past winner of Ernst & Young's "Entrepreneur of the Year" award. Karlgaard's 2004 book, *Life 2.0*, was a *Wall Street Journal* business bestseller. A graduate of Stanford University, Karlgaard lives with his family in Silicon Valley.

For more information, please visit richkarlgaard.com.

Index

Page numbers in italics refer to figures.

A

Aaker, Jennifer, 58
Abacuses, 22–23
Academic credentials, relevancy of, 70, 121, 124
Accountability, 127, 128
Adaptability, 72, 95–98
Adidas running shoes, 141
"Administrative management," 28
Aerodynamic bike design, factors in, 166–168
Aesthetics, 140, 141, 143, 155–164
Age: and diversity, 115, 116, 117, 118, 119, 218; stereotypes about, studies associated with, 119, 228n11; and trust, 218
Alienation: reduction in, 30; rise in, 18
Amazon, 8, 33, 59, 108, 171
American Airlines, 26, 147
American Arithmometer Company, 23
Analytical appeal, 192
Analytical stories, problem with, 196
Analytics, 17, 23, 24, 25–27, 33, 63, 121, 132, 134, 135, 164, 205, 213, 216, 218; social/customer, 61–62; visual, 64, 206, 207. *See also* Data; Metrics
Ancona, Deborah, 104
Anderson, Andy, 48
Andreessen Horowitz, 84, 160, 185, 186
Andreessen, Marc, 100, 185
Android, 186
Angularity, negative response to, 156–157
Apathy, 187, 202
Apple, xii, 7, 13, 19, 22, 32, 59, 116, 120, 125, 141, 148, 149, 150, 157, 159, 160, 161, 194

Apple II, 26
Apple Macintosh, 26, 159, 206–207
Argyris, Chris, 104
ARM, 34
Armstrong, Lance, 139, 167, 171
Artificial intelligence (AI), 91–94
Asian labor, 33
Aspirational goals, conveying, with story, 182
Aspirational purpose, 57
Assembly-line workers, 23–24, 28, 32
Aston Martin, 159, 184
Atlassian, 63
Attraction, mechanics of, 14, 140, 147, 155. *See also* Design, good
Audience: engaged, maintaining an, 204; understanding your, 15, 192–193
Authenticity, 11, 44, 45, 59, 60, 161, 181, 192, 195, 218
Authority, trust creating, 54
Auto industry, 172
Autonomous teams, creating, with boundaries, 126–129
Autonomy, greater emphasis on, call for, 31
Avatar (movie), 147
Aviation industry, 189, 190

B

Baby boomers, 37, 119
Babylonian abacus, 22
Bacon, Francis, 219
Balance, xi, xii, 31–32, 35, 125, 168, 177
Balance sheet, strong, 52

Ballmer, Steve, 54
Bar, Moshe, 156
Barksdale, Jim, 100, 101, 102, 103, 118
Barthes, Roland, 177
Basketball teams, coaching, 12, 55, 66–67, 72–73, 74, 80–81, 87–88, 89, 90–91, 126
Battle between the sexes, 212
Battlefields, military, 86
Bauhaus design movement, 160
Beach, Rick, 198, 199, 200, 201
Beatles, 81
Beauty, 140, 143, 147, 148, 152, 159, 168, 171
Becker, Greg, 71
Bejan, Adrian, 156
Bellini, Mario, 140
Benchmarking, 153
Bennis, Warren, 31, 39
Best-places-to-work lists, 11, 40–41, 45, 46, 62–63, 214
Betrayal: effect of, on trust, 60; risk of, 39
Bezos, Jeff, 59, 108
Bias, 192
Big data, 17, 63, 93, 121, 130, 132, 171
Blogs, 61, 202, 203
Blue-collar workforce, 23 24, 28, 32
BMW, 158, 215
Board chairmen, 10
Board meetings, 210
Boards of directors: building diversity into, 102–103; as mostly hard-edgers, 21
Bono, Edward de, 89
Bottom lines, focused on metrics and, 23, 24, 27. See also Analytics
Boundaries, setting, 127–129
Brain, the, 72, 79, 103–104. See also Intelligence
Brand building, stories and, 14, 176, 179, 183–184, 203–204
Brand recognition, greater, soft edge leading to, 21, 22
Brand value: elevated, 30; lost, 18
Brands: compromising your, 181; knowing your, 161; mediocre, 60; new, launching, stories used for, 14; as promises, 60; standing of, using data analytics for, 61
Branson, Richard, 56, 162
Brase, Jennifer, 53, 123–124
Braun, 160
Bricklin, Dan, 26
Bridge Communications, 102
Brin, Sergey, 70
Broad appeal, 192
Broad ideas, grasping, 179
Budget fights, 212
Building Trust at the Speed of Change (Marshall), 43
Burnout, 125
Burroughs Corporation, 23

Burroughs, William Seward, 23
Business evolution, 32
Business trends, current, 33

C
Cain and Abel, 22
Calculation tools, 22–23
Cambridge University, 211
Cameron, James, 147
Campbell, Bill, 125–126, 150
Cancer Centers of America, 95
Can-do attitude, 69
Capital efficiency: lacking in enduring appeal, 22; metrics for, 21; as a pillar of the hard edge, *8*, 9–10, *16*; and Wall Street, 17
Capitalism, 17, 18
Caring, 55, 108–109, 191
Carnegie, Dale, 38
Carrico, Bill, 102
Causality, 219, 220
Center for Innovation, 76–77, 95
Centre for Contemporary Cultural Studies, 177
Cerf, Vint, 102
Chang, David, 83–84, 89–90, 124
Change: in corporate model, 112; stereotypes about age and, 119, 228n11; story and, 178, 179; surviving and adapting to, chances of, 3; technological, 201
Chaplin, Charlie, 28
Chatter, 62
Cheever, John, 29
Chemistry, team, and getting it right, 121–124
Chicago Bulls, 55
Chicken Little, acting like, avoiding, 193
Chief executive officers (CEOs): comfort level of, with talking in the language of the soft edge, 10; as insufficient to solely sustain greatness, 1–2; as mostly hard-edgers, 21; stories helping, 179, 187–188
Chief information technology officers (CIOs). See CMO-CIO relationship
Chief marketing officers (CMOs). See CMO-CIO relationship
China, 33
Chinese abacus, 22–23
Chouniard, Yvon, 194
Christensen, Clayton M., 5, 31, 44, 95, 219
Cincinnati Bengals, 86
Cinelli, Cino, 165–166
CIO-CMO Forum, 209–210. See also CMO-CIO relationship
Cirrus Aircraft, 176, 188–191, 198–201
Cirrus Owners and Pilots Association (COPA), 176, 198, 199, 200, 201, 202, 204
Cirrus SR20 airplane, 189

Cirrus SR22 airplane, 173–175, 190
Cisco, 34, 110, 203
Citigroup, 32
Clark, Jim, 100
CMO-CIO relationship: divide in, 209–210, 211, 212; healthy, 212–214
Coaches, using, 125–126
Coaching sports teams, 12, 55, 66–67, 72–73, 74, 80–81, 86, 87–88, 89, 90–91
Coca-Cola bottle/cans, 141, 143
Cognition, development of, 156
Cognitive ability. See Intelligence
Cognitive diversity, 115–118, 120
Cognitive systems, networks of, 94
Cognitive tests, 68, 69, 121
Coke Zero, 143
Collaboration: and common ground, 120; and conflict, 119; essentialness of, 13; increased need for, 135; study of, using sociometrics in, 132
Collins, Jim, 31
Collins, Keith, 64, 203, 206
Colnago, Ernesto, 166
Columbia University, 126
Comfort zone, reaching beyond our, 86
Commitment: conviction and, 51; gaining, framework for, 29; increased, soft edge leading to, 21; to team goals, looking for a, 122
Commitments, staying true to, 53
Commodityville, ticket out of, 21, 184
Common ground, 119–120
Communication: corporate, muddle of, getting lost in the, 187; effectiveness of, tracking, 134; improving skills in, software programs for, 135; increased need for, 135; one-on-one versus one-way, 202; patterns of, identifying, 132, 133; story and, 179, 184; style of, choosing team members based on, 134
Communication channels, 133, 201–202, 204
Community building, 179, 183
Company success, lasting. See Long-term company success
Comparison shopping, instant, availability of, 33–34
Competitive Strategy (Porter), 5, 9
Competitors: effect of, on the bar of high performance, 218; intense competition from, increased need arising from, 135; as a pillar of the strategic base, 6, *16*. See also Disrupters
Computers, 25, 26, 27, 34, 91–94, 95, 101, 118, 166, 167, 171, 189, 206, 216, 218
Concern, demonstrating, 53, 55, 213
Conflict: guaranteed, 217; managing, 118–121, 134; in story, 177, 178, 195
Consistency, 14, 22, 60, 161–162, 214
Consumers. See Customers

Context: creating, through story, 206; language of, 64–65
Continuing education, 76
Continuous improvement, 30, 83
Control: extreme, 24, 28, 32; lack of, over trajectory and pace of technology, 34
Conversation economy, shift to a, 203–204
Conviction, 51
Cook, Tim, 7–8
Corporate Cultures (Deal & Kennedy), 30–31
Corporate model change, 112
Corporate-led companies, risk taking and, 151
Cost: fleeting advantage from, 33; as insufficient to sustain greatness, 2; metrics for, 21; as a pillar of the hard edge, *8, 9, 16*; trust and, 43
Cost reductions, 21, 32
Costco, 152
Cost-effectiveness, as a goal, beginning of, 22
Cote, Mark, 167–168
Courage, 17, 69, 70, 72, 150–151, 181
Covey, Stephen M. R., 43
Creativity: celebration of, reasons behind the, 154–155; as a driver, 155; dulling, 58; enabling, 39, 44, 126; greater emphasis on, call for, 31; and intuitive genius, 168; lost, 18; too much focus on, in design, 140; unlocking our, need for, 155
Credibility, 40, 41, 45, 192, 193
Cross-identity realities, 119
Crowdfunding, 130, 203
Crowdsourcing, 130–131, 203
Cultural divide, 211, 212
Cultural DNA, 154
Cultural history, weaving an origination story into your, 194
Cultural training, 97
Culture: broken, common fractures in a, 212; crumbling, 202; of fear, 58–59; of high expectations, cultivating, 124–126; and stories, 177, 179, 180, 182, 183, 184, 202–203; strong, maintaining a, through tough times, 45–47; with a strong soft edge, relationships benefiting from a, 212; of trust, 11, 41, 43, 44, 45, 53–59; values-based, shift from, 18
Curiosity, killer of, 58
Customer analytics, 61–62
Customers: commitment of, 21; connecting with, through story, 183, 184; engagement of, teams and, 134; feedback from, soliciting, 61; as owners, 52; as a pillar of the strategic base, 6, *16*; satisfaction of, measuring, 61, 96; saying "no" to, 164; story-shaping relationship between companies and, 15, 176, 201; and trust, 40, 44–45, 52, 60, 61, 96, 224n8; understanding your, 160, 170; using, for reality checks, 60–61
Cynicism, 37, 39, 187

D

Dali, Salvador, 156

Data: allure of, 21, 33; big, 17, 63, 93, 121, 130, 132, 171; gathering, new technology for, 132; incorporating, into soft-edge tasks, 16; intersection of taste and, example of, 165–168; large quantities of, understanding, framework for, 64; learning about, 213; measurement of, bytes in, 26–27; overlistening to, 152; purchasing, 171; wise use of, to build trust, 60–63

Data management systems, 26

"Data signatures," 132–133, 134

Data storytelling, 205–207

Data truth and human truth, sweet spot between, finding the, xii, 13, 27, 168–172, 218

Data visualization, 63–65, 205

Databases: computerized, rise of, 25–26; earliest, history of the, 22

Data-driven decisions, 171

Davis, Jim, 40–41, 62, 63

Deal, Terry, 30

Decision making, better, 112

Decisions, design, drivers of, 170–171

Deep Blue (supercomputer), 91–92

Delayed gratification, 72

Delegation, 127

Dell, 2, 185–186

Delta Airlines, 147

Deming, W. Edwards, 30, 58–59

Democratization, 202

Design decisions, drivers of, 170–171

Design, good, 14, 22, 139–140, 141–142, 143, 144, 145–146, 148, 149, 152, 153, 158, 161, 168, 169. *See also* Taste

Design Thinking, 139, 153, 160

Desirability, 153, 154, 159

Diet Coke, 143

Differentiation, 143

Digital age, tools of the, trends involving, 33

Digital channels, 212

Digital dashboard, creating a, 134

Digital Equipment, 2, 5

Digital media, exploring more, 153

Digital networking, 130

Digital work, 172

Dignity, 41

Diligence, 51

Discernment, focus on, need for, 140

Discrimination, reduction of, 114

Dishonesty, 60

Disney, 97, 103, 147, 153

Disney, Walt, 159

Disneyland, 159

Disrupters: ability to survive, 21; frequency of, 1; growing disruption from, increased need arising from, 135; in health care, 94–95; industry leaders facing, 19; new, creation of, and the digital age, 33; as a pillar of the strategic base, 6, 7, *16*; quickly adapting to, smarts enabling, 12, 95–98; staying ahead of, by shifting to fast and small teams, 110–112

Distortion, 203

Distrust: rise in, 18, 39, 42, 44, 45; of stories, 180

Diversity: cognitive, 115–118, 120; conflict resulting from, managing, 118–121; issues with teams and, 113–115; tangible benefits of, 115; of the workforce, positive initiatives for, 113, 114

Dot-com boom, 36, 37

Dresner, Howard, 26

Duarte, Nancy, 177, 180, 181, 182, 191, 192, 193, 195, 196, 197, 198, 203

Ducati motorcycles, 162

Duke University, 130, 156

Durability, 181

E

Earnhardt, John, 203

Eastman Kodak, 2, 19

Economy of scale, 150

Edelman Trust Barometer, 42, 44

Edgecumbe, Eric, 122

Edmondson, Amy, 104

Educational diversity, 116, 117

Efficiency, emphasis on, 23–24, 27

Effort, 71, 80, 81

Egger, Robert, xii, 13, 123, 152, 159, 161, 162, 163, 168, 169, 171–172, 214

Electronics Arts, 153

Ellison, Larry, 26, 125

E-mail newsletters, 204

Emotional appeal, 192

Emotional connection, 14, 140, 141, 145, 147, 180, 183, 184, 187, 201

Emotional Intelligence (EI), 69

Emotional manipulation, avoiding, 193

Emotional momentum, 154

Emotional realism, sharing, 194

Empathy, building, 134

Employee surveys, 62, 63, 64

Employees: commitment of, 21, 22; communicating with, teams and, 134; privacy of, 62; recruiting, 11, 179; and trust, 40, 41, 52, 56

Enchantment (Kawasaki), 194

Engagement: creating, through story, 184, 187, 196, 202, 204; emotional, 14; enabling, 39, 44; measuring, 132

Enron, xi

Epic Allez bike, 151

Ericsson, Anders, 81

Espinosa, Roberto, xv–xvii, 11

Estrin, Judy, 102–103, 118
Ethical behavior: believing in a coworker's, 53; standards of, codifying, 128
Ethical lapses, 36, 37
Ethics training, 56
Execution: importance of, 8; perfect, as insufficient to solely sustain greatness, 2; and Wall Street, 17. *See also* Hard edge
Executives: as mostly hard-edgers, 21; openness and trust across all, 64. *See also* Chief executive officers (CEOs)
Exercise, 79
Existing brands, enhancing, stories used for, 14
Expectations, struggle between reality and, displaying the, 195–196
Experience: diversity of, 115, 116, 117, 118; and intuition, combining, 169; shared, 201
Experience, customer, integrated. *See* Integrated experience
Experiential factors, influence of, on behavior, 71–72
Experimentation, trust facilitating, 12, 44
Exploration, quelling, 58
Exposure effect, 159
Expression, freedom of, 129
External market, trust and the, 11–12
External trust, 40, 52

F

Facebook, 19, 56, 57, 61, 70, 202, 204
Factory workers, 23–24, 28, 32
Fadell, Tony, 14, 116–117, 120, 122–123, 125, 135, 148–149, 150, 151, 155, 160–161, 164, 169–170, 170–171, 197, 214
Fads, 60
Failure: disclosing, in stories, 195; learning from, 85. *See also* Mistakes
Fairness, 53
Faith, 181
Faking and posturing, 59
Familiarity, 14, 158–160
Fans, creating, 183
Farley, David, 76, 77–78, 91
Fayol, Henri, 28
Fear, 58–59, 125, 126, 156, 157
Feasibility, 153, 154
FedEx, 4, 8, 13, 20, 32–33, 82, 101, 102–103, 105–108, 118, 127–128, 212
FedEx Corporate Operating Manual, 107, 127
FedEx Corporation, 107–108
FedEx Express, 107
FedEx Express World Hub, 105–106
FedExForum, 107
FedEx Freight, 108
FedEx Ground, 107
FedEx Information Technology and Oversight Committee, 102

FedEx Office, 108
FedEx Services, 108
Feedback, 61, 77, 164
Feedback mechanisms, 62–63
Feelings and emotions. *See Emotional* entries
Fehr, Ernest, 57
Ferrari cars, 159, 162
Fignon, Laurent, 166
Filson Clothing, 194–195
Financial crisis (2007–2008), 42
Financial Times 100, 44
Five Factors Personality Test, 121
Flexibility, 31, 112
Focus and scale, 107
Focus groups, limitations of, 170
Fog of War (documentary), 25
"Fog of war" expression, 86–87
Football teams, coaching, 86, 87–88, 89, 126
Forbes ASAP (magazine), 86
Forbes, Inc., 35, 86
Forbes (magazine), xi, 18, 45, 221
Ford, Henry, 24, 28, 32
Ford, Henry, II, 25
Ford Motor Company, 24, 25, 32
Form, 142, 143, 149, 163
Formula One Racing, 214, 215–218
Forrester Research, 209
Forums, 202
Founder-led companies, risk taking and, 151
Frankston, Bob, 26
Fraudulent prognostications, avoiding, 193
Free digital tools, 33
Free enterprise, 17, 18
Freedom, 56
Function, 142–143, 149, 164, 168, 169
Fundamental considerations. *See* Strategic base
Futures, possible, understanding, story enabling, 176, 181

G

Gallup poll, 42
Gardner, Howard, 69
Gartner Group, 26
Gates, Bill, 26, 54, 59, 81
Gen Xers, 37
Gender battles, 212
Gender diversity, 113, 114, 115, 116, 117, 118, 218
Gender roles, 210
General intelligence (*g*), 68, 69, 70
General Motors, 25, 32
Generational differences. *See* Age
Geometry, 14, 156–157
George Bailey character, 39, 52–53
Georgens, Tom, 41, 45, 46, 70
Gladwell, Malcolm, 81, 82
Glass ceiling, 114

Global economy, 13, 35
Global knives, 144
Global Manager's Guide, 128
Golden rectangle, 156
Goleman, Daniel, 69
Goodnight, Jim, 56, 61, 63
Google, 19, 27, 34, 70, 106, 214
Gossip, 133
Governance, proper, faster learning
    facilitated by, 213
Grace, buying, with a story, 186
Great Depression, 24
Greer, Phil, 101–102, 103, 118
Grit, 12, 17, 50–53, 70, 71–74, 123–124,
    197, 218
Grossman, Jerome, 95
Groups, effectiveness of, trust improving,
    12, 41
Growth and profit: lost, 18; stunting, 58
Guber, Peter, 180–181

H
Haiti earthquake, 173
Hamel, Gary, 31
Hamilton, Ian, 145, 147, 159, 160, 163
Hansei, 83, 84
Happiness, 58
Hard edge, xi; ability to master both the soft
    edge and the, as key, 35; biased toward
    favoring the, xii–xiii, 33; embracing the
    discipline of the, while avoiding extrem-
    ism, 27–28; finding the right balance of
    soft edge and, as key, 31–32, 35; fleeting
    advantages of the, 21, 32, 33–34; impor-
    tance of the, 8, 32–33, 34; investing in
    the, reasons for, 21, 98; master of the,
    7–8; pillars of the, described, 8–10; rela-
    tive value of the, 32; rise of the, and the
    systems view, 23–27; versus soft edge, in a
    fight for resources, 20–21; as starting from
    resource scarcity, 22–23; in the triangle of
    long-term company success, 5, 16; of Wall
    Street, 17
"Hard stuff," x
Hard work, 12, 71, 80
Hardship stories, including, 195–196
Hartness, James, 28
Harvard Business School, 24, 31, 36, 140
Harvard Medical School, 156
Harvard University, 126
Hayes, Bob, 141
Health care industry, 91, 94, 95
Hedonic dominance, principle of, 143
Heiden, Eric, 138, 144
Herrmann Brain Dominance Instrument,
    121
Hewlett, Bill, 18, 182
Hewlett-Packard (HP), ix–x, 18, 182

Hierarchy of needs, 29
Hill, Napoleon, 38
Hitz, Dave, 43, 62–63
Hollerith, Herman, 23
Hollywood, 28
Honesty, 53, 59, 193, 195, 196, 213
Honesty tests, 55
Hornstein, Harvey, 58
Hospitality and service, focus on, 97, 98
How to Win Friends and Influence People
    (Carnegie), 38
HP Way, x, xi, 18, 182
Huawei, 34
Human capability, optimism about, 124
Human Dynamics Laboratory, 132
Human Factor in Works Management, The
    (Hartness), 28
Human nature: accounting for, 218; failing
    to account for, 25
Human truth and data truth, sweet spot
    between, finding the, xii, 13, 27, 168–172,
    218
Human-centered design, 160
Humanism versus rationality, 19, 27–29,
    30–31. See also Hard edge; Soft edge
Humility, 82
Hummer car, 139
Hwang, Jason, 95

I
IBM, 23, 25, 92, 94, 101, 110, 120
Ideas: broad, grasping, 179; celebration of,
    call for, 31; coming up with, source of,
    116; debating, 140; democratization of,
    202; driver of, 155; exchange of, x; flow
    of, tracking, 134; good, rejecting, 120;
    improving, analyzing data for, 164; link-
    ing, with emotion, 180; looking for, 86–88,
    89, 90, 101–102; new, providing people
    with, 131; outside, embracing, 80; selling,
    187; and trust, 44, 57, 59; turning, into
    money, 111. See also Innovation
IDEO, 85, 140, 153
IKEA, 163
Images, language of, 64. See also Data visu-
    alization
Imagination, transforming, into physical
    objects, 14
Immaculate Conception stories, avoiding, 195
In Search of Excellence (Peters & Waterman),
    x, xi, xii, 17, 30–31
India, 33
Indiana University Hoosiers (1975–76), 66–67
Individualization, basis for community and,
    183
Industry leaders, 19, 32–33. See also specific
    companies
Influencers, 61, 203

Information: absorption of, shape accelerating, 156; flow of, ease of, benefits from, 42–43; growth in, 77, 92; sharing, 108, 120; understanding, role of stories in, 179
Innovation: basis for, 155; bedrock of, 43–45; enduring, as the goal, 15; essentialness of, 13; and function, being fanatical about, 168–169; real-time, 217–218; and scale, 111–112; story and, 179; teams catalyzing, 13; trust underpinning, 12, 57, 59
Innovation-to-commoditization life cycle, 34
Innovative response, robust: factors not solely sufficient to create a, 1–2; importance of a, 1; wellspring of a, 3
Innovator's Dilemma, The (Christensen), 5, 31
Innovator's Prescription, The (Christensen, Grossman, & Hwang), 95
Inspiring others, powerful method of, 196
Insularity, 120
Insurance industry, 52
Integrated experience: focus on, at Nest Labs, 148–151; move toward, at Mayo, 97, 98
Integrity, 55
Intel, 34, 110
Intellectual styles, 117
Intelligence: artificial, 91–94; described, 68–69, 74; proxies for, 150; testing for, 68, 69, 121
Internal market, trust and the, 11
Internal trust, 40, 52
Internet, 34, 60, 86, 100, 102, 189, 199, 212
Intuit, 125, 170
Intuition, 116, 166, 168, 169
Invention, 112, 123, 170
Investment bankers, 36
iOS, 186
iPhone, 95, 160, 186, 197
iPod, 116, 144, 148, 160, 161
IQ scores, 69, 121, 124
IQ tests, 68, 69
Irrational things, doing, 149, 151
Iterative design, 158, 169, 170–171
It's a Wonderful Life (movie), 39
iTunes, 171
Ive, Jony, 159–160

J
Jackson, Phil, 55
James Bond character, 159
James, LeBron, 216
Japan, 29–30, 89–90
Jeopardy (television show), 91
Jobs, Steve, 13, 59, 116, 141, 148, 159, 163–164, 197, 206
Johnson & Johnson, x
Johnson, Brooks, 90–91
Johnson, Lyndon, 25

K
Kaizen, 83, 84
Kaltenborn, Jens, 215
Kaltenborn, Monisha, 215–216, 217
Kanter, Rosabeth Moss, 31
Karlgaard, Rich, 220–221
Kasier Group, 215
Kawasaki, Guy, 139, 194
Kelley, Tom, 140
Kennedy, Allan, 30
Kennedy, John F., Jr., 25, 188, 200
Kidd, Jay, 42–43, 63
Kinkos, 108
Kirkpatrick, Curry, 67
Kirton's Adaption-Innovation Theory, 121
Klapmeier, Alan, 188–189, 190, 198, 199
Klapmeier, Dale, 189
Knight, Bobby, 66–67, 72–73, 74, 80, 81, 82
Knowledge: capture and communication of, 179; democratization of, 202; explosion of, 76–79; same, access to, 33; sharing, 44, 113, 114, 203; unlocking, 12. *See also* Learning
Knowledge economy, shift from a, 203
Knowledge industry, 33
Kochan, Thomas, 114

L
Laffley, A. G., 6
Language: common, having a, 64, 213, 217; decision making without, 132; simple, 192; snarky, 36–37, 120; wholesome/earnest, 37, 38
Lascaux Caves, 177
Lasting success. *See* Long-term company success
Lateral thinking, 13, 86, 89–91, 98
Layoffs, handling, 46–47
Leadership, trustworthy, 53–55
Leapfrogging, 33
Learning: from the best, 80–83, 97, 98; contributing to taste, 15; dictating strategy versus driving, 17; by embedding people on other teams, 213; from mistakes, 13, 83–86; proper governance facilitating faster, 213; self-regulated, 72–73; smarts accelerating, 12, 70, 71–74; teams facilitating, 13; and technology, 78, 92–93; in traditional education, 113; trust facilitating, 12, 15, 44
Legacy trap, 34, 101
Legends, creating, 180
LeMond, Greg, 151, 166
Lencioni, Patrick, 31
Leonardo da Vinci, 156
Levi's, 60
LFMN stock, 37
Life span, company, 34
LinkedIn, 61, 202

Listening, 82
Little Tramp character, 28
Lockheed, 5
Logic and intuition, sweet spot between, finding the, 116
Logistics: large-scale, 106; metrics for, 21; military, 25, 106; as a pillar of the hard edge, *8*, *9*, *16*
Longevity, company, 52
Long-term company success: framework for predicting, 4–15, *16*; key to, 35. *See also* Hard edge; Soft edge; Strategic base
Long-term personal health, framework for predicting, 3–4
Lotus 1-2-3, 26
Loyalty: customer, and trust, connection between, 40, 44–45, 60, 61, 224n8; edge provided by, 22; increased, soft edge leading to, 21; story and, 185
Lucas, Amber, 145–146, 146–147, 163
Lucky Peach (magazine), 83

M
Macintosh computer. *See* Apple Macintosh
MacWorld conference, 197
Madonna, 70
Magical feeling, 14, 139, 145, 147, 152, 159
Management trust, 40, 56
Manager control, 23–24. *See also* Top-down management
Managing By Wandering Around (MBWA), x
Mandalay Entertainment Group, 180
Manipulation, avoiding, 193
Manufacturing processes, hard-edge approach to, 24
Marginal gains, xv
Market: as a pillar of the strategic base, 6, *16*; trust and the, 11–12
Market research, traditional, going against, 164
Market share, elevated, 30
Market shifts, 33
Marketing: good, as storytelling, 183–184, 203–204; traditional, 202, 204. *See also* CMO-CIO relationship
Marketing programs, learning about metrics and, 213
Marketplace, crowded, effect of, 140
Marshall, Edward, 43
Martin, Roger, 6
Martin, Tony, 146, 166
Maslow, Abraham, 29, 58
Mateschitz, Dietrich, 215
Maxwell, Brian, 194
Mayer, Marissa, 56
Mayo, Charles, 74–75
Mayo Clinic, 12, 74–79, 91, 95–98, 212
Mayo Clinic Online Learning Program, 75–76
Mayo Graduate School, 75

Mayo Medical School, 75
Mayo School of Continuous Professional Development, 75
Mayo School of Graduate Medical Education, 75
Mayo School of Health Sciences, 75
Mayo, William J., 74–75
Mayo, William W., 74
McDonald's, 60
McGaw Cellular, 101
McGlaughlin, Richard, 173–176, 200
McKinsey, ix
McNamara, Robert, 24–25, 27
Meaning: creating, through story, 182, 184, 203, 206; cultivating, 57, 58, 59, 124; search for, 140; significance of, 140, 141, 144–148, 149–150
Measurement: of data, bytes in, 26–27; ease of, 154; of the soft edge, difficulty of, 10; of trust, 12. *See also* Metrics
Media, immediacy of the, withstanding the, 11–12
Media, social. *See* Social media
Medical technology, 78, 92–95
Medical training, 74–79
Mediocre brands, 60
Meetings: feeling safe in, 59; setting rules for, example of, 127–128
Memorial Sloan-Kettering Cancer Center, 92–93
Memphis International Airport, 105, 106
Mendoza, Tom, 45, 46–47, 54, 55
Mental and emotional health, *3*, 4
Mentors, seeking out, 80–83, 97, 98
Merrill Lynch, 37
Message delivery, importance of, 47
Message deployment, discussing, 214
Metrics: allure of, 21, 33; and bottom lines, focused on, 23, 24, 27; edge most influenced by, 32; learning about marketing and, 213; social, 131–135. *See also* Analytics
Microsoft, 54, 59
Microsoft's Excel, 26
Mind of a Chef, The (television show), 83
"Minus one" philosophy, 109
Miracle Blade, 144
Mirroring, 134
Mistakes: acknowledging your, 83, 84, 85; fear of making, 58; feeling freer to make, 129; honest, tolerance for, 59; learning from, 13, 83–86
MIT Human Dynamics Laboratory, 132
MIT magazine, 106
MIT Sloan School of Business, 114
Mobile devices, 209. *See also* Smartphones
Modern Times (movie), 28
Modernist design, 160

Momofuku, 83, 84, 89, 124
Mondrian, 156
Money, story based on, problem with, 185
Moneyball (movie), 133
Monson, Don, 80
Montana, Joe, 86, 87
Mood contagion, 133
Moore's Law, 189
Morale: sapping, 58; stories and, 179; survey-
  ing, 62
Morito, Akio, 30
Mortality rate, company, 34
Most-innovative-companies list, 214
Motivation: fear and, 59, 125, 126; high
  expectations and, 124–125; in large teams,
  131; skill in fostering, importance of, 135;
  using story for, 178, 180, 186, 187
Motivation and Personality (Maslow), 29
Multiple Intelligences (MI), 69
Multiple sensory inputs, 158
Myers-Briggs Type Indicator test, 121
MySpace, 2

N
NASA, 106
Needs, hierarchy of, 29
Neocortex, 104
Nest Labs, 14, 116–117, 122, 125, 148–151,
  160, 164, 170, 171, 197, 214
Neta, Maital, 156
NetApp, 41, 43, 45–47, 55, 62–63, 70, 213,
  214, 216
Netscape, 100–101
Network analytics, 61
Networking, digital, 130
Networks of cognitive systems, 94
Networks, social. *See* Social media
Neurogenesis, 79
Neuroplasticity, 72, 79
New York Times (newspaper), 69
Newell, Pete, 80–81, 82
Nike shoes, 184
Nordstrom, 60
Norman, Donald, 140
Northface, 194
Northwestern Mutual, xvii, 11, 37, 38–39,
  49–53, 57, 62, 123–124, 180, 212
Noseworthy, John, 75
Novartis, 32
Numbers. *See* Metrics
Nussbaum, Bruce, 140, 141–142

O
Observing, 18, 82, 89
Occam's razor, principle of, 192
Ohio State University, 80
Old La Honda Road (OLH), bicycling the,
  137–139, 144
Ongoing narrative, importance of, 204

Openness, 44, 64
Operational Detachment Alpha, 109
Optimism, 124, 126
Oracle, 26, 110, 124–125
"Organization man," 29
Organizational culture. *See* Culture
Origination story, creating an, 194
Oughtred, William, 23
OutCast Agency, 84–85, 185
Outliers (Gladwell), 81, 82
Owens, Bill, 121–122
Ownership structure, 52

P
Packard, Dave, 18, 182
Paleolithic period, 22, 177
Panke, Helmut, 158
Parrish, Julie, 213, 214
Partners, trusted, in health, 96, 97, 98
Partnerships, supply chain, and trust, 44
Pascal, Blaise, 23
Passion, 17, 21, 122–123, 150, 151, 152, 154,
  179, 181, 197, 218
Past, making sense of the, story enabling,
  176, 181
Patagonia, 194
Patience, 51, 84
Pattek, Sheryl, 209–210
Peale, Norman Vincent, 38
Pentland, Alex, 132–133, 134, 135
Performance: high, constantly raising the bar
  of, factors involved in, 218; organizational,
  trust improving, 12, 41; sapping, 58; of
  teams, 13, 114, 117
Perks, 40, 41, 42
Perseverance, 12, 69, 70, 82
Persian Gulf War, 9
Personal health, long-term, framework for
  predicting, 3–4
Personality tests, 121
Perspectives, different, seeking, and common
  ground, 118–120. *See also* Diversity
Peters, Tom, ix–xi, 17, 30
Phone calls, xvii, 50, 51
Phones, 96, 189. *See also* Smartphones
Physical health, lasting, 3–4
Pickens, T. Boone, 70
Pink, Daniel, 140
Pinterest, 170, 202
Pirelli, 215
Playing to Win (Laffley & Marton), 5–6
Popular culture, 183, 184
Porsche, 110–111
Porter, Michael, 5, 9
Postrel, Virgina, 140
Power of Positive Thinking, The (Peale), 38
PowerBar, 194
Practicing: as an aspect of smarts, 81, 82; for
  good storytelling, 196–198

Predictability, 55, 149
Predictive analytics, 213
PricewaterhouseCoopers, 44
Pricing, trust and, 44, 224n8
Pride, 41
Principles of Scientific Management, The (Taylor), 23
Pritzl, Michael, 57
Privacy, 62
Product design. *See* Design, good
Product development teams, use of, 109–112
Product features, story based on, problem with, 186
Productivity: gossip and, 133; hard-edge approach to, 23–24; of teams, 112; and trust, 11, 41
Profit margins, higher, soft edge leading to, 21
Progressivism, 23
Promises, making and keeping, 60
Purpose: dispersal of, 203; finding your greater, 57–58; importance of, 181, 182; losing your, 181–182; meaningful, 57, 58, 59; as a recurring theme, 17; stories creating, 14, 181–182, 202–203
Pushing and reassuring, simultaneously, 125, 126

Q
Qualcomm, 34, 94
Quality: design, 152; focus on, 30; and reputation, 44
Quantification, ease of, 21. *See also* Metrics
Quantitative analysis, 25–26
Quantitative-only-driven management, 23–24, 28
Questions, asking the right, 213
Quicken, 170

R
Racial diversity, 113, 114, 115, 116, 117, 218
Rams, Dieter, 160
Rationality versus humanism, 19, 27–29, 30–31. *See also* Hard edge; Soft edge
Rayport, Jeffrey, 106
Realism, adding, to stories, 194–195
Realities, cross-identity, 119
Reality: reflection of, 212; struggle between expectations and, displaying the, 195–196
Reality checks, 60–61
Real-world stress tests, 121–122
Reassuring and pushing, simultaneously, 125, 126
Recording, tracking and, 22–23
Red Bull, 215
Rejection, sales, trust in the face of, 48–50
Relationships: beneficial, establishing, as a smart habit, 12; building, trust key

to, 39; effective, trust underlying, 12, 41; story-shaping, between companies and customers, 15, 176, 201. *See also* CMO-CIO relationship
Relative value, 32
Renaissance: early, 22; late, 23
Reputation, 44, 61–62
Research and development (R&D), 2, 9
Reset, time for a, xi
Resilience, 41, 69
Resources: fight for, between the hard and soft edges, 20–21; scarcity of, hard edge starting from a, 22–23
Respect, 40, 41, 57, 59
Retention, 11, 18
Return on investment (ROI): faster, hard-edge investment providing a, 21, 98; measurable, trust creating a, 12; in the soft edge, difficulty attaching a figure for, 10; in story, 181
Rewards, extrinsic versus intrinsic, 29
Risk: huge, of scale, 107; lowering feelings of, in groups, 133; trust as an essential, 39–41
Risk taking: differences in appetite for, 151; encouraging, 85
Ritz-Carlton, 97
Robotics, 33
Roman abacus, 22
Rounded corners, appeal of, 156, 157
Rules, setting, 127–128
Rutgers, 103
Ryun, Jim, 141

S
S&P Index, 34
SABRE, 26
Safe environment, building a, importance of, 58, 59
Salas, Eduardo, 104
Salesforce.com, 62, 71
Samsung, 32–33, 157
San Francisco 49ers, 86, 87–88
San Jose Apaches, 87
Sanford, Curt, 198–199
Santayana, George, 143
SAP, 9, 13, 109–112, 127, 153–154
SAS Institute, 40, 56, 61, 62, 63, 64, 203, 206
SAT math wizards, 18, 52, 70
Sauber Motorsports, 215, 216, 217–218
Sauber, Peter, 215
Scaling up, story based on, problem with, 185
Schein, Edgar, 58
Schlifske, John, 38, 39, 52, 54
Schoon, Todd, 50, 51, 124
Schultz, Howard, 159
Schwarzkopf, Norman, 9

Scientific management, 23–24, 27, 28
Scientific method, 219–220
Sears, 26
Sebanz, Natalie, 103
Seinfeld (television show), 37
Self-actualization, 29, 139
Self-awareness, 54
Self-discipline, 72
Self-disclosure, 195, 196
Self-esteem, 29
Selfishness, 14, 160–161
Self-motivation, trusting in, 56
Self-reflection, 54
Self-regulated skills, 72–73
Sense of Beauty, The (Santayana), 143
Sensibility, universal, 14, 140
Sensing skill, 164, 168. *See also* Taste
Sensors, 63, 132, 146, 166, 167, 216, 218
Sensory attributes/characteristics, 143, 157
Sensory details, sharing, 194
Sensory inputs, 158
Sentiment analysis, 213
Shared context, 64–65
Shared experience, 201
Shared language, 64
Shareholders: versus customers as owners,
    52; as mostly hard-edgers, 21
Sharing information, 108, 120
Sharing knowledge, 44, 113, 114, 203
Sherlock, Ryan, 138, 144
Shiv bike, 165, 166, 167
Shooting from the Outside (VanDerveer), 81
Shrek (movie), 153
Siemens, 32
Signaling, 132, 133–134
Silicon Graphics, 100
Silicon Valley, 17–18, 36, 46, 52, 101, 110,
    118, 125, 153, 184–185
Silicon Valley Bank, 71
Simple stories, as key, 192
Simplicity, 14, 162–164
Sincerity, 44
Singapore Airlines, 214
Singularity University, 92, 94, 95, 112, 130,
    170, 202
Sinyard, Mike, 122, 125, 151, 152, 161, 162,
    165, 169, 194
60 Minutes (television show), 140
Skepticism, 180
Skill diversity, 116, 117
"Sky is falling" stories, avoiding, 193
Skynet, 94
Sloan, Alfred, 32
Sloan School of Business, 114
Sloan-Kettering Cancer Center, 92–93
Smart feeling, providing the experience of
    a, 150, 163
Smartphones, 63, 94–95, 138, 145, 189, 212

Smarts: contributing to stories, 15;
    cultivating, practices/behaviors for,
    80–91; defining, 68; depicted as a pillar
    of the soft edge, *10, 16*; described, 68–71;
    excellence in, attraction provided by,
    98; and grit, 69, 70, 71–74; in a healthy
    CMO-CIO relationship, 213; increas-
    ing, factors in, 79–80; key points about,
    and gaining the edge, 98–99; and the
    knowledge explosion, 76–79; and learning
    fast enough to avoid disruption, 95–98;
    and learning from mistakes, 83–86; and
    learning from the best, 80–83, 97, 98;
    in looking for ideas, 86–88; overview of,
    as an advantage of the soft edge, 12–13;
    significance of, illustration of the, 66–67;
    and supercomputers, 91–94; and thinking
    laterally, 89–91, 98
Smith, Fred, 4–5, 13, 20, 82–83, 102, 103,
    106–107, 108, 118, 127–128, 135
Snabe, Jim, 110–111, 111–112, 154
Snarky lingo, 36–37, 120
Snow, Charles Percy, 211
Social analytics, 61–62
Social health, *3*, 4
Social media, 14, 56, 60, 61, 130–131,
    201–204, 209, 212
Social media analytics, 61, 62
Social nature, 103
Social signals, 133
Socialcast, 62
Sociometrics, 131–135
Soft edge, xi, xii; ability to master both the
    hard edge and the, as key, 35; assessment
    of the, website for, 16; commitment to
    the, importance of, xiii, 218; described,
    10–15; difficulty measuring the, 10; excel-
    ling at the, recurring themes in, 17; as a
    final frontier, 16; finding the right balance
    of hard edge and, as key, 31–32, 35; versus
    hard edge, in a fight for resources, 20–21;
    investing in the, reasons for, 21–22, 98;
    losing sense of the, 152; mastery of the,
    as critical, 35; misunderstanding the, 10;
    neglecting and underfunding of the, xiii,
    10, 20–21, 212; pillars of the, overview of,
    11–15; questions for future exploration of
    the, 221; recurring themes tied to the, 17;
    relative value of the, 32; strong, culture
    with a, relationships benefiting from, 212;
    in the triangle of long-term company
    success, *5, 16*; urgent need for the, reasons
    for, 17–19. *See also* Smarts; Story; Taste;
    Teams; Trust
"Soft stuff," x–xi
Sony, 30
Sony Walkman, 141
Southwest Airlines, 9

Specialized Bicycles, xii, 13, 122, 123, 125, 139, 144, 145–147, 151–152, 158–159, 161–162, 163, 165, 166, 167–168, 168–169, 194, 212, 214

Speed: allure of, 33; fleeting advantage from, 33; as insufficient to sustain greatness, 2; metrics for, 21; as a pillar of the hard edge, 8–9, *16*; trust and, 43; and Wall Street, 17

Speed of Trust, The (Covey), 43

Sports Illustrated (magazine), 67

Stanford Graduate School of Business, 58

Stanford School of Design, 153

Stanford University, 36, 102, 130

Stanford University women's basketball, 12, 72–73, 80, 90, 126

Star Trek tricorder, 94

Star Wars (movie), 141, 161

Starbucks, 22, 159, 214

Stereotypes, 119, 210, 228n11

Stewart, Jimmy, 39

Stock prices, story based on, problem with, 185, 186

Stoddard, Cynthia, 213, 214

Story: allure of, 177; and chances of finding the sweet spot, 218; and changing technology, 201–204; of Cirrus airplanes and customers, 173–176, 188–191, 198–201; contributing to trust, 15; and data, 205–207; depicted as a pillar of the soft edge, *10, 16*; excellence in, attraction provided by, 98; foundational, 187; good, guidelines for telling a, 191–198; in a healthy CMO-CIO relationship, 214; key points about, and gaining the edge, 207; language of, 64, 205; leadership and, 187–188; narrative with conflict, 176–178; ongoing, 204; overview of, as an advantage of the soft edge, 14–15; pillars contributing to, 15; power of, analogy illustrating the, 180–181; significance of, illustration of the, 173–176; that goes wrong, reasons for, 184–186; and trust, 179, 205; universality and ubiquity of, 177–178; value of, in the business world, 179–184; well-told, 180–181; when customers tell a better, 198–201

Story traps, 185–186

Storytelling technique, refining, 15, 191–198

Strategic base, xi; default position favoring the, xii–xiii; essentialness of the, 4–5; pillars of the, described, 6–7; in the triangle of long-term company success, *5, 16*

Strategy: choosing the wrong, 2, 5; classic books on, 5–6; clever, as insufficient to solely sustain greatness, 2; connecting employees to a, 187; dictating, ease of, 17; importance of, 4–5, 20; mistake in, ability to survive a, 21

Strava, 138, 144, 145

Stress, managing, 112

Stress tests, real-world, 121–122

Stumpjumper bike, 151, 158

Suanpan abacus, 22–23

Suarez, Fernando, xvi–xvii

Substitutes, as a pillar of the strategic base, 6, *16*

Supercomputers, 27, 91–94, 95

Supply chain: as insufficient to sustain greatness, 2; lacking in enduring appeal, 22; mastery of, by industry leaders, 32–33; metrics for, 21; as a pillar of the hard edge, 8, 9, *16*; and technology investment, 21

Support systems, 127

Surgical Olympics, 76

Surveys, use of, 62, 63, 64, 96

Sweet spot, finding the, xii, 13, 27, 168–172, 218

Swiss Alps, 159

Synergy, sapping, 58

Systems analysis, 25

Systems view, rise of the, 23–27

T

Tab, 143

Tablets, xvii, 2, 34, 212

Tactile experience, 157–158

Talent, 71, 133

Taste: contributing to stories, 15; and creating an integrated experience, 148–151; defining and describing, 139–141; depicted as a pillar of the soft edge, *10, 16*; essential elements of, 141–148; excellence in, attraction provided by, 98; and finding the sweet spot of, 168–172; in a healthy CMO-CIO relationship, 214; intersection of data and, example of, 165–168; key points about, and gaining the edge, 172; learning, over time, 169; losing, example of, 151–152; overview of, as an advantage of the soft edge, 13–14; pillars contributing to, 15; reclaiming your mojo and, 153–154; remark about, xii; significance of, illustration of the, 137–139; technology and, 146–147, 170; unlocking the secrets of, 154–164

Taste-driven decisions, 170–171

Tattoos, branding and, 184

Tax analogy, 43

Taylor, Fred, 80

Taylor, Frederick, 23, 27, 28, 32

Taylorism, 23–24, 28, 32, 62

Team fit, 121–124

Team members: great, attributes of, 122–124; ideal, data signature of, 134; optimal, identifying, 13, 109, 121–124, 134; satisfaction of, effect of diversity on, 114

Team orientation, 122

Teams: accountability of, 127; basic framework for building and managing, list of,
129; and chances of finding the sweet spot,
218; chemistry of, and getting it right,
121–124; and cognitive diversity, 115–118;
communication in, effect of diversity on,
114; contributing to taste, 15; creating
space for autonomy in, with boundaries,
126–129; depicted as a pillar of the soft
edge, *10*, *16*; effectively implementing, difficulty of, reasons for, 112–113, 129; excellence in, attraction provided by, 98; fast
and small, shift to, example of, 109–112;
and grit, 123–124; in a healthy CMO-CIO
relationship, 213; issues with diversity
and, 113–115; key points about, and gaining the edge, 135–136; magnifying, using
crowdsourcing, 130–131; overview of, as
an advantage of the soft edge, 13; and passion, 122–123; recommended books on,
227–228n10; seeking different perspectives and common ground in, 118–120;
setting high expectations for, 124–126;
shift toward, at Mayo Clinic, 96–97,
98; significance of, illustration of the,
100–103; small, power of, 105–108; and
sociometrics, 131–135; sports, coaching,
12, 55, 66–67, 72–73, 74, 80–81, 86, 87–88,
89, 90–91; success of, predicting, 132–133;
support systems for, 127; taste-driven
culture of, 154; and technology, 130; and
trust, 15, 43, 111, 120, 217; types of, 104,
105; understanding, history of, 103–105
Teamwork: large-scale, using social media
for, 130–131; sapping, 58; science of,
131–135
Technology: analytics, 132; changing, and
story, 201–204; companies commanding
cutting-edge, risk facing, 18; data gathering, new, 132; edge most influenced by,
32; effect of, on the bar of high performance, 218; evolution of, pace of, 34,
91–92, 101; fleeting advantage from, 21,
33, 34; in Formula One racing, 216, 217;
incorporating, into soft-edge tasks, 16;
information, oversight of, team approach
to, 102; instant comparison shopping
through, availability of, 33–34; as insufficient to solely sustain greatness, 2;
investment in, hard-edge gains from, 21,
32; leapfrog, 33; and learning, 78; legacy,
trapped into, 34, 101; in medicine, 78,
92–95; share of investment in, 209; story
traps in, 185, 186; and the supply chain, 9;
and taste, 146–147, 170; and teams, 130.
See also CMO-CIO relationship
Technology Review (magazine), 106
TED talks, 192, 197–198

Tell to Win (Guber), 180
Tenacity, 69, 74
Ten-thousand-hour rule, 81–82
10-3-1 rule, 50
Terminator (movie), 94
Tesla S Model, 159
Text mining, 62
Theodore, Scott, 49–50, 50–51
Think and Grow Rich (Hill), 38
3D programs/printers, 172
3M, x
Time outs, calling, 214
Time reductions, 21. *See also* Speed
Time, taking, to learn, 81, 82
Tompkins, Douglas, 194
Top-down management, 24, 27, 54, 202
Touch appeal, 157–158
Touch blends, 158
Tough times, navigating through, role of
story in, 187–188
Toy Story (movie), 153
Toyota, 30, 106
Tracking and recording, 22–23
Traditional education, problem with, 112–113
Training: cultural, 97; ethics, 56; medical,
74–79, 92–93; military, and testing, to
determine team fit, 121–122; stories used
for, 179
Transformative gains, digging deeper for,
illustrating, xv–xvii
Transparency, 44, 47, 213
Trends: business, current, 17, 33; discussion
of, getting together for, 213; product, new,
147–148
Trojan Horse analogy, 180–181
True north. *See* Purpose
Trump, Donald, 70
Trust: as the bedrock of innovation, 43–45;
begetting trust, 55–57, 62; building,
investing in, as strategic and rare, 41–43;
catalyzer of, 63–65; and chances of finding
the sweet spot, 218; contributing to taste,
15; and customer loyalty, connection
between, 40, 44–45, 60, 61, 224n8;
defining, 39; depicted as a pillar of the
soft edge, *10*, *16*; dictating strategy versus building, 17; edge provided by, 22;
excellence in, attraction provided by,
98; in the face of sales rejection, 48–50;
factors in building, 42–43, 53–59; as
a foundation for greatness, 39–41; as
foundational, 11, 15, 39, 40, 41, 42, 217;
and grit, 50–53; in a healthy CMO-CIO
relationship, 212–213; key points about,
and gaining the edge, 65; lack of, rise in,
18, 39, 42, 44, 45; measurement of, tools
for, 61–63; outcomes linked to, 41–42;
overview of, as an advantage of the soft

edge, 11–12; power of, analogy illustrating the, 43; primary dimensions of, 40; significance of, illustration of the, 36–37; social signals and the formation of, 133; stories and, 179, 205; and teams, 15, 43, 111, 120, 217; during troubled times, 45–47; using data wisely to build, 60–63; value of, company exemplifying, 38–39
Trusted partners, in health, Mayo as, 96, 97, 98
Trustworthy organizations, defining, 53
Turbo bike, 139, 145–147, 158–159, 162, 163
Twitter, 56, 61, 114, 202, 204
"Two Cultures and the Scientific Revolution, The" (Snow), 211
2/5 abacus, 22–23
Two-pizza rule, 108–109

U
Unconscious signaling behavior, 132
Unions, 28, 32
University of Birmingham, 177
University of California at Berkeley, 24, 81
University of Idaho, 80
University of Illinois Supercomputer Center, 100
University of Toyota, 30
University of Wyoming, 30
University of Zurich, 57
UPS, 106
U.S. Army's Special Forces, 109, 121
U.S. Central Forces Command, 9
U.S. Constitution, 127
U.S. Navy SEAL Team 6, 121–122
User groups, 176, 198, 199, 200, 201, 202

V
Value: diversity and, 115; relative, 32
Values: chipping away at, effect of, 18; common core, 119; trust beginning with, 11, 38, 53, 54. See also Soft edge
VanDerveer, Tara, 67, 72–73, 74, 80–81, 82, 90–91, 126, 135
Venture capitalists, 36, 220
Verisimilitude, dialing up, 15, 194–195
Vettel, Sebastian, 216
Viability, 153, 154
Videos online, 204
Vietnam conflict, 25
Virgin America airline, 147
Virgin Group, 56, 162
VisiCalc, 26
Vision (eyesight), development of, 156
Visual analytics, 64, 206, 207
Visual appeal, 156–157
Visualization, data, 63–65, 205
Von Clausewitz, Carl, 86
Vulnerability, showing, 195

W
Wadhwa, Vivek, 95, 112–113, 130–131, 170, 202
Walgreens, 95
"Walk the talk" leadership, 54
Wall Street, 17, 36, 42, 52
Wal-Mart, 26, 32–33
Walsh, Bill, 86, 87–88, 89
Walt Disney Company. See Disney
Walton, Sam, 26
Wang, 5
Warner, Mark, 97
Waste, elimination of, 23, 27
Waterman, Bob, ix–xi, 17, 30
Watson (supercomputer), 91–94, 95
Web. See Internet
Webb, Maynard, 71
Weird actions, 149, 151
Weiss, Peck and Greer, 102
Wennmachers, Margit, 84–85, 160, 170, 179, 184–185, 187, 191
West Coast Offense, 86, 87–88
Western Logic, 30
White-collar work, 28–29
Whitman, Meg, 182
Whiz Kids, 25
Whole New Mind, A (Pink), 140
Whyte, William, 28, 29
Wicher, Chris, 92, 94
Wikipedia, 33
Wilson, Sloan, 29
Wood, Doug, 76–77, 91, 95–96
Woods, Tiger, 216
Workplaces, best, list of, 11, 40–41, 45, 46, 62–63, 214
World War II, 24, 25, 29
WorldCom, xi
Worldport, 106
World's Most Innovative Companies, 45
Worry, 125

X
Xerox Palo Alto Research Center (PARC), 108
X-Prize competition, 94

Y
Yahoo, 56, 71
Yale, 37
Yates, Richard, 29
York, Conrad, 51
Young, John, ix–x
Younger people, 37, 119

Z
Zuckerberg, Mark, 70
Zune, 144

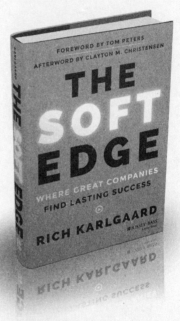